Wilfrid Sellars

Dedicated to Karina

Wilfrid Sellars

Naturalism with a Normative Turn

James R. O'Shea

polity

First published in 2007 by Polity Press

Polity Press
65 Bridge Street
Cambridge CB2 1UR, UK

Polity Press
350 Main Street
Malden, MA 02148, USA

ISBN-13: 978-07456-3002-1
ISBN-13: 978-07456-3003-8 (pb)

A catalogue record for this book is available from the British Library.

Typeset in 10 on 11.5 pt Palatino
by SNP Best-set Typesetter Ltd, Hong Kong
Printed and bound in Great Britain by MPG Books, Bodmin, Cornwall

For further information on Polity, visit our website: www.polity.co.uk

Key Contemporary Thinkers

Contents

Preface

Two decades after his death Wilfrid Sellars has once again become a much discussed philosopher on the contemporary analytic philosophical scene. Accordingly there is no apology needed for the present attempt to lay out clearly and to evaluate his overall views, especially since his writings present quite a challenge for the reader who is not already acquainted with his work. I have attempted to make Sellars' arguments accessible to upper undergraduate students in philosophy. Given the complexity of Sellars' views, however, I am reminded of the late Peter Strawson's remark in the Preface to his book *Analysis and Metaphysics: An Introduction to Philosophy*: "The book, then, may fairly be described as introductory. But though it is introductory, it is not elementary. There is no such thing as elementary philosophy. There is no shallow end to the philosophical pool" (Strawson 1992: vii). I have put a premium on attempting to produce a readable, gradually developing, and interconnected Sellarsian story, while also noting the main points at which Sellars' views are open to criticism. Given this purpose I have not been able to engage in extensive or detailed examination of the secondary literature, although the reader will find appropriate orientation in relation to those debates as well.

I can warmly recommend to the interested reader another introductory book on Sellars that has recently appeared: Willem A. deVries' *Wilfrid Sellars* (2005). Those who know deVries' work know that he is a sure hand in relation to the interpretation of Sellars. The reader will find differences of substance and style between our two books, but mostly, I believe, in a manner which renders them usefully complementary guides to Sellars' philosophy. Although I completed a full draft of the present manuscript before consulting deVries' book, throughout the process I have benefited from our email exchanges and from his encouragement of the present work, for which I thank him.

For bibliographical information, secondary sources, and other useful material, all students of Sellars are indebted to the 'Problems from Wilfrid Sellars' website maintained by Andrew Chrucky (*http://www.ditext.com/sellars/index.html*). Among the most useful items on that website is Jay F. Rosenberg's (1990) *Nachruf* for Sellars, 'Fusing the Images' (also available in Rosenberg forthcoming), an excellent brief overview of Sellars' philosophy. Another very useful secondary source on Sellars is Delaney et al. (1977), listed in the bibliography. Aune (1967) is also still well worth a look for clear Sellars-inspired investigations of a wide range of topics. Finally, a wealth of primary sources relating to Sellars is currently being made available by the helpful people at the Sellars Archive in the University of Pittsburgh Archives of Scientific Philosophy.

I am indebted to the anonymous readers for Polity Press in relation to both my initial book proposal and the final manuscript. I particularly welcome the opportunity to thank Emma Hutchinson and Justin Dyer for their incredibly helpful editorial work and their constant support as the manuscript worked its way to completion. I am also grateful to friends, students, and colleagues who have read various portions of the manuscript: in particular John Callanan, Paul Coates, Jim Levine, John O'Reilly, Vasilis Politis, Jack Ritchie, and all the energetic participants of my graduate seminar on Sellars at University College Dublin (UCD). I am grateful for the continual support of my colleagues in the School of Philosophy at UCD, and also to UCD and the School of Philosophy for granting me time off from teaching during the academic year 2003–4.

Special thanks go to Jeffrey Sicha, a well-known Sellars scholar and the publisher of Sellars' main works (Ridgeview Publishing Company: *http://www.ridgeviewpublishing.com*). Although I have not met Jeff in person, he kindly read the entire manuscript in its final stages and offered many helpful critical comments. I have found the community of philosophers interested in Sellars to be an extraordinarily helpful group of people in general, and this has helped to make the research for this book a pleasure.

By far my greatest philosophical debt is to Jay F. Rosenberg. Over a decade ago Rosenberg was my Ph.D. supervisor at the University of North Carolina at Chapel Hill, and he is himself one of the best-known former Ph.D. students of Wilfrid Sellars. Rosenberg is a systematic Sellarsian and Kantian philosopher who has also rightly earned the reputation among Sellarsians as the philosopher who is most able to render right versions and to offer insightful extensions of Sellars' philosophy. I highly recommend all of Rosenberg's works listed in the bibliography to the reader who is interested in pursuing a more in-depth study of Sellars' philosophy. A new collection of Rosenberg's articles on Sellars, *Wilfrid Sellars: Fusing the Images*, is forthcoming from

Oxford University Press. My thanks to Jay for first introducing me to both Sellars and Kant, and for his detailed comments on drafts of chapters for the present work.

On both the philosophical and the personal sides of life I have had such extraordinary support and benefited from so many insights from my wife, Dr. Karina Halley, that I cannot imagine what it would have been like to take on this task without her strong encouragement all along the way. I thank you from the bottom of my heart for all that you sacrificed for me during the times when I allowed the work for this book to take over just about everything else.

Acknowledgments

The author and publisher gratefully acknowledge the following for their permission to reproduce material in this book: Ridgeview Publishing Company, for quotations from *Naturalism and Ontology* (1997) and *Science and Metaphysics: Variations on Kantian Themes* (1992); University of Pittsburgh Press, for quotations from 'Philosophy and the Scientific Image of Man,' in Robert Colodny (ed.), *Frontiers of Science and Philosophy* (1962); University of Minnesota Press, for quotations from 'Empiricism and the Philosophy of Mind,' in Herbert Feigl and Michael Scriven (eds), *Minnesota Studies in the Philosophy of Science*, Vol. 1 (1956); and *The Monist*, for quotations from 'Foundations for a Metaphysics of Pure Process' (1981). (Copyright © 1981 *THE MONIST: An International Journal of General Philosophical Inquiry*, Peru, Illinois USA 61354.) Every effort has been made to trace copyright holders and to obtain their permission for the use of copyright material. The publisher apologizes for any errors or omissions in the above and would be grateful to be notified of any corrections that should be incorporated in future reprints or editions of this book.

Introduction

There is increasing recognition today that Wilfrid Sellars (1912–89) was one of the most important philosophers in America during the twentieth century. In fact Robert Brandom has recently described Sellars as "the greatest American philosopher since Charles Sanders Peirce. He is the most profound and systematic epistemological thinker of the 20th century" (Brandom 2000b). This introduction will provide a first glance at some of the ideas for which Sellars is best known, followed by a very brief philosophical biography. The substantive issues to be explored in the rest of the book will be introduced more fully in chapter 1.

Sellars is perhaps best known for his attack on what he called the *myth of the given*, as laid out in 1956 in his most important work, 'Empiricism and the Philosophy of Mind' (EPM).[1] It was traditionally (and Sellars thinks mistakenly) argued that since not all of our knowledge can be derived by inference from prior knowledge *ad infinitum*, there must be some basic items of knowledge which are simply 'given' in roughly the sense that they are (allegedly) known directly or immediately without presupposing our possession of any other knowledge. Such presuppositionless knowledge would constitute the given element in our knowledge, the rest of our knowledge being built upon that foundation. Different conceptions of the given have been proposed by philosophers working within the assumptions of this basic *foundationalist* structure (although we shall see in chapter 5 that there are also non-foundationalist versions of the given). *Empiricists* such as John Locke held that the data of immediate sensory experience and introspection are among the items that constitute these fundamental starting points for knowledge; while traditional *rationalists* and classical metaphysicians such as René Descartes have held that certain primary principles of reason or intellect are the self-evident 'givens' on which rests the superstructure of our knowledge.

Sellars' EPM launched a powerful attack on the entire "framework of givenness" that he argues is shared by all foundationalist approaches to the structure of our knowledge. His most prominent criticisms in EPM helped to bring about the demise in particular of influential empiricist *sense-datum* epistemologies at mid-century, but his general critique of the whole idea of the given remains at the center of much discussion in epistemology today. In place of foundationalism Sellars offered an account of our knowledge as characterized by *holism* and *fallibilism*: it is the whole structure of a conceptual scheme that ultimately meets the test of experience, and any belief or presupposition, whether it is an intellectual 'first principle' or a 'direct empirical observation', is open to rejection and replacement if an alternative conception and better explanation presents itself.

This is closely related to what has been called Sellars' *explanationist* epistemology: his emphasis on the role of 'inference to the best explanation' as the primary source of epistemic justification, whether such explanatory inferences are explicitly proposed in scientific theories or only implicitly available in our reason-giving practices in everyday life. On Sellars' holistic account of our knowledge, as he puts it in the following well-known passage, "in characterizing an episode or a state as that of *knowing*, we are not giving an empirical description of that episode or state; we are placing it in the logical space of reasons, of justifying and being able to justify what one says" (EPM VIII.36). We shall explore Sellars' famous views on the myth of the given and the logical space of reasons in detail in chapter 5, although the argument there will be seen also to depend in part upon his 'inferentialist' conception of meaning and his 'functional role' account of conceptual thinking as developed in chapters 3 and 4.[2]

The reason the rejection of the idea of the given was so important to Sellars is that it forms a crucial part of his overall approach to resolving the most fundamental problem that he argues confronts the contemporary philosopher. As Sellars conceives it, this task is to successfully overcome, by fusing together into one coherent "synoptic vision," the apparent clash between what he called the *manifest image* and the *scientific image* of 'man-in-the-world' (PSIM, 1962).[3] Like the myth of the given, Sellars' distinction between these two 'images' or all-comprehensive conceptions of the nature of the human being and the world has become a familiar one in contemporary philosophy, at least by name. The nature of the manifest and scientific images, the sources of their ostensible clash, and the philosophical tasks that this clash generates will be outlined in chapter 1, and the resulting set of problems will form the structure of the rest of the book.

The clash between the manifest and scientific images pertains to certain *prima facie* conflicts between the world as perceptibly manifest to and conceived by sophisticated common sense, in contrast to the conception of the world developed in modern scientific theories from the seventeenth century to the present. The revolution in physics represented most famously by Galileo and Newton gradually led to the triumph of the idea that all natural phenomena should in principle (if not yet in fact) be explainable in terms of physical laws governing mere matter-in-motion, without the need to resort to 'teleological' explanation in terms of purposes, essences, or designed goals in nature. With the subsequent chemical and Darwinian biological revolutions, along with the development of quantum and relativity physics as well as neurophysiological and cognitive research into the mind/brain, Sellars contends that it has become a *regulative ideal* or rational goal of the scientific enterprise that not only inanimate matter but also all living things should in principle be entirely explicable in terms of the postulated entities and laws of the various natural sciences.

As a result, however, this omnivorous scientific image of the world has continued to raise the sorts of questions that were pursued by all the early modern philosophers, most strikingly by Descartes himself and by Immanuel Kant. What is the nature of my own consciousness, of my thinking self, in the midst of all this complex atomic and subatomic matter-in-motion? How are we to imagine that conceptual thinking could be explainable in such physicalistic terms? And are the qualitative aspects of our sensory consciousness – our subjective experiences of color, for instance – also entirely explainable in terms of the swarms and fields of *colorless* microphysical particles that physics assures us exhaustively compose all things? How are free will, norms of rationality, intentional action, and moral responsibility possible in the purposeless world of matter described by science?

As we shall see in chapter 1, Sellars articulates his account of the clash between the manifest and scientific images of the human being in the natural world in terms of questions concerning the very possibility of these three fundamental dimensions of human experience: the nature of conceptual thinking, sensory consciousness, and rational willing. And as we shall see throughout subsequent chapters, Sellars developed often radically new ways of thinking about our own nature as sensing, thinking, knowing, valuing, and rationally active beings, which will enable us finally (or so he argues) to understand how that same human nature is also entirely and exhaustively explainable in terms of the picture of the natural world that is currently developing and is ideally projected within the scientific image. Sellars' task, then, is to envision how we could explain our own human nature naturalistically without 'explaining it away' altogether, in what will be characterized in this book as Sellars' *naturalism with a normative turn*.

We shall find that in the course of exploring and attempting to advance this overall meta-philosophical aim, Sellars originated many other conceptions that have since become highly influential notions that are vigorously debated within contemporary academic philosophy. He has correctly been credited by Daniel Dennett (1987) with being the originator during the 1950s of the subsequently dominant *functionalist* account of the nature of thinking (chapter 4), which Sellars built upon a conceptual role or inferentialist account of meaning along with a novel nominalist account of abstract entities (chapter 3). Yet early on Sellars simultaneously raised what has come to be known as the 'hard problem' of sensory consciousness as an insuperable difficulty for any such functionalist account, arguing that this problem necessitates a radically different approach to that aspect of consciousness (or so he argues; see chapters 5 and 6). Sellars also, as Ernest Sosa (2003) has recently noted, clearly anticipated already at mid-century the basic structure of the recent disputes between 'internalism' and 'externalism' in contemporary epistemology (chapter 5); and he defended a robust *scientific realism* during a time when the scene was largely dominated by logical positivists and empiricists (chapter 2). There is no doubt that Sellars was a highly original and systematic philosopher, among the most significant thinkers of the twentieth century.

So who was Wilfrid Sellars?[4]

Wilfrid Stalker Sellars was born in Ann Arbor, Michigan on May 20, 1912 to two first cousins and Canadians by birth, Helen Maud (Stalker) Sellars and Roy Wood Sellars. Soon after followed the birth of Wilfrid's sister Cecily in 1913. His father Roy Wood Sellars (1880–1973), who was raised in Michigan and taught philosophy at the University of Michigan when Wilfrid was born, was a well-known founder of the critical realist movement in early twentieth-century American philosophy, as the author of *Critical Realism: A Study of the Nature and Conditions of Knowledge* (1916). It is worth saying a few words about the philosophy of Sellars *père* here at the start, since there are instructive continuities and differences between the philosophical outlooks of the father and the son.[5]

Roy Wood Sellars' anti-skeptical philosophy insisted that we should start from a presumption in favor of both our ordinary knowledge and our reflective scientific knowledge of the world. Critical realism is the view that, as common sense rightly insists, we do have referentially direct perceptual knowledge of the external material world as it is in itself; however, scientific and philosophical reflection also reveal that this knowledge is both causally and substantively mediated by the sensory contents that are produced in the knower by the object. The result is that philosophical accounts that ascribe experienced sensory qualities to the external objects themselves can in various crucial respects be highly misleading or mistaken regarding the true nature of our perceptual knowledge.[6] Two of Roy Wood Sellars' other most important books, *Evolutionary Naturalism* (1922) and *The Philosophy of*

Physical Realism (1932), outline a conception of the human being as a complex 'emergent' product of organic evolution, engaged in a dynamic and multi-levelled cognitive, causal, and valuational relationship with its environment. With respect to the mind–body problem, Roy Wood Sellars developed what he called the *double knowledge* approach. We have knowledge of our biological brain-mind from the 'inside', as it were, in our awareness of the experienced contents of our own qualitative states of consciousness. But we know the *same* biological brain-mind from the 'outside,' scientifically, as a functionally adaptive cognitive mechanism or structure that is geared to its environment.

Roy Wood Sellars' non-reductively materialist naturalism also extended to a refreshingly frank and morally committed atheism. (Son Wilfrid would later report that "as a second generation atheist, I was completely at ease about the subject [of religion] and over the years I have taken great intellectual pleasure in exploring abstruse issues in theology in the classroom and in private discussion," AR 281.) Sellars and many other like-minded thinkers called for a reorientation of religious values in the direction of what he called a "religious humanism," based essentially on common moral values and the aspiration of increasing human welfare. Roy Wood Sellars was in fact the author of the first draft of the *Humanist Manifesto* of 1933, which was signed by many leading intellectuals of the time, including Sellars' more famous philosophical contemporary, John Dewey.

Wilfrid Sellars' philosophy exhibits both obvious and not so obvious continuities with all of the above themes in his father's work. The substance of these views, however, was quite radically transformed by the son's immersion in the 'linguistic turn' that took place in twentieth-century philosophy, which was inspired in particular by British and European thinkers such as G. E. Moore, Gottlob Frege, Bertrand Russell, Ludwig Wittgenstein, and Rudolf Carnap. This fundamental change in philosophical method and approach was central to the development throughout the century of what came to be known as *analytic philosophy*, which continues to flourish as a leading style of philosophizing today.[7]

Already an avid and somewhat solitary reader, from the age of nine Sellars attended schools first in New England and then in Paris, where he learned French (his mother translated Célestin Bouglé's *Evolution of Values* in 1926). He then attended the junior high and high schools run by the University of Michigan at Ann Arbor, graduating in 1929 with a strong interest in mathematics. This was followed by further studies at the Lycée Louis Le Grand while he was in Paris with his mother and sister, during which time the stock market crashed and young Sellars read "the philosophical and quasi-philosophical polemical literature which is the life blood of French intellectuals," including a strong dose of Marxist political philosophy (AR 279). Sellars later reported that about this time it "suddenly hit me that my father was a philosopher and that I knew nothing about this dimension of his existence. [. . .] Needless to say, I found his views congenial from the start and [. . .] a dialogue was initiated which has continued for some forty-two years" (AR 280).

After six months at the University of Munich, where he learned German and "soon became convinced that Hitler would in one way or another gain power" (AR 280), he returned to attend the University of Michigan in 1931. At Michigan Sellars studied mathematics, economics, and philosophy, graduating two years later. He tells us that at this time his "first serious work in philosophy was in C. H. Langford's course on Locke, Berkeley, and Hume. Actually, it was at least as much on G. E. Moore and Cambridge Analysis as it was on the Empiricists" (AR 281). He also studied the metaphysics of time and was inclined toward a 'substance ontology' as opposed to an 'event ontology' – a position he would also later defend as the ontology of the manifest image, in contrast to the 'absolute process' ontology that he would eventually defend in relation to the emerging scientific image (cf. Sellars TWO, MP, and FMPP, and chapter 6 below). At Michigan Sellars also studied C. I. Lewis and C. H. Langford's *Symbolic Logic*, and while he was deeply impressed by the new mathematical logic of Russell and Whitehead's *Principia Mathematica*, he was and remained "convinced that most transcriptions of philosophically interesting concepts into logical forms were wildly implausible" (AR 282). Somehow the new formal insights would have to be put to use within a more realistic account of the rich structure of human cognition and of the causal and logical 'modalities' (of necessity, possibility, etc.).

In 1933 Sellars went to the University of Buffalo as a graduate teaching assistant, where he received his MA with a thesis on 'Substance, Change, and Event' in 1934 (available on Chrucky's Sellars website). There he studied Kant's *Critique of Pure Reason* and Husserl with the phenomenologist Marvin Farber, whose "combination of utter respect for the structure of Husserl's thought with the equally firm conviction that this structure could be given a naturalistic interpretation was undoubtedly a key influence on my own subsequent philosophical strategy" (AR 283). In the fall of 1934 Sellars entered Oriel College, Oxford on a Rhodes Scholarship, two years later receiving his first class honors BA (later officially an MA) in philosophy, politics, and economics.

While at Oxford Sellars was influenced in different ways by H. A. Prichard, Cook Wilson, C. D. Broad, and H. H. Price, overall in directions that led him toward realism in perceptual epistemology and toward Prichard's 'deontological intuitionism' in ethics. However, somehow Prichard's realist interpretation of moral obligation and the logic of 'ought' would have to be combined, Sellars thought, with insights from the naturalistic account of moral motivation that was emerging in the new 'emotivism' (AR 284–5; see chapter 7 below).

It was reflection on Kant's critical philosophy, however, that would above all continue to occupy Sellars' thinking, in particular Kant's contention "that a skeptic who grants knowledge of even the simplest fact about an event occurring in Time is, in effect, granting knowledge of the existence of nature as a whole. I was sure he was right" (AR 285). But how could one appropriate Kant's insights without sliding all the way into Kant's own 'transcendental idealism'? "It wasn't until much later that I came to see that the solution of the puzzle lay in *correctly locating the conceptual order in the causal order* and correctly interpreting the causality involved" (AR 286, italics added). We shall see in every chapter of this book that questions concerning the complex relationships between reasons and causes, between the normative and the natural, were to remain at the center of Sellars' philosophical reflections.

In 1936 Sellars embarked on a D.Phil. thesis at Oxford on Kant (with T. D. Weldon), but he moved to Harvard the next year and never would end up completing a Ph.D. thesis. It might have been thought impossible to match or better the list of his teachers at Oxford, but at Harvard his teachers formed an equally impressive All-Star line-up, amongst them D. W. Prall, C. I. Lewis, R. B. Perry, C. L. Stevenson, and W. V. O. Quine. Through Quine, Sellars was introduced to the work of Rudolf Carnap, who over the next decade was to become a powerful influence on his own way of doing philosophy. In 1938 Sellars decided that he wanted to pursue ethical intuitionism as the topic for his Ph.D., until he discovered "how thoroughly and lucidly William Frankena [. . .] had mastered it" (AR 288).

Having married his first wife Mary Sharp in 1938 (Mary died after a long illness in 1970; later his long-time companion and second wife was a former student, Susanna Felder Downie), Sellars was anxious to find employment, and his first academic appointment was at the University of Iowa in the same year. He was responsible for teaching a wide variety of history of philosophy courses and he developed expertise in ancient and medieval philosophy. Sellars and the logical positivist Herbert Feigl at Iowa shared a basic scientific naturalist philosophical outlook, but Feigl (comparable in this respect to Quine) apparently did not share Sellars' uniquely reconciliationist metaphilosophical aims. Writes Sellars of Feigl:

We hit it off immediately, although the seriousness with which I took such ideas as causal necessity, synthetic *a priori* knowledge, intentionality, ethical intuitionism, the problem of universals, etc., etc., must have jarred his empiricist sensibilities. Even when I made it clear that my aim was to map these structures into a naturalistic, even a materialistic metaphysics, he felt, as many have, that I was going around Robin Hood's barn [i.e., taking the long way around to the right conclusion]. (AR 290)

Sellars was also in dialogue at Iowa with Gustav Bergmann and Everett Hall, and in the intellectual neighborhood of the behavioral psychologists Kenneth Spence and Kurt Lewin.

Despite his growing reputation, Sellars had neither finished a Ph.D. nor published anything by 1943 when he applied for a commission and saw active duty in Air Combat Intelligence in the Atlantic Fleet Anti-Submarine Development Detachment at Quonset Point, Rhode Island. After the war, he and his wife Mary, who was now successfully writing short stories, resolved to write for up to ten hours every day to get Wilfrid over his writing block. Eventually in 1947 there appeared the first of what was thereafter to be a steady outpouring of deep and challenging journal articles for the remainder of his highly successful academic career.[8]

In 1946 Sellars had followed Feigl to the University of Minnesota, where he subsequently flourished for thirteen years: as full professor from 1951, as chair of the philosophy department from 1952 to 1959, and as a vigorous participant in the highly respected Minnesota Center for Philosophy of Science founded by Feigl in 1953. Feigl and Sellars co-edited the long-standard anthology *Readings in Philosophical Analysis* in 1949, which was followed by Sellars and Hospers' similarly influential anthology *Readings in Ethical Theory* in 1952. In 1950 Feigl and Sellars co-founded *Philosophical Studies*, the first journal in America explicitly devoted to the new 'analytic' approach to philosophy. These were all significant events in the development of analytic philosophy in America.

From 1959 to 1963 Sellars was professor of philosophy in a divided department at Yale, until he was lured to the University of Pittsburgh, where he happily remained for twenty-six years until his death in 1989. Pittsburgh quickly became and has remained one of the top departments of philosophy in America.

The list of influential philosophers who either were students of Sellars or whose views he strongly influenced is very impressive indeed. Hector Neri-Castañeda (Ph.D. 1954) at Minnesota, and Jay Rosenberg (Ph.D. 1966) and Paul Churchland (Ph.D. 1969) at Pittsburgh were among those who wrote Ph.D. theses under Sellars' supervision. Sellars' philosophy plays an important role in the thought of such well-known philosophers as Bas van Fraassen, Ruth Millikan, Richard Rorty, Daniel Dennett, John McDowell, Gilbert Harman, David Lewis, William Lycan, Robert Brandom, Patricia Churchland, Laurence Bonjour, Michael Williams, and Keith Lehrer. By all accounts Sellars was at his best in dialogue as a teacher and colleague, and he clearly made a lasting impression on his former students.

I will not attempt a chronological or thematic survey of Sellars' philosophical writings here, but will rather let their importance show through the discussions to follow. As to his personal characteristics, Sellars was apparently a rather private person who enjoyed gardening, baseball, and politics. Most of all, however, all who knew him recount how he thrived on the sort of animated dialectical philosophical discussions with students and colleagues which were, as he saw it, a participation in the same ongoing dialogue that he maintained in his writings with his historical philosophical colleagues – Plato and Aristotle, Hume and Kant, Russell and Wittgenstein – the dialogue which, for Sellars, constitutes philosophy itself.

Our exploration of Sellars' conception of the nature and aims of philosophy, however, begins in chapter 1.

1

The Philosophical Quest and the Clash of the Images

There is no better entryway into Sellars' philosophical system than to begin with his reflections on what he characterized in 'Philosophy and the Scientific Image of Man' (1962) as "the philosophical quest" (PSIM 1). This first chapter will include a hefty sampling of quotations from Sellars in order to convey a sense of the shape of the key problems as he characterized them. Later chapters will provide the more detailed and critical analyses.

The quest for a stereoscopic fusion of the manifest and scientific images

In one of his most frequently quoted passages, Sellars wrote that the "aim of philosophy, abstractly formulated, is to understand how things in the broadest possible sense of the term hang together in the broadest possible sense of the term" (PSIM 1). In his 1971 Matchette lectures on 'The Structure of Knowledge' he put it this way:

> The ideal aim of philosophizing is to become *reflectively* at home in the full complexity of the multi-dimensional conceptual system in terms of which we suffer, think, and act. I say 'reflectively', because there is a sense in which, by the sheer fact of leading an unexamined, but conventionally satisfying life, we are at home in this complexity. It is not until we have eaten the apple with which the serpent philosopher tempts us, that we begin to stumble on the familiar and to feel that haunting sense of alienation which is treasured by each new generation as its unique possession. This alienation, this gap between oneself and one's world, can only be resolved by eating the apple to the core; for after the first bite there is no return to innocence. There are many anodynes, but only

one cure. We may philosophize well or ill, but we must philosophize. (SK I.3)

The aim of this stage-setting chapter is to gain a sense of what Sellars means by the "alienation, this gap between oneself and one's world" that comes to light only as a result of philosophical reflection, and which he thinks "can only be resolved by eating the apple to the core": that is, only through further sustained and systematic reflection in which "no intellectual holds are barred" (PSIM 1).

Sellars has chosen his words carefully in referring to "the multi-dimensional conceptual system in terms of which we *suffer*, *think*, and *act*." As we shall see, he wants to structure the issues raised by our loss of intellectual innocence in terms of certain difficulties that stand in the way of our becoming "reflectively at home" with our understanding of our own nature as (1) passively *sensing*, (2) conceptually *thinking*, and (3) rationally *active* beings. Ironically, it is one of our greatest intellectual achievements in opening up the nature of reality to us – the development of the modern natural sciences since the sixteenth century – which has by its very success threatened to alienate us intellectually from that same natural world. Sellars' overarching philosophical aim is firstly to articulate the nature and sources of our loss of intellectual innocence, and then to cure our resulting sense of intellectual alienation by eating the apple to the core.

The philosopher or the philosophically inclined, according to Sellars, strives for "a reflective insight into the intellectual landscape as a whole," attempting to grasp in one overall "synoptic vision" how it *all* hangs together (PSIM 2–3). Since it is clearly impossible for any thinker to competently know her way around all the different specialized fields of human knowledge, Sellars recognizes that the idea of "the synoptic vision of true philosophy" is what Kant would have called a *regulative ideal of reason*. We seek "to approximate to the philosophical aim" (PSIM 2–3) through a sustained 'second-order' reflection on the general principles, methods, and assumptions that characterize the 'first-order' practices and results of the various other disciplines and dimensions of human experience.

In fact, however, Sellars argues that the most important tasks facing the synoptic philosopher may be brought together in terms of two idealized conceptual frameworks that he calls the *manifest image* and the *scientific image* of 'man-in-the-world.' Thus he contends that there is

a crucial duality which confronts the contemporary philosopher at the very beginning of his enterprise. Here the most appropriate analogy is stereoscopic vision, where two differing perspectives on a landscape are fused into one coherent experience.

For the philosopher is confronted not by one complex many-dimensional picture, the unity of which, such as it is, he must come to appreciate; but by *two* pictures of essentially the same order of complexity, each of which purports to be a complete picture of man-in-the-world, and which after separate scrutiny, he must fuse into one vision. Let me refer to these two perspectives, respectively, as the *manifest* and the *scientific* images of man-in-the-world. (PSIM 4–5)

one vision

general view of the whole

The synoptic vision aimed at by the philosopher may in this way be conceived as the achieving of a synoptic, stereoscopic fusion into one coherent picture of two global or all-comprehensive 'images' of the nature of the human-being-in-the-world. What we need to consider now is in what sense and why Sellars holds that this is so.

Does it have to be "human"?

Sellars indicates that he is "using 'image' in this sense as a metaphor for conception" (PSIM 5). Contemporary philosophy thus has as its primary aim a comprehensive understanding of how the two different *conceptual frameworks* of the manifest image and the scientific image may be integrated into one coherent conception of the nature of the human person within the natural world.[1] While the manifest image and the scientific image both exist concretely in the form of various actual historical conceptual practices ("as much a part and parcel of the world as this platform or the Constitution of the United States"), Sellars explains that they

with a.i???

are both 'idealizations' in something like the sense in which a frictionless body or an ideal gas is an idealization. They are designed to illuminate the inner dynamics of the development of philosophical ideas. [. . .] The story is complicated by the fact that each image has a history, and while the main outlines of what I shall call the manifest image took shape in the mists of pre-history, the scientific image, promissory notes apart, has taken shape before our very eyes. (PSIM 5)

a.i is taught on both images

Sellars regarded it as an indispensable method in philosophy to attempt to construct relatively clear, ideal types or models – for example, 'empiricism' and 'rationalism' as types of approach in the theory of knowledge – while recognizing that one will gradually need to complicate and significantly revise the initially oversimplified, tidy distinctions as the investigation proceeds to the details. The manifest and scientific images are idealized conceptual frameworks that reflect real historical intellectual developments, each framework offering a characterization of the nature of reality that may be evaluated as to its ultimate adequacy as a representation of how things really are.

In upcoming chapters we shall be examining in greater detail the complex and evolving conceptual structure of Sellars' manifest and scientific images themselves. However, in order to introduce in a general way the fundamental question of the ostensible conflict or 'clash' between the two images, we may begin with Sellars' characterization of the manifest image as "the conceptual framework in terms of which man experienced himself and the world long before the revolution in physics was even a twinkle in the eye of Democritus," the ancient Greek 'atomist' philosopher (SK I.22). It is potentially misleading but useful for many purposes to think of the manifest image as the world of 'common sense' (Sellars himself often uses the two phrases interchangeably, as at *SM* V.64). It is misleading because Sellars intends the manifest image to include various highly sophisticated conceptual refinements that have been painstakingly articulated within what he calls the "perennial" tradition in philosophy.[2] Another respect in which it is misleading simply to equate the manifest image with common sense is due to the fact that the former is conceived to include whatever observational or empirical refinements have been generated by the inductive statistical methods of the natural and social sciences. The story of the emergence and development of the manifest image would be the story of humanity's own complex and evolving intellectual history (see PSIM parts I–III, about which more in a moment).

Granting these and other important qualifications, however, it will be useful to begin by thinking of Sellars' distinction between his two global images in terms of what philosophers have often contrasted as the world as conceived by common sense in terms of *manifest sense-perceptible properties* – the colors and shapes (or, more generally, the 'proper and common sensible properties') of ordinary persisting physical objects, for example – as opposed to the often strange and colorless scientifically postulated world of swarming microphysical atoms and subatomic particles that is *imperceptible to our unaided senses*.[3] Thus the key distinction between Sellars' idealized manifest and scientific images ultimately turns out to be the following:

> There is [. . .] one type of scientific reasoning which [the manifest image], by stipulation, does *not* include, namely that which involves the postulation of imperceptible entities, and principles pertaining to them, to explain the behaviour of perceptible things. [. . .] And, indeed, what I have referred to as the 'scientific' image of man-in-the-world and contrasted with the 'manifest' image, might better be called the 'postulational' or 'theoretical' image. (PSIM 7)

In our investigation of Sellars' scientific realism in chapter 2 we shall explore in detail the nature of *postulational theoretical explanation* in science that is appealed to in this passage. The general idea, however, may be brought out by considering the philosophical reaction by Descartes and other early modern philosophers to the "revolution in physics" that had been initiated by Galileo and other 'natural philosophers' since the sixteenth century (cf. PSIM part V). In broad form consideration of this simplified atomistic or 'corpuscularian' scientific picture will bring out the central issues with which we shall be grappling throughout this book.

The clash of the images and the status of the sensible qualities

Following Sellars, let us take as our central case one of the most famous difficulties that arose within the new Galilean and Newtonian scientific frameworks, according to which, we shall suppose, every material object is entirely composed of complex swarms of very tiny, imperceptible atoms. This was the problem of the place of *color* and other sensible qualities within this new 'particulate' or atomistic ontology.[4] In 'Philosophy and the Scientific Image of Man' Sellars refers to the British physicist Arthur S. Eddington's famous description, in his book *The Nature of the Physical World* (1931), of the 'two' very different 'tables,' so to speak, which he is led to conceive in relation to the *one table* at which he is sitting. As Eddington writes of his 'two tables':

> One of them has been familiar to me from my earliest years. [. . .] It has extension; it is comparatively permanent; it is colored; above all it is *substantial*. [. . .] Table no. 2 is my scientific table. It is a more recent acquaintance and I do not feel so familiar with it.[5] It does not belong to the world previously mentioned – that world which spontaneously appears around me when I open my eyes, though how much of it is objective and how much subjective I do not here consider. [. . .] My scientific table is mostly emptiness. Sparsely scattered in that emptiness are numerous electric charges rushing about with great speed; but their combined bulk amounts to less than a billionth of the bulk of the table itself. [. . .] There is nothing *substantial* about my second table. It is nearly all empty space – space pervaded, it is true, by fields of force, but these are assigned to the category of 'influences', not of 'things'. [. . .] I need not tell you that modern physics has by delicate test and remorseless logic assured me that my second scientific table is the only one which is really there – wherever 'there' may be. (Eddington 1931: 70–2)

Eddington's example of the 'two tables' brings out dramatically – if somewhat problematically[6] – the central philosophical problem-space that Sellars epitomizes in the phrase *the clash of the images* (PSIM 25). Sellars himself frames the issue and the main resulting philosophical options, as he sees them, as follows:

> The initial challenge of the scientific image was directed at the manifest image of inanimate nature. It proposed to construe physical things, in a manner already adumbrated by Greek atomism, as systems of

imperceptible particles, lacking the perceptible qualities of manifest nature. Three lines of thought seemed to be open: (1) Manifest objects are identical with systems of imperceptible particles in that simple sense in which a forest is identical with a number of trees. (2) Manifest objects are what really exist; systems of imperceptible particles being 'abstract' or 'symbolic' ways of representing them. (3) Manifest objects are 'appearances' to human minds of a reality which is constituted by systems of imperceptible particles. (PSIM 26)

The sort of 'instrumentalist' and 'anti-realist' empiricist approaches to the nature of scientific explanation characteristic of (2), and against which Sellars launches strong independent arguments, will be among the topics examined in chapter 2. Let us focus here, then, on introducing Sellars' general attitude toward (1) and (3).

Sellars argues against (1) by means of what has come to be known as his *grain argument* ('grain' here basically refers to the 'particulate' ontology of microphysics), which he articulates in terms of his well-known example of a pink ice cube.[7] While it is of course true, he points out, that "systems [can] have properties which their parts do not have," the "case of a pink ice cube, it would seem clear, cannot be treated in this way":

> *Pink* does not seem to be made up of imperceptible qualities in the way in which being a ladder is made up of being cylindrical (the rungs), rectangular (the frame), wooden, etc. The manifest ice cube presents itself to us as something which is pink through and through, a pink continuum, all the regions of which, however small, are pink. It presents itself to us as *ultimately homogeneous*; and an ice cube variegated in colour is, though not homogeneous in its specific colour, 'ultimately homogeneous', in the sense to which I am calling attention, with respect to the generic trait of being coloured. (PSIM 26)

A few preliminary clarificatory comments on this passage are in order.

Sellars chooses the example of a transparent pink ice cube looking smoothly pink through and through, in all its perceptible parts – *homogeneously* pink, to use Sellars' technical term – in part because it vividly illustrates his claim that our manifest conception (or equivalently, for Sellars, the 'phenomenology') of ordinary perceptible physical objects takes them in general to have colors as their intrinsic contents.[8] We 'see of' an apple its smooth reddish surface, for example, and we vividly imagine the juicy whiteness (to mix sense modalities) of its insides. Sellars calls these intrinsic sensible features of objects their *occurrent* sensible qualities, as opposed to their 'dispositional' and causal properties. A given pink cube might appear to be ice, but whether it is in fact a piece of ice or not depends on its 'iffy' causal properties:

if you put it in your drink, for instance, it will cool your drink. The cube's iciness is a dispositional or causal property of the cube, whereas the pinkness is an occurrent sensible property of the cube.

Many scientists and philosophers have been tempted to interpret the colors of objects, too, as causal or dispositional ('iffy') properties rather than intrinsic contents or features of those objects. Galileo, Descartes, Locke, and many other thinkers influenced by scientific considerations argued that the colors, sounds, tastes, and other proper sensibles that we ascribe to objects are mere *secondary qualities* or causal 'powers' of those objects to produce the corresponding experiences or sensations of color, sound, etc., in the perceiver. These causal powers were conceived to be based on the *primary qualities* or common sensible properties of size, shape, motion, etc., that were taken to be properly ascribable to the matter (ultimately, the imperceptible atoms, etc.) that makes up the physical world as it is in itself. However, while Sellars will eventually contend that *something* like such an account is ultimately correct (along the lines of (3) above), such views are badly mistaken if they are put forward as an account or analysis of the conceptual structure of our ordinary or manifest experience of the world. As Sellars puts the phenomenological point, "Only a theory-intoxicated philosopher can look at a pink ice cube in daylight and suppose that *to see it to be pink* is to see it to have the power to cause normal observers to have sensations of pink when they look at it in daylight" (SK I.26). As conceived within the manifest image or in ordinary experience, the colors of objects are as much intrinsic properties of them as their shapes, which, as Bishop Berkeley rightly pointed out in his critique of Locke, occur seamlessly together as the *form and content* of the objects of our manifest experiences.

Sellars' so-called 'grain argument' in the passage above is very roughly that, contrary to the suggestion in (1) above, the "*ultimately homogeneous*" occurrent pinkness that is intrinsic to the manifest-perceptible pink ice cube as presented to us cannot plausibly be identified with or reduced to any properties or relations of the *system of imperceptible objects* of which science informs us the ice cube is nonetheless entirely composed.[9] In reflecting on this point Sellars puts forward what he takes to be a plausible "*principle of reducibility*" (PSIM 35, italics added; cf. SSIS), "which can be formulated approximately as follows":

> If an object is *in a strict sense* a system of objects, then every property of the object must consist in the fact its constituents have such and such qualities and stand in such and such relations or, roughly,
>> every property of a system of objects consists of properties of, and relations between, its constituents. (PSIM 27)

According to Sellars, once the scientific image ontology is on the table, and every physical object is thus conceived to be "*in a strict sense* a system of objects" in the form of swarms of colorless, imperceptible microphysical particles, our innocence is lost. We can no longer account for the sensible qualities of objects in the way that we can explain their structural and functional properties (recall the ladder example), namely in terms of "properties of, and relations between" their ultimate constituent parts.

It was considerations such as these that led Galileo, Descartes, Locke, and the other thinkers to conclude "that manifest physical objects are 'appearances' *to human perceivers* of systems of imperceptible particles which is alternative (3) above" (PSIM 27). This is not the absurd claim that the objects of common sense lack color – *of course* bananas are yellow – but rather the philosophical claim that the significance of the entire framework conception or manifest image of physical objects must be *reconceived* if it is to be properly integrated or 'stereoscopically fused' with the emerging scientific image of the nature of reality:

> It is familiar fact that those features of the manifest world which play no role in mechanical explanation were relegated by Descartes and other interpreters of the new physics to the minds of the perceiver. Colour, for example, was said to exist only in sensation; its *esse* to be *percipi*. It was argued, in effect, that what scientifically motivated reflection recognizes to be states of the perceiver are conceptualized in ordinary experience as traits of independent physical things, indeed that these supposed independent coloured things are actually conceptual constructions which ape the mechanical systems of the real world. (PSIM 29)

Again, this "is not the denial of a belief *within a framework*, but a challenge to the framework" (PSIM 27). Sellars' own ultimate view, despite his many sharp disagreements with Descartes, will share much in common with the broadly Cartesian view expressed in the passage quoted above. The road will be a long one, however, for many of the subsequent bites into the apple after the initial loss of innocence led the early modern philosophers from Descartes to Hume down certain tempting dark corridors out of which philosophers are still attempting to find their way today.

Sensing, thinking, and willing: persons as complex physical systems?

Once the proper sensible qualities attributed by common sense to the objects of the 'external world' had in this way been reconceived by the majority of modern natural philosophers to be in fact sensory *states of the perceiver* – as the contents of what were variously called 'perceptions,' 'sense impressions,' or 'ideas' – the focus of philosophical attention naturally shifted to the question of the nature of the human mind itself. The problem now, however, is that *"unless thinking and feeling are capable of interpretation as complex interactions of physical particles"* (PSIM 29, italics in original), the original problem of the 'ultimate homogeneity' of the experienced sensible qualities has simply been reintroduced in the context of inquiry into the nature of the human mind. Living human bodies and brains, like everything else in nature, are conceived within the scientific image as complex systems of microphysical particles. The difficulty in this new context, then, is

> that the feature which we referred to as 'ultimate homogeneity', and which characterizes the perceptible qualities of things, e.g. their colour, seems to be essentially lacking in the domain of the definable states of the nerves and their interactions. Putting it crudely, colour expanses in the manifest world consist of regions which are themselves colour expanses, and these consist in their turn of regions which are colour expanses, and so on; whereas the state of a group of neurons, though it has regions which are also states of groups of neurons, has ultimate regions which are *not* states of groups of neurons but rather states of single neurons. And the same is true if we move to the finer grained level of biochemical process. (PSIM 35)

In addition to this vexed issue concerning sensory qualities, having now turned our attention to the nature of the human subject we are also immediately confronted with further questions concerning how *conceptual thinking, rationality, free will, intentional action,* and all the other dimensions of human cognition and agency could conceivably be interpreted in accordance with Sellars' 'principle of reducibility' as consisting of "properties of, and relations between" the constituent microphysical entities of which the evolving scientific image informs us the human animal is entirely composed.

The deep difficulties involved in trying to conceive of how sensing, thinking, and willing might in principle be explainable in terms of the properties and relations of the complex swarms of material 'atoms in the void' posited in the new 'mechanical philosophy' were vividly illustrated by Leibniz's famous thought experiment in 1714 against the very idea of such a thinking and perceiving material 'machine':

> [W]e must confess that perception, and what depends on it, is inexplicable in terms of mechanical reasons, that is, through shapes and motions. If we imagine that there is a machine whose structure makes it think, sense, and have perceptions, we could conceive it enlarged, keeping the same proportions, so that we could enter into it, as one enters into a mill. Assuming that, when inspecting its interior, we will only find parts that

push one another, and we will never find anything to explain a perception. And so, we should seek perception in the simple substance and not in the composite or in the machine. (Leibniz 1714, §17)

Leibniz's mill-sized 'thinking machine' analogy is intended to suggest, to put it in more recent terms, that nowhere in the complex physical circuitry and patterns of firing neurons will you find a *thought*, or an act of *will*, or a *perception* (which is not to deny that there are systematic *correlations* between those physical and mental phenomena). Leibniz, Descartes, and many other modern philosophers thus concluded, as indeed Plato had long ago in the *Phaedo*, that it is only in a 'simple' or perfectly indivisible *immaterial soul* that conceptual thinking could conceivably be found. And once the 'soul + body' dualistic conclusion had been drawn, the puzzles above concerning the homogeneity of the experienced sensible qualities could be addressed by seeking to assign their most problematic features to the same non-physical home.

As every first-year student of philosophy learns, however, the soul–body dualism imported from the ancients rested uneasily (to put it mildly) with the new mechanistic ontology of the scientific image of the world, according to which the natural universe is conceived as a *causally closed physical system* (see chapter 6, however). Roughly put, all physical effects, including those involving the redistribution of the atoms making up one's own body and brain, were conceived by the new mechanistic physics to have necessary and sufficient physical causes. If the causal efficacy of one's thoughts, perceptions, and willings required the non-physical, immaterial soul's production of physical effects in the brain and body, then the prospects for an intellectually satisfying stereoscopic integration of the manifest and scientific images of 'man-in-the-world' seemed to have been rendered no less problematic as a result of these particular bites into the apple.

On the other hand, if we reject all of the philosophically and scientifically problematic variations on soul–body dualism, how are we to explain the ultimate homogeneity of our sensory experiences, not to mention our capacities for rational thought and purposive action, compatibly with the materialistic scientific image of the world? Even if we should not be tempted down the road of soul–body dualism, Sellars contends that there are additional reasons beyond those canvassed so far why it might seem an impossible task to successfully integrate the manifest and scientific images of 'man-in-the-world.' To bring out these further challenges to any such attempt at a synoptic vision we need to look more closely at the sophisticated manifest image conception of the nature of the human being as Sellars takes this to have been refined within the perennial philosophy from Plato to Kant and Wittgenstein.

Standing out among all its other aspects, the manifest image is centrally conceived as the framework of the human being's *self-conception*. Sellars believes that there is a profound truth, but also a paradoxical element, in the manifest image conception that there is a radical difference in kind between human beings as *thinking selves* in contrast with every other kind of being in the natural world. The paradox consists in the fact, as Sellars puts it one way with an existentialist turn of phrase, "that man couldn't be man until he encountered himself" (PSIM 6). As a *rational* animal, the human being is capable of conceptual thinking; but

> anything which can properly be called conceptual thinking can occur only within a *framework* of conceptual thinking in terms of which it can be criticized, supported, refuted, in short, evaluated. To be able to think is to be able to measure one's thoughts by *standards of correctness*, of relevance, of evidence. In this sense a diversified conceptual framework is a whole which, however sketchy, is prior to its parts, and cannot be construed as a coming together of parts which are already conceptual in character. The conclusion is difficult to avoid that the transition from pre-conceptual patterns of behaviour to conceptual thinking was a *holistic* one, a jump to a level of awareness which is irreducibly new, a jump which was the coming into being of man. (PSIM 6, all italics added)

Sellars will argue (as we shall see in chapters 3 through 5) that the ability to think in terms of concepts – which he contends, following Kant, is itself required in order to have the distinctively human conceptual awareness *of oneself as experiencing a world* – is an ability that can only be acquired against the background of a larger network of normative 'standards of correctness.' The general idea will be that self-awareness, the distinguishing characteristic of human beings, is possible only within a wider system of conceptual rules or norms that constitutes what it is, for instance, to apply a concept correctly as opposed to incorrectly, or to reason validly as opposed to invalidly.

It will be an important point to remember that Sellars *agrees* with this aspect of the manifest image and the perennial philosophy. Sellars' own philosophical outlook will turn upon his conception of the holistic, systematic nature of human conceptual thinking, as well as the importance of distinguishing the *normative* level of human experience from all the other, 'lower' levels of nature, for which (as the above passage suggests by contrast) the parts are in some sense prior to the whole. The crucial question, as we shall discover in subsequent chapters, concerns the nature and status of this distinction.

As conceived within the manifest image and the perennial philosophy (or the 'broadly Platonic' tradition, as Sellars also calls it), human rationality is *sui generis* and its emergence is in a sense inexplicable.

Ultimately as conceived within the manifest image alone, we cannot explain *mind* except, ultimately, in terms of *mind*, or at any rate in terms of some ultimate reality that is conceived to be akin to mind (for example, a God or Spirit, Forms or Ideas, the Absolute). What we certainly cannot do from within the perspective of the manifest image alone is somehow explain mind as the product of complex, piecemeal interactions of matter-in-motion. On Sellars' analogy of the 'stereoscopic view,' by contrast, in the final analysis the scientific image and the manifest image will be fused – contrary to the essential *discontinuity* posited within the manifest image and analyzed by the perennial philosophy – into a *single* systematic account of the human-being-in-nature, involving no such inexplicable or irreducible discontinuities:

> There is a profound truth in this conception of a radical difference in level between man and his precursors. The attempt to understand this difference turns out to be part and parcel of the attempt to encompass in one view the two images of man-in-the-world which I have set out to describe. For, as we shall see, this difference in level appears as an irreducible discontinuity in the *manifest* image, but as, in a sense requiring careful analysis, a reducible difference in the *scientific* image. (PSIM 6)

In one sense irreducible, in another sense reducible: this is what will require especially careful analysis throughout our investigations. In accordance with how Sellars originally framed these issues back in 1953 in his pioneering but less well-known article, 'A Semantical Solution of the Mind–Body Problem' (SSMB), it will turn out that the phenomena of mind, meaning, truth, and knowing are all – "in a sense requiring careful analysis," of course! – what he calls *logically* (i.e., *conceptually*) *irreducible* yet at the same time *causally reducible* phenomena (SSMB; see also O'Shea 2006b). Figuring out what this distinction really amounts to in each case will require diving into the detailed discussions of subsequent chapters. (As we saw Strawson put it, there is no shallow end to the philosophical pool.)

Since Sellars stresses that "man is *essentially* that being which conceives of itself *in terms of the [manifest] image which the perennial philosophy refines and endorses*" (PSIM 8), perhaps the most important challenges for his own stereoscopic fusion will cluster around the question: "to what extent does manifest man survive in the synoptic view which does equal justice to the scientific image which now confronts us?" (PSIM 15). This is due to the fact that "in any sense in which this [manifest] image, in so far as it pertains to man, is a 'false' image, this falsity threatens man himself, inasmuch as he is, in an important sense, the being which has this image of himself" (PSIM 18). This, then, is another steep challenge for the integrating, synoptic philosopher, a conceptual tangle concerning the explanation of the very possibility of rational, conceptual thinking itself – the epicenter, as it were, of the ostensible conflict between the manifest and scientific images of 'man-in-the-world.'

Finally, in addition to the problems facing the synoptic philosopher in relation to the sensible qualities, human sensory consciousness, and conceptual thinking as briefly sketched above, we shall also be faced with "the task of showing that categories pertaining to man as a *person* who finds himself confronted by standards (ethical, logical, etc.) [. . .] can be reconciled with the idea that man is what science says he is" (PSIM 38). The human person is an agent who is capable of acting intentionally, freely, and as guided by rational principles. How can the human animal, understood within the scientific image as a complex bio-physical system, be recognized to be the sort of autonomous rational agent that we take ourselves to be? The distinctions required to tackle these last questions will not have come fully together until the final concluding chapter.

In this chapter we have seen Sellars articulate the clash between the manifest and scientific images of the human-being-in-the-world in terms of certain difficulties that face any account of our capacities for sense perception, for conceptual thinking, and for intentional action. On the idealized scientific image of the human being as "a complex physical system" (PSIM 25), how do we find a place in nature for those qualitative states of sensory consciousness such as our sensations of color, which do not seem to be explainable as functional or structural features of complex systems of the colorless microphysical entities that compose all natural things, including ourselves? Again, how do we find a place for free, rational agency, and for the normative bindingness of rules and prescriptive principles ("To say that man is a rational animal, is to say that man is a creature not of *habits*, but of *rules*," LRB ¶16, 298), within a scientific world of physical processes that seems to harbor no *ought* but only what *is, was,* and *will be*? And finally, how do we explain our capacity for conceptual thought and the grasp of meanings, and for the rational as opposed to merely associative connections characteristic of logical, rule-governed thinking? How do we explain these capacities compatibly with our scientific understanding of the human animal as in principle exhaustively describable – to put it bluntly – as a certain kind of complex physical tissue of tissues, a fleshy coagulation gradually clotted out of the purposeless evolutionary processes of random mutation and natural selection ('ugly bags of mostly water,' as a less fleshy alien on *Star Trek* recently described us)?

These are the challenges to be addressed in upcoming chapters. First, however, they will be posed more sharply by means of a thorough investigation of Sellars' conception of the developing scientific image itself.

2

Scientific Realism and the Scientific Image

At the core of Sellars' account of the clash between the manifest and scientific images is a particular conception of the nature of scientific explanation. More specifically, Sellars contends that the proper analysis "of scientific thought is essential to the *appraisal* of the framework categories of the common-sense picture of the world" (EPM IX.41). The manifest image, as we know, is an empirically and conceptually refined picture of persons acting within the common-sense perceptible world of colored, persisting material objects. The scientific image, by contrast, postulates a largely 'unseen,' multi-dimensional world of colorless micro-particles and fields of force.[1] Sellars' fundamental philosophical quest, as we have seen, is to achieve a unitary, synoptic understanding of how these two apparently conflicting conceived 'worlds' are to be stereoscopically integrated within one coherent conception of our one world.

How this quest is conceived depends to a large extent upon a controversy that is of ancient philosophical lineage but which has taken a particularly revealing shape in the philosophy of science over the last half-century. The debates in this area are highly technical and complex, but the fundamental issues at stake can be streamlined without being oversimplified. The key dispute may be presented as one between two broadly contrasting approaches to the nature of scientific theoretical explanation: *scientific realism* and (as we may call it somewhat arbitrarily to begin with) *standard empiricism*. While each approach will of course attempt to take due account of the role of both observation and theory in scientific explanation, the standard empiricist in the sense I am using the term tends to argue for the primacy of the manifest observable domain, while the scientific realist contends for the primacy of the theoretical domain of unobservables. Questions concerning the relevant senses of 'primacy' involved will of course turn out to be part and parcel of the issues to be investigated.

In the first section we shall lay out in some detail the standard empiricist account of the structure of scientific theories, using as our lead example the kinetic-molecular theory of gases. As our discussion proceeds, 'standard empiricism' will gradually be refined from a *reductive* empiricism into a more nuanced philosophical attitude to our central dispute which we shall call *irenic* empiricism; and eventually by the second section we shall find Sellars engaging in controversy with the *constructive empiricism* of his well-known former student, Bas van Fraassen (whose position differs in important ways from previous empiricist views). Sellars' central objection as I reconstruct it in the second section, however, will be taken to apply to all of these versions of empiricism. The main issue we shall focus upon concerns the complex relationship between theory and observation in scientific explanation. The final section will then bring out the consequences Sellars sees his defense of scientific realism to have in relation to the wider task of achieving a stereoscopic vision of the manifest and scientific images.[2]

'Empiricism' and 'realism' are prime examples of technical philosophical terms with many actual and possible meanings, and although Sellars defends scientific realism, he himself would also take his own view to be a properly *corrected empiricism*. In a nice metaphor, Sellars once called terms such as these "*accordion words* which, by their expansion and contraction, generate so much philosophical music" (SRII 158, italics added). Nonetheless there is a real dispute between these two broad '-ism's once each outlook is appropriately clarified. The result is a complex philosophical dialectic that Sellars in 'Is Scientific Realism Tenable?' (1977) characterized as "one of the most significant dialogues of our time" (SRT 307). Although in this chapter we shall not attempt to explore the latest controversies and standard objections concerning scientific realism in general, the classic disputes and distinctions examined here will find ready application to those ongoing debates.

Empiricist approaches to the interpretation of scientific theories

When Sellars began articulating his novel conception of scientific realism in the 1950s the standard empiricist outlook in the form of *logical positivism* was by far the dominant source of interpretations of the nature of science in Britain and America. Let us begin by considering how a classic example of successful scientific theorizing, the kinetic-molecular theory of gases, would have been reconstructed on a standard logical empiricist or positivist account of scientific explanation.[3] Sellars characteristically holds that the latter 'received empiricist view' is a complex mixture of insights misshapen by certain subtle misconceptions.

Let us suppose that we have observational data suggesting that there are certain empirical regularities that obtain between the pressure, volume, and (absolute) temperature of gases. More particularly, the empirical data confirm the hypothesis that the pressure exerted by a gas varies inversely with the volume of the container at constant temperatures (bigger volume, less pressure, etc.). During the seventeenth and eighteenth centuries the *Boyle–Charles ideal gas law* successfully formulated these empirical relationships between the pressure, volume, and temperature of a gas more precisely as $PV = kT$, where k is a constant. This law is an example of an *observational generalization*, in this case a highly confirmed *empirical law*. Following Sellars, however, let us symbolize observational generalizations in general by putting them in the form of an 'if–then' conditional and observation–kind variables, '$O_i \supset O_j$,' where this is understood as "a generalization which relates two kinds of situation definable in the observation framework" (PH 95–6). The idea is that observational generalizations are observed constant correlations between properties or kinds such that *if* there is a case or instance of O_i, say, O_1, *then* (*ceteris paribus*, and in appropriate circumstances) there will also be a case or instance of O_j, say O_2.

In the nineteenth century the *kinetic theory of gases* was subsequently gradually developed to better explain the behavior of gases by means of the following sorts of *theoretical postulations*. The theoretical model assumed that gases consist of tiny, unobservable, perfectly elastic, spherical molecules in rapid motion, and that these motions are governed by the laws of Newtonian mechanics (along with further assumptions). Furthermore, the pressure exerted on the walls of the container is assumed to be produced by the impacts of these rapidly moving molecules. Finally, it is postulated that the temperature of a gas is proportional to the mean kinetic energy of the molecules that are assumed to compose it. On these theoretical assumptions it turns out that we can in some sense – in *what* sense, exactly, will be examined in this chapter – *'derive'* the empirical Boyle–Charles ideal gas law from the theoretical principles of Newtonian mechanics as applied specifically to these postulated unobservable molecules-in-motion.[4] In short, by postulating a domain of unobservable micro-entities that are assumed to obey certain postulated theoretical laws, the empirical regularity or law concerning the observable phenomena is fully accounted for (and in fact corrected for accuracy) in terms of fundamental theoretical principles that also apply across a wide range of other empirical domains.

Let us label this kinetic-molecular theory 'T' and symbolize the postulated theoretical laws of T by '$T_i \supset T_j$.' The standard empiricist view of scientific explanation may accordingly be symbolized at the most abstract level by 'T $\rightarrow$ ($O_i \supset O_j$)' (cf. PH 95–6), where the arrow '$\rightarrow$' is meant to symbolize the fact that the relevant observational generalizations or empirical laws are supposed to be *logically derivable* from theory T as a whole, in a manner that we must now flesh out in more detail.[5]

Already at this stage, however, we can see how theoretical explanation is conceived on the standard logical empiricist view in terms of a hierarchy of *levels*:

[3]   *Theories* (e.g., T and its postulated theoretical laws, $T_i \supset T_j$)
[2]   Empirical *laws* or observational generalizations (e.g., $O_i \supset O_j$)
[1]   Particular *observations* and measurements (e.g., $O_1, O_2, O_3, \ldots O_n$).

Supposing we have confirmed the generalization or empirical law $O_i \supset O_j$, then on the occasion of observing O_1 (for example, we measure the temperature of a gas), we can proceed to use simple 'if–then' logic either to *predict* the future occurrence or to *explain* the past occurrence of O_2 (say, a rise in pressure). So on this *standard empiricist view of explanation as logical derivation by subsumption under general laws*, we explain or predict particular observations by deriving them as instances of established empirical laws; we explain the empirical laws themselves by logically deriving them from theories; and theories are in turn incorporated within or subsumed by still more embracing theories as scientific knowledge advances.[6] As Sellars conveniently epitomizes this logical empiricist 'levels' account of explanation, we thus have:

[3]   Unexplained Explainers [i.e., fundamental theories]
[2]   Explained Explainers [i.e., observational generalizations, empirical laws]
[1]   Explained Nonexplainers [i.e., particular empirical observations] (cf. LT 120).

So far, however, our discussion has abstracted from a crucial component of the standard empiricist account of theoretical explanation, one that Sellars will proceed to zero-in on. This concerns the role in theories of *correspondence rules* (sometimes also called, with varying emphases, 'bridge principles,' 'coordinating definitions,' 'operational definitions,' or 'rules of interpretation'). In our lead example, correspondence rules are what enable the scientist to make the crucial moves between the theoretical laws concerning posited unobservable kinetic motions of molecules ($T_i \supset T_j$), on the one hand, and the corresponding situation concerning the observable phenomena as described by the

Boyle–Charles gas law ($O_i \supset O_j$), on the other. Sellars in fact makes a further distinction between two kinds of correspondence rule, *substantive* vs. *methodological*, which he illustrates in terms of the postulated connection between temperature and molecular activity which we have been discussing (cf. TE 150):

Substantive correspondence rule:
   Temperature of gas in region R is such and such $\leftrightarrow$
      Mean kinetic energy of molecules in region R is such and such.

Methodological correspondence rule:
   Spectroscope appropriately related to gas shows such and such
      lines $\leftrightarrow$
   Atoms in region R are in such and such a state of excitation.

The above *substantive* correspondence rule in the kinetic-molecular theory in some sense 'identifies' or 'associates' (again, this is a key issue to be explored in this chapter) the empirical temperature of a gas with certain theoretically posited molecular states of the gas. The *methodological* correspondence rule, by contrast, does not pretend to tell us what the temperature of a gas itself theoretically consists in, but only how we may empirically *detect* the presence of that molecular state, which is unobservable to the naked eye, by means of some appropriate instrument (and this assumes a theory as to how the instrument is able to register such unobservable goings-on).[7] This distinction marks the fact that the kinetic-molecular theory is supposed to be a substantive theory about the nature and properties of *gases*; it is not intended to be a theory about *spectroscopes* or any other instruments or methods that might be used to measure or register the properties of gases.

With these distinctions in place we can now add some further detail to our idealized account of how correspondence rules, as the standard empiricist view plausibly has it, enable the scientist to use theories as instruments for the prediction and control of observable phenomena. We have the kinetic-molecular theory T in hand. Using T's methodological correspondence rules in the lab we observe a gas to have a certain temperature (O_1). Using T's substantive correspondence rules we in some sense 'interpret' that observed temperature in terms of a certain theoretically characterized molecular state of the gas, an interpretation which we may represent by '$O_1 \leftrightarrow T_1$' (again, let us leave open for the moment the question as to how to understand the 'bridging' biconditional or two-way 'if–then', '$\leftrightarrow$' – including whether it should really be interpreted as a biconditional). Leaving the lab for the armchair, so to speak, we now use our purely theoretical laws ($T_i \supset T_j$) to calculate that this molecular state T_1 must lead to the subsequent molecular state T_2. T's correspondence rules then tell us, in turn, that T_2 corresponds to the observable property O_2 of the gas (say, a rise in pressure), which we thus confidently predict and subsequently successfully observe in the lab. In broad terms this is how theories are plausibly viewed as enabling the derivation of empirical laws and observational generalizations in accordance with the overall empiricist schema '$T \rightarrow (O_i \supset O_j)$' from which we started.

The steps above that particularly grab the philosopher's attention, however, are those in which observable empirical entities or properties are 'linked' by correspondence rules with unobservable theoretical entities or properties. What is the nature of this connection or bridge between the empirical observables and the theoretical unobservables? This question, as well as prior questions concerning what the 'observable/unobservable' distinction itself amounts to, will turn out to be crucial to Sellars' defense of scientific realism and thereby to his account of the overall ontological primacy of the scientific image.

First, however, we must pursue the matter a bit further from the standard empiricist perspective. Some strongly 'reductive' versions of empiricism in twentieth-century philosophy of science attempted to interpret the relevant correspondence rules ($O_i \leftrightarrow T_i$) in such a way that all so-called 'unobservable theoretical entities' (T_i) were supposed to be *directly definable* in terms of – and hence logically 'reducible' to – various actual and hypothetical observations and measurement operations (O_i). The idea was that such 'operational' definitions or 'instrumentalist' interpretations of theoretical terms, as they were variously called, would allow reductive empiricists to maintain that those theories which *seem to go beyond* possible sense experience in speaking of exotic unobservable entities (subatomic particles, gravitational fields, and the like) are in fact merely useful shorthand calculational devices or instruments for generating generalizations concerning the *observables* ($O_i \supset O_j$). A strict empiricist of this sort might for this and other reasons hold that observables are the only entities that we are strictly speaking justified in believing to exist. And we may note here in particular that if strictly reductive empiricist approaches of this kind were to succeed they would thereby also neatly resolve the overall ostensible clash between the manifest and scientific images – namely, by stripping the purely theoretical postulational image of any real ontological significance (cf. *SM* VI.54–6). One would not have to hold that there *really* exist any unobservable theoretical entities on such a view.

Unfortunately for reductive empiricism, however, it turned out that there were persistent difficulties with all such attempts to strictly reduce the theoretical to the observable, and this eventually led positivist and logical empiricist thinkers to develop various more subtle and holistic empiricist outlooks along roughly the following lines. These developments will also provide our transition to Sellars' critical response to the empiricist picture and its more recent variations in the next section.[8]

Most logical empiricists by the 1950s, in light of the sorts of difficulties just mentioned, came to regard it as sufficient to argue that the interpreted theory *as a whole* (hence, 'holism') has testable empirical consequences due to the transitions or bridges afforded by the correspondence rules between the language of the theory and the language of observation. What the correspondence rules thus seemed to provide was something along the lines of what Carnap called a 'partial interpretation' of the theory in terms of its empirical consequences.[9] How exactly to interpret the cognitive status of the theoretical terms that *seem* to refer to unobservable theoretical entities, however, remained a controversial and delicate issue for leading logical empiricists such as Rudolf Carnap, Ernest Nagel, and Carl Hempel, whom we may briefly take as examples (with apologies to Hans Reichenbach and Herbert Feigl) of philosophers whose views on the nature of scientific explanation were at the center of Sellars' attention in the late 1950s and early 1960s. During this period these three thinkers seemed to converge on an outlook that Sellars, specifically in relation to Nagel's approach but with wider applications, called *irenic instrumentalism*. The general outlook might just as well have been called *irenic realism*, however, for the basic irenic or conciliatory contention of these and other more recent thinkers as well, as we shall now see, was essentially that the scientific realism vs. (instrumentalist) empiricism debate is not such a big deal after all. As long as the *empirical* consequences are accommodated or 'saved,' these thinkers argue, *both* the scientific realist and the 'anti-realist' empiricist outlooks can be accepted *as alternative manners of speaking that are convenient for certain purposes.*

The central issues here were self-critically explored in impressive technical detail in the philosophy of science of the period.[10] For present purposes, however, it will be convenient to make use of Sellars' own statement of the nub of the dispute in the following passage from his 1959 article 'Phenomenalism.' Here Sellars is considering some of the classic logical empiricist or positivist objections that might be made to what we shall shortly see to be his own scientific realist view – that is, his view that "to have good reasons for espousing a theory which postulates the existence of unobservable entities is to have good reason for saying that these entities really exist" (PH 95–6, 97n). This scientific realist view, Sellars explains using the terms we have introduced above,

> runs up against the objection that the entities postulated by theories of this type are and can be nothing but 'computational devices' for deriving observation framework conclusions from observation

framework premises, and that even this role is 'in principle' dispensable. For, it is argued, every success achieved by the theory has the form
$$T \rightarrow (O_i \supset O_j)$$
where '$O_i \supset O_j$' is a generalization which relates two kinds of situation definable in the observation framework, and which, though derivable from the theory (including its correspondence rules), must in principle be capable of *independent* inductive confirmation or disconfirmation. (PH 95–6; cf. Hempel 1958, ch. 8: 'The Theoretician's Dilemma')

The standard empiricist contention here that theories might in principle be *dispensable* is basically the idea that if theory T really does its job successfully, then it enables us to derive all the relevant empirical generalizations and empirical laws that cover all of the phenomena we wanted to explain and predict in the first place. And since the latter observable generalizations ($O_i \supset O_j$) could on this empiricist view (allegedly) *in principle be established by empirical-inductive procedures alone without the use of the theory postulating unobservables*, any such theory that really does its job thereby shows itself to be a useful but in principle merely dispensable calculational device. That is, the theoretical posits of predictively successful theories would on this view seem to be in principle dispensable though perhaps in *practice* indispensable tools for usefully organizing and simplifying the observable phenomena. An empiricist might therefore conclude that nothing about good scientific theories logically or epistemologically *compels* us to construe the apparent references in such theories to unobservable entities as really referring to anything beyond the observable domain.

In fact, however, such thinkers as Nagel, Hempel, and Carnap strained to achieve a more conciliatory or irenic philosophical perspective, one which would allow us to accept this (alleged) result concerning the in principle dispensability of theories while *also* somehow preserving the compelling realist intuition that there are indeed theoretical entities that correspond to the theoretical terms in accepted scientific theories. Their general strategy was to cast the standard empiricism vs. scientific realism controversy as a *pseudo-dispute* that really only amounts to a question of convenience between alternative linguistic forms: as Nagel put it, "the opposition between these views is a conflict over preferred modes of speech" (Nagel 1961: 152); or as Carnap likewise suggested, "the conflict between the two approaches is essentially linguistic" (Carnap 1966: 256). Hempel, too, seemed to seek an irenic compromise that would straddle both sides of the fence.[11]

Sellars himself was also by nature a methodologically conciliatory philosopher, arguably far more so, when viewed in historical perspective, than the logical empiricists Carnap, Hempel, or Nagel. By philosophical temperament Sellars sought to uncover and preserve elements of truth within apparently diametrically opposed positions by means of appropriate philosophical distinctions. Nonetheless, in the next section we shall discover why he was firmly convinced that the irenic peacemaking style of approach to this particular problem is fundamentally mistaken, not only in relation to the scientific realism vs. empiricism controversy in particular, but also more generally in relation to the overarching philosophical question concerning the ostensible clash between the manifest and scientific images of man-in-the-world introduced in chapter 1.

The 'irenist,' if we may coin such a term, is basically one who argues (whether in defense of common-sense realism or in defense of some variety of what would later be called 'anti-realism') that ostensible conceptual conflicts can be satisfactorily resolved and intellectual peace restored through a strategy of segregation or insulation – a kind of conceptual apartheid, as a particularly harsh critic might describe it. ('Pluralism' and 'quietism' would be two more sympathetic terms for closely related philosophical attitudes.[12]) P. F. Strawson's characteristically admirable article, 'Perception and its Objects' (1979), is a clear and pertinent example of this general irenic strategy as applied to the overall clash between the manifest and scientific images. Strawson suggests that we should regard the common-sense and the scientific-theoretical accounts of the world, which he admits do ostensibly conflict with one another, as simply "*two discrepant descriptions, each valid from its own viewpoint*" (italics added):

> I acknowledge the discrepancy of the two descriptions, but claim that, once we recognize the *relativity in our conception of the real*, they need not be seen as in contradiction with each other. *Those very things which* from one standpoint we conceive as phenomenally propertied [e.g., as physical objects possessing color] we conceive from another as constituted in a way which can only be described in what are, from the phenomenal point of view, abstract terms [e.g., as systems of colorless microphysical particles]. (Strawson 1979: 58–9, italics and bracketed material added)

Strawson argues that in these sorts of cases of conflict what we in fact do is "shift our standard" for what may be taken really to exist; but he contends that such shifts nonetheless do not "condemn us to internal conflict. The appearance of [. . .] conflict vanishes when we acknowledge the *relativity of our 'reallys'*" (Strawson 1979: 57, italics added). Interestingly, almost two decades earlier in 1961 Ernest Nagel had himself drawn his overall irenic conclusion in a similar way. Like Strawson, Nagel appealed to allegedly different "senses of 'real' or 'exist'" in order to peacefully fence off the apparently conflicting instrumentalist-empiricist and scientific realist accounts of theoretical explanation (Nagel 1961: 151).[13]

So the irenic attempt to relativize truth or reality to different linguistic or conceptual frameworks is one time-honored way of attempting to sidestep the ostensible clash between the manifest and scientific images. It is supposed to be the case that both images can 'win,' according to the irenic philosopher, once we properly relativize our descriptions and give up the demand for one unified, fully comprehensive categorial account of the structure of reality.[14]

Sellars' argument will be that such irenic empiricist and other 'separate-but-equal' pluralist and quietist approaches cannot, on close inspection, really succeed the way they are supposed to in the case of the dispute concerning the interpretation of scientific theories. This is because the attempted peaceful segregations in this case fail for quite specific, though rather complex reasons, as we shall now see.[15] *A fortiori* such approaches will inevitably fail to provide an adequate solution to our wider problem concerning the ostensible clash of the images. (These conclusions will later be important to keep in mind during the second half of chapter 6 below.) To take up the former specific contention concerning scientific theories, however, we must now critically re-examine the empiricist approaches to theoretical explanation outlined above. Sellars' criticism of the standard empiricist reconstruction of scientific theories, if sound, will be seen to be applicable not only to both the classically reductive and the more irenic empiricist approaches discussed above, but also (as we shall see) to the importantly different 'constructive empiricism' that has recently been ably defended by van Fraassen.

Sellars' critique of empiricism and his defense of scientific realism

For convenience let us put before us again in summary form the standard empiricist 'levels' approach to scientific explanation. This was the idea that

[3]   *theories,* with their postulated theoretical laws ($T_i \supset T_j$) and correspondence rules ($T_i \leftrightarrow O_i$)
                explain-by-deductively-entailing

[2]   the *lawlike observational generalizations* or empirical laws ($O_i \supset O_j$), which themselves (given initial conditions)
                explain-by-deductively-entailing

[1]   particular empirical *observations* ($O_1, O_2, O_3, \ldots O_n$).

The general empiricist interpretation of this structure was then that the non-observational theoretical level [3] need not be construed as literally referring to unobservable theoretical *entities*, since its real job is simply to summarize accurately and conveniently the level [2] empirical laws which are themselves the direct generalizations and hence explainers of our level [1] observations. The sophisticated irenic refinements of this picture then contended that as long as the observational phenomena of levels [2] and [1] are 'saved' or 'covered,' we can interpret the theoretical level [3] along either realist or non-realist lines as we wish, depending on the context – as long as we understand our claims to be appropriately relativized to the separate purposes and perspectives of our theoretical descriptions of unobservables at level [3] as opposed to our empirical descriptions of observables at levels [2] and [1].

Sellars' most important line of argument against these empiricist and irenic outlooks, and in favor of scientific realism – as he clarified his view in 'Scientific Realism or Irenic Instrumentalism' (SRII 1965) and later in relation to van Fraassen in 'Is Scientific Realism Tenable?' (SRT 1976) – will turn on his claim that there is a crucial ambiguity between "two importantly different types of candidates which satisfy the general criterion for being an observation framework counterpart [which is] correlated with theorems in the theory by correspondence rules" (SRII 179; see also SRT 319; more on 'counterpart concepts' in chapter 6). More specifically, there are two different sorts of observational generalization both of which cover the same observational evidence for a theory at a given time. For reasons that should soon become clear, we shall distinguish these as *manifest* observational generalizations ($O_i \supset O_j$) as opposed to *theory-contaminated* observational generalizations, where the latter will be marked with asterisks: $*O_i \supset *O_j$. The asterisks are intended to mark the "ingression" of theoretical concepts into the language of direct empirical observation itself.

Both theory-contaminated observations ($*O_i$) and manifest observations (O_i) are perceptual observations insofar as they are *reliable noninferential classificatory responses to an object*. (We shall have much more to say about the nature of perceptual observation in general in chapter 5.) Intuitively, the difference between them will be that manifest observations are restricted to the colored and shaped objects of the manifest image, whereas theory-contaminated observations are of theoretically postulated objects such as electrons. On Sellars' view, then, appropriately trained people can have theory-contaminated perceptual observations ($*O_i$) of 'manifest imperceptible' entities. For example, '*This electron* is doing so and so,' as judged by a physicist looking at a certain electron cloud chamber, would constitute a theory-laden or theory-contaminated observation ($*O_1$) of a 'manifest imperceptible' entity in the relevant sense. 'There is a grey streak in the middle of the white cloudy stuff in this chamber' (O_1) would be the corresponding manifest observation.

To anticipate, the general idea below will be that both theory-contaminated observational generalizations (*$O_i \supset$ *O_j) and corresponding manifest observational generalizations ($O_i \supset O_j$) will in general be *compatible* with or 'cover' the observational evidence for an accepted theory at any given time. However, manifest observational generalizations are such that they "were accepted and would still be accepted on purely inductive grounds – i.e., in the absence of theoretical considerations," while in a crucial respect this is not the case with the theory-contaminated generalizations, *$O_i \supset$ *O_j (SRII 179; SRT 319). Further below our earlier gas law example from chemistry and physics will be used to illustrate this distinction. By the end of this section I contend that Sellars will have clarified this distinction in such a way as to put significant critical pressure on empiricist accounts and simultaneously in favor of his own scientific realist understanding of the nature of scientific theories.

The first step at this stage, however, is to clarify Sellars' unusual but I think plausible views on what philosophers of science call the *theory/ observation distinction*. As we shall now see, Sellars bases the above distinction between theory-contaminated observations (*O_i) and manifest observations (O_i) on a phenomenological distinction between (to take the case of visual observation) what we see an object *as* – for example, what kind of thing we see the object *to be* – as opposed to what sensible qualities we *see of* the object which we see, whatever kind of thing we might see it as. Let us consider how Sellars explains these distinctions and mobilizes them against the various empiricist outlooks we have been considering.

Many scientific realists take it to be essential to their scientific realism to *reject* the idea, which Sellars will defend, that there is any generally sustainable, principled distinction between entities that are observable and entities that are unobservable (see Maxwell 1962 for an early example). This rejection is entirely understandable, and according to Sellars it is in fact the correct attitude in one important sense of the 'theoretical/observable' distinction. For suppose the case can convincingly be made, as Sellars emphatically agrees that it can, in favor of the claim that theoretical entities at level [3] can in the legitimate 'theory-contaminated' sense be *observed* (i.e., *O_i), for example by means of physicists using spectroscopes, or electron microscopes for observing molecules, or cloud chambers for detecting electrons, and so on. '*That* is an electron' is how the trained physicist can directly and reliably perceptually respond by pointing to a streak of droplets in a cloud chamber, without having to cautiously *infer from* anything 'more immediately' perceptible such as the shape-and-color characteristics of the streak – although she *may* retreat to those 'manifest' observations, too, if need be (cf. chapter 5). Sellars therefore certainly wants to insist, along with most scientific realists, that a physicist who knows the appropriate theory-cum-correspondence rules governing a certain theoretical term T_1 (say, 'electron') can come to be able to use that concept as an observation term in her direct (i.e., non-inferential) perceptual responses to the appropriate physical circumstances in front of her. In short, she can have the theory-contaminated but nonetheless genuinely perceptual observation report (*O_1): '*This electron* is doing so-and-so.'

So on Sellars' understanding of perceptual observation in general as any appropriately reliable non-inferential classificatory response to an object, including the physicist's theory-contaminated, instrument-assisted observations, the 'observable vs. theoretical' distinction does not classify *kinds of entities*, since *any* entity can in principle become observable in this way. In this respect the theory/observation contrast marks not an ontological but rather an epistemological and methodological distinction. That is, it basically has to do with whether or not, at a given stage of our knowledge, our justified beliefs concerning a certain kind of entity are supportable *only* by means of inferences from other beliefs (including various observations), or whether, to the contrary, such beliefs have *themselves* come to be able to function reliably in certain circumstances as non-inferential perceptual judgments which are causally elicited directly by the appropriate situations in the environment. Finally, the scientific realist might understandably take this correct account, as Sellars see it, of the theory-laden or theory-contaminated observation of (previously) postulated 'theoretical' entities to show, all by itself, that the standard empiricist way of distinguishing between level [3] 'unobservables' and the domain of empirical observables at levels [2] and [1] is entirely misguided, and for that reason alone has none of the usual phenomenalist, irenic, or constructivist consequences an empiricist might claim for it.

Sellars, however, was a scientific realist with a difference. He does indeed defend the above account of observations as reliable non-inferential responses in the widest sense that includes theory-contaminated observations (this is part of his rejection of the myth of the given). As anticipated above, however, he also distinguished within this wider framework, as part of his defense of scientific realism, what he calls an *absolute* conception of the observation framework. The latter is restricted to the "*perception proper*" of manifest-perceptible physical objects as conceived within the manifest image (SRT 318). Sellars develops this latter conception with considerable care, but our discussion of the manifest image in chapter 1 has prepared us for the basic account.

The general idea is that while recognizing, as against the myth of the given, that *all* perceptual cognition involves conceptualization – for example, all cognitive seeing is seeing something *as* some kind of thing or other, if in some cases only inchoately or indeterminately – Sellars argues that we must also recognize a phenomenological sense in which what we *see of* a given physical object at any given time is (roughly speaking) its *shaped-and-colored facing side*. Suppose that a physicist, a twelve-year-old student, and a three-year-old toddler all stand looking at a certain object on a table. In one sense, what they all *see of* the object is likely to be fairly similar for each of them, insofar as they all perceive the facing side of a certain greyish, tube-shaped object on a white surface; that is, they all see roughly the same "occurrent sensible properties" of the object (SRT 317). However, what they each see that object *as*, or what they see it *to be*, will depend on what "concepts of *causal* properties" they each are able to bring to bear on their perceptual experiences (SRT 317–18). And in relation to the latter, people of course differ with respect to what concepts they may at any given time have acquired of the non-occurrent *dispositional* properties or 'if–then' behavioral tendencies of objects. In this particular case, for example, perhaps the physicist sees the object on the table to be a 1980s-vintage spectroscope, the twelve-year-old sees it as some kind of telescope-like scientific instrument, and the three-year-old toddler sees it pretty much as just a grey object (though see chapter 5 for more precision on these matters). In drawing this 'seeing *of*' vs. 'seeing *as*' distinction, Sellars accordingly notes that

> if we look at these two types of conceptual resource belonging to the framework of perception, we notice that whereas the resources of the *first* type [i.e., seeing *of*] can be said to be constant, those of the *second* type [i.e., seeing *as*] change. Our classifications of physical objects can become more complex and sophisticated. Old pigeon holes can be subdivided, change their shape, and even disappear. (SRT 317–18)

While it is important for Sellars' view that the physicist can come to "see an object *as* a conglomerate of molecules," namely in the theory-contaminated sense explained above, the conceptual framework of manifest perceptibles is more narrowly conceived to be one in which the relevant concepts pertaining to thing-kinds and causal properties, however sophisticated the latter may become, are all "built out of [. . .] concepts pertaining to the occurrent sensible properties of physical objects" (SRT 318). In short, our manifest observations are always of the phenomenologically colorful world of physical objects in space and time, however much we may change our conceptions of their natures and causal dispositions. In this sense, then, the 'theoretical vs. *manifest* observable' distinction is a constant one between the domain of perceptible objects as conceived within the manifest image (with their occurrent sensible properties, etc.) as opposed to any domain of postulated theoretical entities that are imperceptible in the sense of not being *manifest* perceptible entities.

What the above distinctions enable us to account for, according to Sellars, is the fact that in the practice of science there are really two crucially different ways in which our observational generalizations – the empirical 'data' for our theories – are conceptualized. In what he calls the "tough" sense, Sellars is "equating the observational frame-work with the perceptual framework proper" (SRT 320) – that is, the framework of manifest observables (O_i). As Sellars remarks during his published exchange with van Fraassen:

> Since the conception I have advanced of the observation framework is, in a legitimate sense, an 'absolute' one, based on what might be called 'perception proper', it is important to note that I have assumed that inductive generalizations in the observation framework take place in [manifest] perceptual terms. (SRT 318)

In this sense our manifest observational generalizations are inductively supported by perceptual data (O_i) of the sort that would be welcomed by classical empiricists. However, when one looks at the empirical data that are actually appealed to in the development, testing, and predic-tive use of mature scientific theories, it becomes clear that the empirical data in this latter sense are not only concept-laden – as indeed *all* our observations are for Sellars; more specifically, such data are typically laden or contaminated with postulational *theoretical concepts* of entities that are not manifest-perceptible (i.e., $*O_i$). This of course is thanks to the fact that in the use of well-confirmed theories various correspond-ence rules will have become second nature to those scientists whose routine empirical observations now include non-inferential percep-tions of highly theory-contaminated states of affairs ($*O_i$). If one asks a chemist or a physicist in the lab, 'What are the established observa-tional generalizations or empirical laws – whether they be exception-less laws or only statistically highly probable generalizations does not matter – that I may take for granted and rely upon as bottom-level [1] or *hard empirical data*?', the answer will typically *not come in the form of manifest observational regularities* ($O_i \supset O_j$) *but rather as theory-contaminated observational generalizations* ($*O_i \supset *O_j$). If one wants to make the most accurate predictions in the lab concerning the measur-able volume, pressure, and temperature of gases in containers, for example, one had better observe the gas's temperature by means of a spectroscope that has been theoretically constructed to detect tempera-ture as consisting in the mean kinetic energy of molecules (i.e., $*O_i$). If one conceives temperature and pressure as observable properties of manifest-perceptible empirical kinds of physical object (O_i), one's observable generalizations ($O_i \supset O_j$), it turns out (as we shall see), are inevitably *falsified* under certain empirical conditions. Most impor-tantly, adequate *insight* into what those conditions are can be had only in light of the theoretical identifications and resulting theory-laden observational generalizations ($*O_i \supset *O_j$) discussed above. Sellars argues that "the distinction is crucial," for when the empirical data supporting a theory takes the form of a theory-contaminated observational generalization ($*O_i \supset *O_j$), such a generalization

> need not be the lawlike statement [namely, $O_i \supset O_j$] which it would be reasonable to accept on purely inductive grounds, nor even contain the [manifest] empirical concepts which it would be reasonable to construct and use in the absence of theoretical considerations. It is characteristic of good theories to show their observational counterparts in sense (b) [i.e., manifest observational generalizations, $O_i \supset O_j$] to be false. (SRT 319–20; also at SRII 179; bracketed material added)

What we need to explore further is what exactly Sellars is getting at in this pregnant passage.

The point here is not that our manifest observable generalizations are merely crude or inexact and simply need to be sharpened up by using finer instruments. The point is rather that we have discovered through postulational theorizing that objects conceived as being of manifest perceptible empirical kinds *are ultimately not empirically lawful* as so conceived (where this includes merely statistical lawfulness); and that they are so, in these sorts of cases, only if they are *reconceived* as being categorially different empirical kinds of thing – namely, as being identifiable with complex systems or 'swarms' of non-manifest, microphysical objects. Microphysical theories in such cases thus

> *explain empirical laws by explaining why observable things obey to the extent they do, these empirical laws;*[16] that is, they explain why individual objects of various kinds and in various circumstances in the observation framework behave in those ways in which it has been inductively established that they do behave. Roughly, it is because a gas is – in some sense of 'is' – a cloud of molecules which are behaving in certain theoretically defined ways, that it obeys the *empirical* Boyle–Charles law.[17]
>
> Furthermore, theories not only explain why observable things obey certain laws, they also explain why in certain respects their behaviour obeys no inductively confirmable generalization in the observation framework. (LT 121)

In order to see what Sellars is arguing in these passages it will help to consider how a sophisticated empiricist might reasonably respond to the claims he seems to be making (for some of these lines of response, see van Fraassen 1975, 1976, and 1980). The empiricist might be prepared to grant to Sellars, as van Fraassen does in his constructive empiricism, that theories are indeed often the practically indispensable means for generating improved observational generalizations and hence for establishing more accurate empirical laws than our 'manifest' observations and inductions would generate by themselves. The kinetic-molecular theory of gases certainly did lead to more accurate, highly refined generalizations and predictions concerning the observable behavior of gases, and it certainly did so by in some sense construing gases to be composed of unobservable molecules-in-motion, etc., as explained above. Theories are wonderful, perhaps even indispensable, aids in this way. But the constructive empiricist insists that we can *accept* such theories without regarding their talk of unobservable entities as being *true* (hence van Fraassen: "To my mind, theoretical entities are fictions," van Fraassen 1976: 334). What is required of a good theory, on this view, is that it be *empirically adequate*: that it successfully cover the (manifest) observations. As such, however, the empiricist will insist that we can always in principle accept such theories while restricting our beliefs to the ever more refined observable generalizations *themselves*, however much theorizing might be involved in their conception, discovery, or establishment.[18] We can make full use of our correspondence rules and we can even engage in theory-contaminated talk of 'observing molecules,' if we wish; but the constructive empiricist argues that the final empirical upshot will always be some more refined empirical generalization or other that may in principle always be reformulated *as an improved 'manifest' observational generalization*, $(O_i \supset O_j)$. As van Fraassen concludes: "The only thing we need to believe here is that the theory is empirically adequate, which means that *in its round-about way* it has latched on to actual regularities in the observable phenomena. Acceptance of the theory need involve no further beliefs" (van Fraassen 1976: 337–8, italics added).

There are many ways in which van Fraassen's own wider story, briefly hinted at here, might be challenged. At a minimum we would need to look very carefully at what this notion of 'accepting' theories without believing them to be true really amounts to.[19] For our present purposes, however, the important point is that this general empiricist style of response to Sellars does seem to put pressure on his own argument, for Sellars must surely grant that the empiricist is always capable in this way of interpreting any such theory-improved observational generalization as in *some* sense 'saving the same phenomena.' That is, we can in principle always reformulate such a generalization, after the fact, as a more refined observation concerning *manifest* observables (thus correcting the previous, now falsified manifest generalization which we started with prior to the theorizing). For instance, suppose (as is roughly historically the case) that using the kinetic-molecular theory we generate and confirm predictions about gases at extremely high pressures which falsify the older Boyle–Charles gas law. The empiricist will suggest: why not just take this more precise empirical result and simply believe only in the resulting corrected *manifest* observable generalization about gases at very high pressures, while maintaining a serene, irenic diffidence as to the truth or falsity of theoretical molecule-talk itself? Thus, even if theories are indispensable pragmatic aids in our explanatory practices, the empiricist might insist nonetheless that the question as to the truth of the theoretical "postulates becomes quite irrelevant" (van Fraassen 1976: 337). As we just saw van Fraassen suggest, "the autonomy of the [manifest] physical thing language is preserved if we say that these improved generalizations are also expressed in that language" (van Fraassen 1975: 610; cf. SRT 320).

Sellars' basic reply to this empiricist line of response represented by van Fraassen is to insist that this is "to confuse two concepts of 'improved generalization', and in an important sense, beg the question" (SRT 320). The ultimate issue here is admittedly a subtle one, but Sellars' key point is this. It is true, as the empiricist suggests, that we generally can, after the fact, generate a *corrected manifest-perceptible* generalization, $O_i \supset O_j$, which takes in the new predictions we have confirmed in a "round-about way," as van Fraassen put it above, by using theories. Taking our example, we can now simply help ourselves to the confirmed observations about gases at extremely high pressures, which had been expected only in light of the kinetic-molecular theory. But van Fraassen has missed the point that despite all of this there still remains a crucial difference in the nature of the case between *that* improved generalization, formulated in terms of manifest image empirical concepts (i.e., the more refined $O_i \supset O_j$), and the 'same' set of improved observations (so to speak) when they are formulated *using the relevant theoretical concepts*, as in the intrinsically theory-contaminated observational generalization, $*O_i \supset *O_j$.[20] The reason is that, as conceived using manifest observational concepts, there is *no reason why* gases should violate the Boyle–Charles gas law at very high pressures in the way that they have now been observed to do. Not that there is anything wrong in principle with 'brute facts' *per se* (van Fraassen mistakenly thinks that this might be the point regarding the need for explanation that Sellars is making: see SRT 314–15). The point is rather that when the gas's pressure, temperature, and so on, are reconceived as empirical phenomena directly in terms of the relevant molecular-theoretical concepts (i.e., $*O_i \supset *O_j$), then only *as so conceived* does it follow *lawfully* that such particular results at very high pressures will be observed. And it *this* comparison between these two subtly different types of (coextensive) *empirical* generalizations that finally does reveal the refined generalization that is restricted to manifest concepts (i.e., $O_i \supset O_j$) to be of an unstable or accidental nature. It is clear that the latter manifest generalizations will 'project' lawfully to new cases *only as a result of their being the 'round-about' or parasitic manifest counterpart of the theory-contaminated successor observational generalization, $*O_i \supset *O_j$.*[21]

The manifest observational generalizations will, as Sellars puts it, thus "exhibit an incorrigible variance with respect to fresh cases which is not a matter of their being statistical and which can not be attributed to experimental error" (SRT 320). What he characterizes as the "instability" that is inherent in the manifest generalization is due to the fact that it is only the theory-contaminated generalizations that have succeeded in picking out those *empirical kinds* which turn out to afford an intrinsically lawful (as opposed to a merely parasitic or 'piggy-backing') projection to "fresh cases," as he phrased it above. The key question in the end, therefore, is the question of whether or not the manifest observational framework is "autonomous – not just methodologically – but *with respect to its very conceptual content*" (SRT 316, italics added) – and Sellars' argument has just been that it is not. This is what Sellars was driving at when he claimed earlier that "it is because a gas *is* [. . .] a cloud of molecules which are behaving in certain theoretically defined ways" that the gas obeys the empirical laws that it does obey, to the extent that it does (SRT 314; LT 121).[22]

Sellars' argument for scientific realism has much to be said for it, or so it seems to me. It is no doubt true that in a more complete account the dispute would have to be pursued 'one step up,' as it were, for despite Sellars' remark above that van Fraassen has begged the question at issue, it is perhaps not entirely clear just who might be begging the question against whom. It would be characteristic of a standard empiricist, for example, to have initial qualms about the entire distinction between *lawful* and *accidental* generalizations or 'projections' which manage to cover (extensionally) the same observational data, which Sellars' argument, as I have reconstructed it, turns upon. In Sellars' favor, however, the notion of causal lawfulness would certainly seem to be central to our conception of the goals of good scientific theorizing. So if Sellars has indeed succeeded in connecting the thesis of scientific realism with the very possibility of adequate causal explanation, he has made at least a strong *prima facie* case for scientific realism in the form sketched here.

The ontological primacy of the scientific image

The most direct consequence of Sellars' argument examined in the previous section is that the empiricist account of scientific explanation is mistaken, not only on its older 'levels' versions but arguably on van Fraassen's more recent constructivist version as well. Put in terms of Sellars' critique of the older 'levels' empiricism, we do not explain particular observable matters of fact (O_i) by deductively subsuming them under (manifest) observational generalizations ($O_i \supset O_j$), and then seek to explain the latter generalizations by deductively deriving them in turn from more general theories (T). As has just been argued, *"the behaviour of macro-objects [is not] even statistically lawful in a way which leaves to theories only the job of deriving these laws from its postulates and correspondence rules"* (PH 96). Rather, the role of substantive correspondence rules, as we have seen, is in fact to boldly reconceive and thereby *identify* individual manifest observable states of affairs with individual theoretical states of affairs directly, which results in the reliable theory-contaminated observational generalizations or corrected 'counterpart' empirical laws, $*O_i \supset *O_j$ (see TE and chapter 6 below for more on these issues). "To sum up the above results, microtheories explain why inductive generalizations pertaining to a given domain *and any refinement of them within the conceptual framework of the observation language* are at best approximations to the truth" (LT 123).

What is striking and not usually emphasized about Sellars' main argument for scientific realism as reconstructed in the previous section is how tightly he has connected scientific realism to the possibility in principle, if not necessarily in methodological practice, of *perceiving the world directly in scientific-theoretical terms*, i.e., at the rock bottom level [1] of singular empirical observations (which are what ultimately succeed in directly 'mapping' or 'picturing' the environment, as we shall see in chapter 6). As Sellars frames the realism issue (see, for example, PH 97; SRII 163, 188–9; TE 155; and *SM* 145, 147), unless we can coherently envision that our theory-contaminated observations ($*O_i$) of the microphysical world in the scientific image *"in principle, at least, could serve all the functions, and, in particular, the perceptual functions of the framework we actually employ in everyday life"* (PH 97, latter italics added), we would always be forced back in the end to a merely irenic view that restricts our primary empirical concepts to the observational concepts and generalizations of the manifest image.[23]

For Sellars, the plausibility of the scientific realist interpretation of the reference of theoretical terms is thus *essentially* connected to the possibility that concepts which, as things currently stand, have the methodological status of being 'merely' theoretical concepts (T_i) that are linked to manifest observations in a 'round-about way' by correspondence rules could in principle *take over entirely* the "first-class" fact-reporting role of basic singular observation statements ($*O_i$).[24] (The latter, as we shall see in chapter 6, ultimately constitute the ideally projected, matter-of-factual *truth* in the form of the most accurate 'maps,' 'pictures,' or isomorphic *representations* of the objects, events, and regularities occurring in the natural world.) As Sellars puts it:

> Thus, to say that theoretical statements are capable of factual truth in the full sense is to say that a stage in the development of scientific theory

(including the theory of sentient organisms) is conceivable in which it would be reasonable to abandon mediation by substantive correspondence rules in favor of a direct commerce of the conceptual framework of theory with the world. Such direct commerce exists already in limited contexts, and, to the extent that it does exist, theoretical frameworks enjoy in anticipation the first class status which would be theirs in that 'long run' in terms of which, according to Peirce, we conceive the scientific enterprise and the 'truth' about 'what really exists,' which is its formal, final, and efficient cause. (SRII 189)

As Sellars has conceived the matter, his argument for scientific realism thus has the consequence that our common-sense conceptual framework of manifest-perceptible objects, properties, and kinds must in an important sense be regarded as strictly speaking *false*. However, the degree to which such manifest empirical laws ($O_i \supset O_j$) *approximate* to the truth can be rigorously accounted for in terms of the improved scientific conceptual frameworks and postulational ontologies which generate their corresponding successor observational generalizations, $*O_i \supset *O_j$ (again, more on this in chapter 6). The most important consequence in relation to later chapters and the general clash of the images, therefore, is the two-sided one that, by comparison with the ongoing scientific image:

1 the manifest image has been shown ultimately to lack the conceptual resources for an adequate explanation even of the manifest perceptible phenomena that fall within its own domain; and
2 it is only by radically reconceiving the nature of the empirical phenomena in the successor terms of the postulational scientific image that increasingly more adequate explanations are achieved.

On this view, scientific theorizing is in this way gradually uncovering the matter-of-factual truth about the nature of the empirical world, and in so doing it is providing better explanations of the appearances within the manifest image than the manifest image could give of itself.

This is the basis for Sellars' well-known *scientia mensura* remark in 'Empiricism and the Philosophy of Mind' (which transforms the ancient Greek sophist Protagoras' *homo mensura* dictum, "Of all things the measure is man, of the things that are, that they are, and of things that are not, that they are not"):

[S]peaking as a philosopher, I am quite prepared to say that the common-sense world of physical objects in Space and Time is unreal – that is, that there are no such things. Or, to put it less paradoxically, that in the dimension of describing and explaining the world, science is the measure of all things, of what is that it is, and of what is not that it is not. (EPM IX.41)

Whether Sellars' view here is ultimately correct or not, this passage has frequently been misunderstood due to a lack of careful attention to its several implicit contrasts: (i) between "speaking as a philosopher" who is attempting to achieve a view *across* different conceptual frameworks, as it were, as opposed to speaking from *within* the framework of common sense; (ii) between "the dimension of describing and explaining the world" as opposed to all the other important dimensions of discourse, such as those pertaining to rational action, practical methodology, social communication, and normative evaluation;[25] and (iii) between the "common-sense world of physical objects in Space and Time" as opposed to possible radical reconceptualizations (or in some cases abandonment) of those objects within successor conceptual frameworks, which result from the often 'revolutionary' categorial ontologies that are generated over time by theoretical science in its increasingly refined attempts to explain the phenomena.

As indicated, we shall re-encounter these important issues concerning *conceptual change* at a later stage, including Sellars' controversial claim above that the manifest image is strictly speaking false. In this chapter, however, we have been abstracting from one further aspect of Sellars' account that must at least be mentioned before bringing this account of scientific realism and the scientific image to a close.

In the discussion so far we have been focusing on cases in which the substantive correspondence rules build bridges between *empirical* observables (O_i) and postulated *theoretical* unobservables (T_i). As we have seen, Sellars' view is that the substantive correspondence rules that 'link,' for example, observed temperature with the mean kinetic energy of molecules should be read as *identifications* ($O_i = T_i$). The resulting theory-contaminated measurements or observations ($*O_i$) of temperature are thereby *reconceived*, in principle, as direct encounters with molecular states of affairs. This idea of improved explanation by means of *theoretical identification as conceptual change* is involved not only in what might be called 'theory/observation' substantive correspondence rules of the kind discussed so far; it is also involved in the cross-theory or 'theory/theory' substantive correspondence rules which, as scientific theorizing progresses, successfully reconceive the nature of the phenomena in one scientific theory in terms of the concepts and laws of some more fundamental scientific theory (see TE and LT). In the latter cases

> it is not a question of 'identifying' [manifest] empirical properties with the corresponding theoretical properties, but rather properties defined in one theoretical framework with properties defined in a second theoretical framework to which the first theory is said to be 'reducible'. The stock example is the reducibility of the objects of current chemical theory to complexes of the objects of current atomic physics. (TE 151–2)

Similar to our previous discussion as to how the observable behavior of gases is ultimately best explained by reconceiving the nature of gases in molecular terms (it is because a gas *is* a complex system of molecules-in-motion that it obeys the empirical laws it does to the extent that it does), so too the behavior of *chemically* conceived molecules themselves in turn, for instance, turns out to be more adequately explained at an even deeper level by making use of atomic physics to reconceive chemical objects as being *complex systems of subatomic particles*. "Ions behave as they do because they *are* such and such configurations of subatomic particles" (LT 124). Again, as in the Boyle–Charles law and kinetic-molecular theory case, so too in this case there is a crucial sense in which atomic physics is able to beat chemistry *even at its own game*, so to speak (cf. LT 126), by uncovering the real (sub)atomic physical kinds and laws that enable more accurate projections and predictions of the full range of phenomena at issue.[26]

It is important to recognize in this connection, however, that Sellars does not hold that such comparatively 'higher-level' sciences or 'special sciences' as chemistry or biology would be put out of business *as sciences* by the successful ontological reduction-by-identification of the *objects* of those sciences with systems of the sorts of objects treated in atomic physics. The 'reduced' science will normally continue to "use different experimental techniques, and will gain access to concepts in the unified [physical] theory by different operational routes and at a different level of the theory" (TE 152). For example, the chemist will still be concerned with important methods and laws pertaining to, among other things, chemical elements understood as substances that cannot be decomposed into simpler substances by chemical means (where the latter notion would then have to be further elucidated). But as far as the ontological 'furniture of the world' is concerned, the successful theoretical re-identifications that have already been achieved make it reasonable to reconceive these chemical elements and their properties as being identical with complex (sub)atomic physical goings-on of definable kinds. The atomic theory of physics could thus *in principle*, on Sellars' view, be made to do the substantive explanatory work if not the methodological work that chemistry does – and the same is true of the scientific image in relation to the manifest image as a whole (cf. SSIS 438–9). Our predictions and projections in terms of the empirical concepts and 'stances' (to borrow Daniel Dennett's useful notion) of the higher-level sciences and the manifest image will always have enormous utility insofar as the relevant empirical generalizations ($O_i \supset O_j$) are approximately true, well-founded phenomena. But the nature and extent of this approximation to the truth of these 'predecessor' generalizations is adequately explained only by means of their ontological identification with their theoretical successor generalizations, $*O_i \supset *O_j$.

These last issues concerning reducibility and the 'levels of nature' are very complex and currently controversial. As indicated earlier we shall also eventually grapple with further questions concerning conceptual change, truth, and ultimate ontology in chapter 6. In the three central chapters now to follow, however, we shall be returning to explore the questions that were opened up in chapter 1 and have now been made all the more pressing. In particular, how is this vision of the ontological primacy of the scientific image to be integrated with a coherent account of *our own* human capacities as sensing, thinking, and rationally active beings? In what sense could it be possible that we, too, like everything else in nature, are ultimately to be identified with complex systems of subatomic particles?

In this chapter we have seen that on Sellars' view the clash between the manifest and scientific images of man-in-the-world can be successfully resolved only by turning the empiricist and irenic conceptions of science radically upside-down, as it were, in favor of a strong version of scientific realism. It is far from being the case that in principle we may irenically resist believing in the real existence of (manifestly) unobservable theoretical entities and stick with regularities among manifest observable phenomena. Rather, a coherent and explanatory synoptic vision is achievable only if – in principle if not throughout our daily practice – we can leave the cave of manifest phenomenal appearances behind and reconceive the world that we directly perceive in terms of the concepts of the 'invisible' world, as it were, that is slowly being revealed in the evolving categories and theory-contaminated observations of the postulational scientific image. In the end, then, Sellars' radical conclusion regarding the clash of the images will be that it is the 'unobservable,' non-manifest world of scientifically postulated entities that is ultimately properly conceived as *our* world, as the one world that we truly encounter in our most reliable level [1], theory-contaminated empirical observations (*O_i). Making sense of this is the goal of upcoming chapters, but Sellars paints the resulting big picture as a synoptic vision in which "the world of theory and the world of observation would be one":

> From the standpoint of the methodology of developing science, it might seem foolish to build physical theory into the language of observation and experiment. A tentative correlation of theoretical and empirical terms would seem more appropriate than redefinition [i.e., reconceptualization]. But this is a truism which simply explains what we mean by developing science. But the perspective of the philosopher cannot be limited to that which is wise for developing science. He must also attempt to envisage the world as pictured from that point of view – one hesitates to call it Completed Science – which is the regulative ideal of the scientific enterprise. As I see it, then, substantive correspondence rules are anticipations of definitions which it would be inappropriate to implement

in developing science, but the implementation of which in an ideal state of scientific knowledge would be the achieving of a unified vision of the world in which the methodologically important dualism of observation and theoretical frameworks would be transcended, and the world of theory and the world of observation would be one. (TE 155; cf. chapter 6)

3

Meaning and Abstract Entities

We have seen Sellars articulate the clash between the manifest and scientific images of 'man-in-the-world' in terms of the challenges that face any account of our capacities for sense perception, conceptual thinking, and intentional action, while remaining strictly within the limits of our projected scientific-naturalist ontology. The linchpin issue that connects these three domains concerns the nature of thought. Both perceiving and willing are themselves forms of conceptual thinking, according to Sellars, which are linked causally to the world in certain reliable ways that will be explored in later chapters. So, given the scientific realist image of the human being as "a complex physical system" (PSIM 25), how in the first instance do we find a place in nature for what philosophers call the basic *intentionality*[1] of conceptual thought, which includes our capacity to grasp meanings and to understand the rational as opposed to merely associative connections that are characteristic of logical, rule-governed thinking?

This chapter and the next one will accordingly address fundamental questions concerning the ultimate nature of conceptual thinking, and for Sellars, as for so many other thinkers since the nineteenth century, that means beginning with language. Sellars is well aware that some philosophers will think that approaching thought through language is putting the cart before the horse. By the end of chapter 4, however, we shall see that Sellars thinks the relationship between inner thoughts and outer linguistic behavior is a complex one. While inner thoughts will indeed turn out to be ontologically prior to their overt expression in speech, for example, Sellars will argue that it is our pattern-governed linguistic behavior that initially provides the conceptually autonomous and methodologically prior 'model' for our understanding of what inner thoughts are in the first place.

That is the road ahead. Our first steps down it will begin by exploring two broadly contrasting general approaches to the theory of
meaning in the next two sections. In the final two sections of this
chapter we shall then be in a position, on that basis, to introduce Sellars'
novel *nominalist* theory of abstract entities, which represents a crucial
plank in his overall naturalist ontology.

Approaching thought through language: is meaning a relation?

As we saw very briefly in chapter 1, the predominant perennial conceptions of the relation between the rational intellect and the abstract
meanings or concepts which the intellect grasps have generally conceived it to be a unique or *sui generis* 'intentional relation' or 'meaning
relation' (PSIM 16). While rejecting that relational picture, Sellars will
agree that there are compelling reasons to regard meaning and conceptual cognition as in *some* sense having an 'irreducible' status, in that
such phenomena are not fully explainable in 'bottom-up' fashion in
terms of the sorts of complex spatio-temporal-causal relations and
processes that are attributed to things by the natural sciences. This, in
fact, is the heart of the philosophical problem of 'aboutness' or intentionality, a problem that is still very much with us – as are all the related
problems that are involved in understanding what it is for something
to have (or be) a *meaning*. From the early twentieth century to the
present time the problem as to whether or not, and if so in what
sense, intentionality can be *naturalized* has been one of the most
fundamental questions both in contemporary analytic philosophy
of mind and language and in the phenomenological tradition. It is also
a debate to which Sellars made a major, arguably groundbreaking,
contribution.

Let us once again begin with a simplified and tidied-up philosophical distinction in order to get an initial handle on a complex philosophical issue. In the present connection Sellars develops a rather
sweeping but useful distinction between what we may call *relational*
(or 'world-relational') as opposed to *non-relational* approaches to semantics or the theory of meaning. Sellars took himself to be defending a
non-relational view of meaning, and in so doing he succeeded in developing in the early 1950s what is now recognized to have been a seminal
functional role (or 'inferential role,' 'conceptual role') conception of
meaning and of conceptual content generally.[2]

The 'relational' in 'relational theories of meaning' is here meant
to refer primarily to specific kinds of relation that have been held to
obtain between linguistic and non-linguistic entities, not to complex

(inferential) relations between linguistic entities themselves. (Sellars' non-relational view will emphasize the latter.) The central question is this: is meaning a relation of some kind between language and the world (or between thoughts and the world – but recall that we are making a methodological start with language)? In exploring this question a variety of classical philosophical approaches to meaning will be encountered during the course of this chapter. For instance, do meaning and reference ultimately consist in complex *empirical relations* of causality or similarity that obtain between linguistic items and physical objects in the world? Or does meaning perhaps derive from certain *intelligible relations* to Platonic or other abstract entities (as will be explained further below)? Or is there some other broadly world-relational manner in which meaning might be a matter of interpreting linguistic items by assigning them corresponding objects or classes of objects in a 'semantic model' of some kind?

In what follows we shall take the *truth-conditional* style of approach to meaning as our basic example of a world-relational semantics. It will be convenient to select Rudolf Carnap as the philosopher who was most on Sellars' mind in this respect, while keeping in mind that truth-conditional approaches to semantics have taken on ever more sophisticated forms in recent decades.[3]

First, however, it will perhaps be helpful here to indulge in one final anticipation of upcoming discussions. Crucial to Sellars' own naturalistic synoptic vision will be his claim that meaning and intentionality do not involve the sorts of basic, irreducible relations between mind/language and the world that philosophers have characteristically posited. By contrast, Sellars' *naturalism with a normative turn,* as I have called it, will ultimately be seen to be based on the following key idea. While meaning, reference, intentionality, knowledge, and even truth itself are not *themselves* problematic relations between mind or language and the world, for Sellars, such phenomena do 'presuppose' or 'convey the information' (as he puts it) that various highly complex but unproblematic empirical-causal relations and natural uniformities have come to characterize our linguistic behavior both in its own internal patterns and in its relationship to entities in the world. That this is so will itself be a result of the social-normative guidance that is involved in learning a language, and in particular as governed by what I call Sellars' *norm/nature meta-principle*: "Espousal of principles is reflected in uniformities of performance" (TC 216). Enough foreshadowing, however – let us move on to the theory of meaning and build gradually to these conclusions in this and the next chapter.

What is it, then, for someone to grasp a meaning or for something to have a meaning? Starting more simply, what is it for a *word* to have a meaning? Befitting his heritage as a dyed-in-the-wool analytic philosopher, Sellars takes one step back and adopts the strategy of first reflecting upon the meaning of 'meaning'; and for a start, upon the nature of those basic meaning statements in which we say that a word has a certain meaning.

Someone who knows what the word 'horse' means (in English), or what 'caballo' means (in Spanish), is someone who has the *concept* of a horse. Knowing the meaning of a word is something that comes in degrees, of course, ranging from the two-year-old child's capacity to point to a horse in response to hearing the word, to a lexicographer's or a zoologist's definition: ' "horse" means a hoofed, herbivorous mammal of the family *Equidae.*' Such definitions, to be of any use, obviously presuppose that one already knows the meanings of the words in the definition. If someone learning English was unsure and looked up the meaning of 'hoofed,' she might find 'having hoofs; ungulate'; and then a look at 'ungulate' would bring her back to 'having hoofs.' Dictionaries only take you so far. Defining words in terms of other words is an indispensable practice, of course, but surely, one wants to say, understanding the meanings of words and sentences is ultimately a matter of understanding what they are directly *about* or *refer to* or *designate* in the world. It is at this point that classical relational conceptions of meaning in terms of truth-conditions unfold quite naturally, in the following way.

It seems plausible to say that we know the meaning of a sentence when, to take a simple type of case, we know which individuals, properties, and relations are designated or denoted by the referring and characterizing components of the sentence. For example, the meaning of 'Paris' is the particular place in France to which it refers; the meaning of 'city' is a certain complex property that characterizes and is shared by, among others, Boston, Paris, and London; and one understands the meaning of the sentence 'Paris is a city' (having the symbolic logical form, 'Fa') when one knows which individual (Paris; a) must exemplify what property (being a city, or cityhood; F or F-ness) in order for the sentence to be true. This is the sentence's *truth-condition.* Using straightforward truth-functional and quantificational logic, one can then systematically generate the truth-conditions for more complex sentences in terms of logical relations over the basic terms and sentences: 'Either Paris is a city or Paris is a town,' 'Fa or Ga'; 'There are some cities,' '$\exists x(Fx)$,' and so on. In this way the meaning of any given sentence is *compositionally* determined by the meanings of its parts, both sentential components and sub-sentential parts (names, predicates), which accounts for our striking capacity to grasp a potentially infinite number of novel sentences. Following the pioneering leads in formal logic of Frege, Russell, Wittgenstein, Tarski, and others, of particular influence on Sellars were Carnap's impressive attempts spanning four decades from the late 1920s onwards to systematize these logical and semantic insights into a clear and powerful formalized theory of meaning. The following are some basic elements in Carnap's approach to formal semantics.

In a major collaborative work of the logical positivists entitled the *International Encyclopedia of Unified Science* (1939), Carnap in his contribution entitled the 'Foundations of Logic and Mathematics' sketched a semantics for a simple fictitious language in which there are: (1) *designation rules* for the basic terms: names designate things (Carnap remarks that here there "is to be given a complete list of rules for all the names" of the language), and predicates designate properties of things; and then there are (2) *semantical rules* specifying the truth-conditions for sentences: for example, a sentence of the general form, '[name] is [predicate]' is true if and only if the thing designated by the name has the property denoted by the predicate. The semantical rules also include the usual truth-conditions for sentences that are constructed from the former basic sentences by the standard logical truth-functional connectives and quantifiers: for example, a sentence 'not p' is true if and only if the sentence 'p' is not true, and so on (Carnap 1939: 9–10). Carnap sums up this clear and subsequently highly influential basic approach to meaning as follows:

> Since to know the truth conditions of a sentence is to know what is asserted by it, the given semantical rules determine for every sentence of [the language] what it asserts – in usual terms, its 'meaning' – or, in other words, how it is to be translated into English. [. . .] Therefore, we shall say that we *understand* a language system, or a sign, or an expression, or a sentence in a language system, if we know the semantical rules of the system. We shall also say that the semantical rules give an *interpretation* of the language system. (Carnap 1939: 10–11)

Applying this outlook to natural languages, we know (roughly speaking) that 'Schnee ist weiss' in German means that snow is white if and only if we know that the common noun 'Schnee' designates snow and the predicate '___ ist weiss' denotes the property of being white (or perhaps the class of white things). Provided we know or stipulate for a given language which names designate which things and which predicates designate which properties and relations (this is the basic 'relational' foundation in Carnap's account of meaning), then this sort of truth-conditional semantics appears to give us all we need in order to explain the meaning of *any* sentence that might be generated, however complex, in that language. We 'interpret' a language in this sense when we provide it with a logical 'model' (hence the term 'model-theoretic' approaches to semantics). The semantic model is a certain kind of logically structured or ordered list of the objects, properties, relations, and other entities which correspond to the names, predicates, and sentences of the language.[4]

Of course, matters are not as simple as the above picture suggests, as Carnap and all other formal semanticists are well aware. The above gives the basics of what logicians call a purely *extensional* semantics, where the meaning (in the truth-conditional sense) of any given sentence depends only on the extensions or designations of its constituent terms, and the truth-values of compound sentences and other sentential contexts are a function of the truth-values of their constituent sentences, and so on. From the start, however, the founding figure Frege (1892) stressed that a more complex account would have to be given to account for the various non-extensional or *intensional* contexts in which, for example, two co-referential names, i.e. names that designate the same object, nonetheless cannot be substituted for one another in a given sentential context without changing the truth-value of the resulting sentence. In such cases the meaning or 'sense' of a word or sentence seems to depend on more than just its extension (the entity or entities to which it refers). For example, there is a well-known sense in which 'Sally admires Cicero' can be true yet 'Sally admires Tully' false, despite the fact that those names designate the same individual – if, for example, Sally is unaware of that fact. As in this particular case, many examples of non-truth-functional, intensional contexts (with an 's') are provided by intentional contexts (with a 't') in which meaning, to put it loosely, depends not just on *things* referred to or conceived but on *how* they are referred to or conceived, or what psychological attitude is taken toward them.

These cases and others of non-extensional, intensional contexts have generated a rich variety of technical philosophical research programs in the philosophy of language over the past century in the attempt to retain the intuitively plausible 'relation-to-entity' truth-conditional model of meaning of the sort sketched above. Such views characteristically build upon a basic language/world semantic relation of designation or reference, while constructing theories to account for what is going on in the various non-extensional contexts. In many cases, not surprisingly, the most convenient strategies in relation to the latter have involved populating reality with additional entities, so to speak, to serve as the referents for the various designation relations in the problematic intensional contexts. In this spirit, for example, is Carnap's remark during his informal introduction of his own intension/extension distinction in his seminal work, *Meaning and Necessity*: "Then we look around for entities which might be taken as extensions or as intensions for the various kinds of designators" (Carnap 1947: 1).

One characteristic, indeed perennial, way of pursuing this general sort of relational strategy in semantics – the 'look-for-an-entity' approach, as it might be called – has been to posit a so-called 'third world' of *abstract entities* ('third' in the sense of being an addition, perhaps outside of space and time, to the two familiar 'inner' and 'outer' worlds that are the spatio-temporal subject matters of psychology and physics). Thus Frege (1892) distinguished *sense (Sinn)* from *reference (Bedeutung)*, where the sense of a sentence, for instance, is a *thought* or *proposition* understood as a shareable abstract meaning (not merely some particular person's psychological 'idea') that may itself be grasped by many different minds and be instantiated in different sentences in different natural languages. Such views in general will be further reinforced by the various other plausible grounds philosophers have perennially adduced for the apparent need to posit the existence of "a world of universals," as Russell called it in *The Problems of Philosophy* (1912), involving the recognition of such abstract entities as properties, relations, propositions, states of affairs, classes, and so on. Sellars characteristically thinks that there are important philosophical insights to be preserved in this perennial conception of abstract entities, as we shall see later in this chapter.[5]

In very general terms, then, whether the leading logical idea behind the sort of truth-conditional semantics sketched in this section is modified in the direction of a Fregean sense/reference distinction or not, the picture of meaning in either case might be said to offer us a fundamentally *world-relational* conception of meaning. Such views conceive of meaning in terms of basic semantic relations holding between linguistic items and non-linguistic realities, whether directly by understanding meaning in terms of truth-conditions in the one sort of case (perhaps including the postulation of other 'possible worlds,' on many accounts),[6] or as mediated by Fregean senses or other abstract intensional entities in the other sort of case. Varieties of world-relational semantics of these kinds are currently flourishing in nearly every philosophical hedgerow. A Sellarsian *non*-relational, conceptual role account of meaning and reference has its work cut out for it if it is to convince current philosophers of language.

With this sketch of the spirit of relational approaches to semantics as background, let us now to turn to Sellars' alternative conception of meaning. As we have indicated, Sellars thinks that his view differs fundamentally from the approaches described above in his firm "denial that meaning is, in any but the most superficial sense, a *relation*" (EAE 279). He thus wants to reject the basic assumption "that meaning is a relation between a word and a nonverbal entity" (EPM VII.31); or as he elsewhere puts it, he wants to reject "the 'matrimonial' or 'bow and arrow' theory of meaning" (SRLG §67) according to which the semantics of basic descriptive terms, as with Carnap above, "is constituted by the fact that they are associated with (married to) classes of objects" (ITSA 314). To the contrary, Sellars contends, the resulting lists or pairings of linguistic and non-linguistic items in such model-theoretic accounts, while very useful for certain purposes in formal logic, give us as little insight into the *nature* of meaning and truth as a correct list of married couples would give us into the nature of a wedding ceremony or the matrimonial bond.

For Sellars the crucial first step toward an adequately naturalistic synoptic vision of mind-and-meaning-in-the-world will be the recognition that, except in a trivial sense, *meaning is not a relation*. What Sellars will now defend is a view of meaning that is in many ways similar to, and was roughly contemporaneous with, the later Wittgensteinian notion that the meaning of a word is – in a sense requiring careful elucidation – its *use* or *role* within the language (or within a 'language game,' as Wittgenstein developed the latter analogy).[7] On the whole Sellars will attempt to mark out a conception of rule-governed meaning and closely corresponding conceptions of intentionality and of abstract entities that will finally show how to naturalize and integrate, within a holistic, pragmatic, and corrected-empiricist outlook, the 'irreducible' cognitive dualism which we saw in chapter 1 is endemic to the perennial philosophical account of the nature of human conceptual thinking.

After these last general remarks, let us return to ground and consider Sellars' own *non-relational* explication of such modest but crucial semantic sentences as those of the general form, 'word *x* means *y*.'

Sellars' alternative functional role conception of meaning

How could meaning *not* be some sort of fundamental relation between words and non-linguistic entities? Is not the meaning or at any rate the reference of a name precisely the person, place, or thing for which it stands, so that the name 'Paris' stands to the city of Paris in the naming or designation relation? And surely 'red' in English, 'rot' in German, and 'rouge' in French all mean the color *red* precisely because of how standard uses of those words are *related to red things* or to the shareable quality of redness. Indeed, explicitly semantic statements such as " 'Paris' refers to *Paris*" and " 'Rot' (in German) means *red*" do apparently have the surface logical form of a relation holding between two terms, '*aRb*,' and thus seem to state that a linguistic item and a non-linguistic item stand in the (asymmetrical, or one-way) reference or meaning relation.

On the other hand, as Sellars remarks,

> if all one meant by saying that a sentence asserts a relation between two items were that the sentence can be represented by the grammatical form '(a) R (b),' then both '(Jones) ought (to run)' and '("rot") means (red)' would assert relations. Yet philosophers today know how misleading

such appearances can be, and the primary source of this error lies elsewhere. (EAE 280)

The primary source of the error of treating meaning and cognition as fundamental kinds of relations-to-entities is, according to Sellars, a misunderstanding of the significance of what is otherwise a perfectly sound idea. This is the idea that, in standard cases of successful empirical reference at any rate, in order for names and basic descriptive predicates to name or mean what they do, various "empirically definable relations" (EAE 280) must obtain between the relevant linguistic and non-linguistic items involved in the given meaning statement. Sellars thus agrees, for example, that *of course* the word 'red' would not mean what it does if it were not regularly used in statements made in perceptual response to red objects, such as 'that stop sign over there is red.' Meaning statements thus do indirectly convey the information that "appropriate psychological-social-historical (PSH) relations" (TTP 318) – in particular certain reliable causal relations – do indeed obtain in this way between utterances of 'red' and red objects (what sort of relations these are, we shall see presently). But it is a fundamental mistake, according to Sellars, to infer from this that semantic statements such as " 'rot' means *red*" are themselves functioning to *assert* a relation of any kind between 'red' and red things (or the property of redness). Rather, the role of 'means' might be such that the truth of a meaning statement entails that there must *be* certain kinds of empirical-causal relations established between persons' utterances (and thoughts) and various entities, without there being any such thing in the world as a philosophically problematic *meaning relation* holding between those utterances (and thoughts) and those entities. What we need to see now is how Sellars conceives of meaning in just such a manner.

Earlier we saw the plausibility in the idea that 'means' is a relation between words and entities, or between linguistic and non-linguistic entities more generally. It might give us pause, however, if we consider that when we actually use idioms having the abstract form, '[linguistic expression] *x* means *y*,' what occurs on the right-hand side of the meaning statement is often clearly a certain kind of reference to another linguistic expression. This is especially clear in cases where the meaning of a word is being explained to a student of a foreign language, for example, and so to begin to get a feel for Sellars' alternative view let us consider such cases of *translational* meaning. And as a further aid to opening up new lines of thinking, let us take as our initial example not the meaning of a name or a descriptive predicate but rather the meaning of a *logical* word, such as the conjunction 'and.' (This is not to suggest that classical relational semantic theories are insensitive to the unique status of logical vocabulary, which indeed they are not.)

Picking up one of Sellars' oft-used examples, let us then consider in some detail an English speaker's use of the sentence (M):

(M) 'Und' (in German) means *and*.

The *'and'* is italicized to reflect the fact that the word is not being used in this sentence in the normal way as a conjunction (we do not normally end a sentence with an 'and'). In a certain way sentence (M) is exhibiting or displaying the word 'and,' and calling upon our prior knowledge (as English speakers) of its meaning. Now, we are obviously less tempted in this case than in the case of names and descriptive predicates ('Paris,' 'red') to hold that what (M) asserts is that the word 'und' stands in the *designation relation* to an entity, whether to an alleged abstract logico-grammatical entity named *Conjunction* or to a possible ordered list of conjoined items. Rather, the most natural interpretation in this case is that (M) is asserting that 'und' functions in German in the same way that 'and' functions in English, where someone asserting (M) *assumes* that one already has a grip on the role in English of 'and' as a sentential connective.[8] It is as if one were to say: "You know how 'and' works? Well, that's how 'und' functions in German." Essentially what a meaning statement like (M) does, according to Sellars, is to *functionally classify* a given linguistic item (here, 'und' in German) by identifying the role that it plays with a type of linguistic role with which one is already familiar (in this case, with how 'and' is used in English). Here we begin to see one sense in which what Sellars will be offering is a version of the so-called 'use' theory of meaning: the meaning of a term is its use, role, or function within the language (bearing in mind the qualifications on this claim noted earlier). But here we get ahead of ourselves, for first there is more to be said about how sentence (M) conveys this information concerning functional role.

It is important to note the use of such devices as quotation marks and italics in sentences such as (M), for quotation marks in some sense form a name of what falls between them (although as Sellars' story unfolds, such devices in the case of (M) are eventually revealed to be 'functional role classifiers' rather than names). For example, Paris has millions of inhabitants, but 'Paris' has five letters. The quotation marks here serve to *mention* the word itself, rather than *using* the word to refer to a city. It is often important to be clear on this use/mention distinction in contexts where part of what we are talking *about* are linguistic items themselves (and similar points hold when one is discussing *concepts* as well). Similarly, the use of two embedded pairs of quotation marks, " 'und'," is a way of mentioning or referring to *a quoting* of the word 'und,' rather than simply being a mention of the word 'und' itself. It turns out that in "the New Way of Words" in philosophy, as Sellars called it in the late 1940s, one often wants not only to take a step back and talk about words, but to take two steps back and talk about *talk about* words – for example, about the implicit or explicit *quoting* of words, perhaps even in various different senses of 'quoting.' In fact this turns out to be of crucial significance in Sellars' theory of meaning.

The quoting of the word 'und' in (M) might also look to form a kind of name insofar as 'und' is a grammatically *singular term* appropriately followed by 'is,' as for example in " 'und' is a German word" (cf. 'John is a sailor'). However, in giving the meaning of the word 'und' in (M) we intend it to cover *any* appropriately functioning instance or *token* of that German word-*type* (to follow Sellars' use of C. S. Peirce's 'type/token' terminology). The three differently shaped sign-designs '**Und**', 'ᴜɴᴅ' and '*und*' all mean *and*, when appropriately used in German statements and sentences (by contrast, for example, with the sense in which the 'und' in 'Grund' does not so function). But now it might look as if we are referring to or naming an abstract entity again: in this case the *linguistic universal* or type to which a quoting of the word 'und' refers, and of which the three tokens of 'und' in the previous sentence are *instances*. This would land us back with the relational 'word-designates-entity' model of meaning which we are seeking to replace.

Sellars argues, however, that the quoting device is not functioning here as the name of a linguistic universal or abstract object, as the 'name/object' model would have it. Rather, the quoted " 'und' " functions here like certain other singular terms, such as 'the lion' or 'the pawn,' not as the name of an object, but as a way of *generalizing* about (normal) lions or (standard) pawns. When one says that 'the lion is a tawny beast,' one is referring neither to the light-brown color of this particular roaring lion, nor to the tawny color of the shareable attribute of *lionhood* or of *the class* of lions (abstract entities, whatever they are, are presumably not colored). Rather, one is referring to lions in general: take any lion, and in normal cases it will be tawny. 'The lion' is thus functioning, according to Sellars, as what he calls a *distributive singular term* (AE 52n, *SM* 96), in that what is predicated of the lion distributes over or is true of any given individual lion. (This is true despite the existence of cases of painted lions. Compare 'the human animal is a biped,' which is true despite the existence of amputees.)

Sellars' idea is that the " 'und' " in sentence (M) is functioning as a distributive singular term, one that generalizes over particular 'und's as they function appropriately in the speech and writing of competent speakers of German. Instead of saying, for example, that " 'und' (in German) is a word," we could say "The 'und' (or an 'und', or any 'und') (in German) is a word" (compare "The lion is a mammal"); or as we could also put it, " 'Und's (in German) are words" ("lions are mammals"). This opens up the prospect of understanding the role of the quoted word " 'und' " in (M), not on the relational name-of-an-entity model, but rather as a way of saying something about the typical functioning of any of the countless 'und's that might be 'tokened' or produced in the normal way by competent German speakers and writers. (In chapter 4 we shall address the key issue of the *normativity* or rule-governed nature of the idea of a typical, normal, standard, or correct usage.) So, then, what does the 'means' statement (M) tell us about the various 'und's that get typed and printed and uttered by German speakers?

As indicated above, what the meaning statement (M) accomplishes is to call upon the English speaker's antecedent knowledge of how 'and's are used in her own language, in order to convey the information that 'und's in German play the same or a relevantly similar role in the German language.[9] This reference to the role of 'and's in English brings us finally to the idea that the italicized *'and'* in 'means *and'* on the right-hand side of (M), like " 'und' " on its left-hand side, is also functioning to indicate a certain functional role shared by each of the countless cases of 'and' produced by English speakers in normal conversation and writing. An 'and' in English (normally and in a context-relative manner) plays approximately the same role as an 'und' in German. This parallel functioning could be put by saying that 'und's (in German) are 'and's, or an 'und' (in German) is an 'and,' again on the assumption that we already know the use of the latter as speakers of English. What it is to be an 'and' would (as we shall see) be specified functionally in terms of its *role* in the language, not in terms of the empirical shape or size or sound or structure of the various token sign-designs which play that role in different instances ('AND,' *'and,'* etc.).

Sellars developed his well-known device of dot quotation (e.g., •and•) to explicitly register this idea of so mentioning or illustrating a word, as he is arguing we do when we say '*x* means *y*,' that we call attention to the known *functional role* in the language of the word that is illustrated between the dot-quotes. An '•and•' is thus a sortal term – a term applying to all things of a specific sort or kind – covering any item in any language which plays *that* role (or a relevantly similar role). In short, an •and• is any item in any language which functions as 'and's normally do in our language. The *'and'* in 'means *and'* is thus shown to be what Sellars calls an *illustrating* (i.e., a kind of quoting) *functional classifier*; and the 'means' in (M) is correspondingly really an 'is' of a certain kind, a specialized form of the copula. That is, 'means *and'* has the underlying logical form: 'is an •and•' (*NAO* IV.62–8).[10]

In sum, then, a proper understanding of the role of meaning statements such as (M) reveals the 'means' in " 'und' means *and*" to be not a *relation* term, strictly speaking, but rather a functional classifying idiom conveying the information, roughly, that those German 'und's are •and•s. That is, the underlying logical form of (M) is not '*aRb*' but is rather of the general classificatory or sortal form '*a* is an F.' Or finally, picking up on the role of the distributive singular term on the left-hand side (recall 'the lion is a mammal'), meaning statements such as (M) are in effect of the non-relational form: 'The G is an F,' or simply 'Gs are Fs.'

In those of his undergraduate lectures of the 1970s that have been published as *The Metaphysics of Epistemology* (*ME*), Sellars neatly summed up the matter in this way:

> Meaning statements do not talk about relations between words and entities; they classify words within languages with respect to our own base language. A meaning statement takes a word in our own language which functions in a certain way and from that word it forms a classifier which can then be applied to German words, French words, Italian words, Russian words, and so on. Thus [the sentence:
>
>   (M) 'und' (in German) means *and*]
>
> has the form
>
>   'und's (in German) are •and•s
>
> What else would one expect a meaning statement to do? All we are doing is de-mystifying meaning statements: a very fashionable activity in which I indulge with pleasure. (*ME* 245)

On "this functionalist theory of meaning" (MEV III.37), to have a meaning is to play a certain kind of functional role within a wider system. But what sorts of role, and in what kinds of system? And how is the above analysis of the logical or grammatical word 'and' supposed to generalize to cover the cases of names and descriptive predicates, •Socrates•s and •red•s? For surely, it will be said, the meanings of the latter terms involve 'word/world relations' (to things and properties) more directly and essentially than in the case of a sentential connective such as 'and,' where it is perhaps easier to suppose that meaning might solely be a matter of intra-linguistic functional classification and inter-linguistic comparison.

To understand what this functional role conception of meaning thus really amounts to we shall need in the next chapter to examine in some detail Sellars' conception of language as rule-governed and his analysis of what he calls "norm conforming behaviour" more generally (SRLG §1). However, at this point we can introduce the basics of that account as follows.

"Essential to any language," Sellars argues, "are three types of pattern-governed linguistic behavior" (*NAO* IV.31), which he calls:

1   *language entry transitions* (world → language; perception);
2   *intra-linguistic transitions* (language → language; inference);
3   *language departure transitions* (language → world; volition, intention).

What makes something a •red• in any language will be constituted by the uniformities that characterize the learned, holistic, pattern-governed linguistic behaviors of speakers of that language. Accordingly, a child learning the English word 'red' must, through norm-governed social training, come to be such that *ceteris paribus* (i.e., 'other things being equal', 'c.p.'):

1   she reliably responds to the presence of red objects by uttering 'this is red' (for example, when queried as to their color, etc.);
2   she is disposed to make certain sorts of inferences, as from 'this is red' to 'this is colored,' and *not* to make certain others, as from 'this is entirely red' to 'this is also entirely green'; and
3   she reliably responds to her own utterances of 'I will now lift the red one' by lifting the red one.

That 'rot's (in German) mean *red* (i.e., are •red•s) is not constituted by 'rot's standing in putative designation relations either to an abstract entity *redness* or to concrete red objects. Rather, it is by 'rot's (for Germans) being systematically caught up in the sort of rule-governed pattern of perceptual responses, inferences, and volitions as in (1), (2), and (3). (Note in particular the parallel between the three basic types of pattern-governed linguistic behavior outlined here and the three fundamental problem areas for a synoptic vision of the human-being-in-the-world: it is no accident that they both concern *perceiving*, *thinking/inferring*, and *willing*.)

Here we can also see the key *'norm/nature'* relationship anticipated earlier. It is true that for the word 'red' to mean what it does certain naturalistically specifiable and reliable language/world relations must obtain between, say, utterances of 'red' and red objects. (This fact will have crucial implications for Sellars' theory of perceptual knowledge discussed in chapter 5, and his theory of mental and linguistic representation or 'picturing' in chapter 6.) However, the word/world relations that are involved in the transitions or uniformities that are thus *prescribed* by the language entry and exit rules above are ordinary empirical-causal natural relations, not basic semantic or intentional relations. This general distinction between extensional, naturalistic information that is implicitly conveyed or entailed by, but is not explicitly asserted or described in, a semantic statement such as '*x* means *y*' hearkens back to a fundamental meta-philosophical strategy of Sellars' as it was set out in particular in four articles in 1953–4: 'A Semantical

Solution of the Mind–Body Problem' (SSMB), 'Inference and Meaning' (IM), 'Is There a Synthetic A Priori?' (ITSA), and 'Some Reflections on Language Games' (SRLG). These articles laid the blueprint for a conception of mind, meaning, and normativity in which such phenomena were ultimately to be characterized as in some sense *logically (i.e. conceptually) irreducible* yet at the same time *causally reducible* to certain complex extensional, non-normative patterns or regularities in the natural world. (For this particular way of putting the distinction, see SSMB.) The crucial point is that there are complex language/world causal correlations established in nature as a result of the normative communal commitments that are made explicit in the linguistic rules mentioned above. These causal uniformities include, for example, that between utterances of 'this is red,' considered merely as what Sellars calls a *natural-linguistic object* (i.e., as a certain pattern of noises or inkmarks), and the presence (c.p.) of red objects in the nearby environment.

Normative principles, then, are for Sellars conceptually irreducible to the corresponding causal patterns and behavioral uniformities which – learned *oughts* having the default motivational force that they do – they nonetheless systematically generate and generally sustain due to their widespread embrace by the members of the relevant community. There is thus a complex interplay between the *ought* and the *is* in Sellars' theory of meaning and his philosophy generally, which is summed up in the norm/nature meta-principle: "Espousal of principles is reflected in uniformities of performance" (TC 216; more on this in upcoming chapters).

The first step toward making sense of this overall picture of the interdependence of the natural and the normative has been provided by Sellars' non-relational, functional role account of meaning. It is the essential first step, that is, toward understanding what he may have meant when in chapter 1 we saw him assert that the "difference in level" between self-conscious, concept-using human beings and the rest of animate and inanimate nature "appears as an irreducible discontinuity in the *manifest* image, but as, in a sense requiring careful analysis, a reducible difference in the *scientific* image" (PSIM 6). This, I suggest, will turn out to be the same 'logical irreducibility yet causal reducibility' that he had developed in relation to normative concepts a decade earlier in SSMB, and toward the understanding and assessment of which we shall have more to say in later chapters. In the next chapter we explore in particular the conception of linguistic rules and verbal behavior that has been appealed to in this account, and there we shall also finally consider Sellars' theory of the nature of *inner* conceptual thinking in terms of his famous 'myth of genius Jones.'

Before moving on to examine those topics, however, we have opened up just enough of Sellars' functional role conception of meaning in this chapter to take a look at how he uses that theory to address one of the traditional stumbling blocks in the way of a properly naturalistic synoptic vision of mind-in-the-world: the problem of abstract entities.

The problem of abstract entities: introducing Sellars' nominalism

Sellars once wrote, "Philosophers have a peculiar form of the Midas touch. Everything they touch becomes a puzzle, and eventually a problem" (*NAO* II.1). In this case there are common-sense distinctions between concrete individuals, on the one hand, and matters that are more general or abstract, on the other, which when touched by philosophers from Plato to the present have generated various versions of the perennial problem of 'the one and the many,' most notably the problem of *universals* and of abstract entities more generally. Our discussion here will be designed to introduce the basic problem and to bring out the key initial stages of Sellars' novel nominalist approach to abstract entities.

A 'universal' in this context refers to something that by its nature can be exemplified by or instantiated in many individuals or particulars. Suppose that on a table there are three wooden triangles, *a*, *b*, and *c*: an isosceles, an equilateral, and a right-angled triangle. Each particular concrete triangle has a different location in space and a different history in time. Each, however, exemplifies (or perhaps approximates to) the same shareable property of *triangularity* or *being triangular*. The philosophical problem of universals and of abstract entities concerns the existence and nature of such *shareables* as triangularity. Does 'triangularity' denote some reality that exists in addition to or perhaps 'abstracted from' the concrete triangular objects *a*, *b*, *c*, in which it is instantiated? What is it about reality that *makes it true* that all three differently shaped and located objects are *triangular*?

Arguably the two main contrasting positions in relation to the problem of universals are Platonism (platonic realism) and nominalism, with conceptualism representing an important but unstable mediating position. I will focus primarily on the contrast between platonism and nominalism (using 'platonism' with a small 'p' to generalize beyond, and to avoid interpretive controversies concerning, Plato's own views).

In Plato's dialogues, a dialectical examination of the nature of mathematical knowledge, moral ideals, and other universal conceptions leads to the conclusion that in knowledge we pass beyond the 'visible and tangible' world of changing particular perceptible things to the 'invisible' intelligibles or 'Forms.' Plato characterizes the forms as the pure, eternal, uniform, divine, non-composite and unchanging objects of knowledge (Plato 1961: *Phaedo* 68–81, *passim*). In the *Phaedo* Plato has Socrates offer a model of explanation according to which, taking beauty as his example, "whatever else is beautiful apart from absolute beauty" – that is, apart from 'the beautiful itself,' or the form of beauty – "is beautiful because it partakes of that absolute beauty" (100c).

It is helpful to look at the logico-linguistic phenomena that mirror Plato's insights here. Singular terms are terms that are used to refer to one item, while adjectives, general terms, and common nouns are used to denote properties and kinds that are shared by many things. Let 'F-ness' be shorthand for the various abstract terms that are formed from adjectives in the way that 'beauty' is from '*x* is beautiful' ('*x* is F'), or 'wisdom' from 'wise,' 'triangularity' from 'triangular,' and so on. Suffixes such as '-hood,' '-ity,' '-kind,' '-dom,' '-ness,' etc., thus serve to form *abstract singular terms*, as in 'Wisdom is a virtue,' the surface grammar of which suggests a reference to an individual abstract object, *wisdom*. A particular perceptible thing, *a*, is F, on the general platonist view, due to *a*'s partaking of or participating in *F-ness itself* (or because of the 'presence,' in some sense, of F-ness 'in' *a*).

A platonic realist thus seeks to explain how it is that many individuals can be characterized by the same one quality or be of the same general kind, by appealing to the real existence, independent of the mind, of the abstract entity *F-ness*. In addition, the intersubjectivity of concepts and the objectivity of knowledge, as well as the sameness of meaning across different languages, would similarly be explained by the fact that the same abstract, unchanging platonic entity, F-ness, is grasped by (or comes to 'in-form') the minds of all those different thinkers and speakers who in their different mental and linguistic media assert or judge *that a is F*.

Very briefly, conceptualism is similar to platonism in accepting the objective reality of abstract universals, but differs in holding that the being of a universal is essentially *being conceived by some mind*: by our finite minds, or, on many medieval views, ultimately as conceived in God's divine intellect. Finally, the nominalist contends that ultimately there are no objectively real universals or abstract entities; all that exists are individuals. Universal concepts and general truths concerning individuals, for the nominalist, are ultimately a matter of how those individuals are represented in thought or in language (hence the term 'nominalism,' from the Latin '*nomina*': words or names). The burden on the nominalist is to explain how exactly it is that *general* conceptual representation is possible without illicitly reintroducing precisely the sorts of abstract entities to which the platonist and conceptualist had understandably appealed. It will be convenient for our purposes to focus on certain well-known twentieth-century controversies between platonists and nominalists.

Variations on platonic realism with respect to universals and abstract entities have in particular been ably defended over the last century or so by mathematical logicians such as Russell (explicitly), Frege (on standard readings), and more recently Quine, whose naturalism, as we shall see, reluctantly embraced platonism with regard to sets as abstract entities that he contends are required for mathematics. Russell, for instance, argued in 'The World of Universals' chapter of his classic introductory book *Problems of Philosophy* that "no sentence can be made up without at least one word which denotes a universal. [. . .] Thus all truths involve universals, and all knowledge of truths involves acquaintance with universals" (1912: 96). He consequently character- ized his own theory as "largely Plato's, with merely such modifications as time has shown to be necessary" (1912: 91). In this general connec- tion Sellars also cites what he calls "a recent formulation of the Platonic thesis" by the well-known mathematical logician Alonzo Church, in 'The Need for Abstract Entities in Semantic Analysis' (1951). Sellars remarks that this formulation "is the more valuable in that it is taken from a paper by one of the central figures in the current controversy over abstract entities" (EAE 258). Here, then, is Church on the mind's 'grasp' of abstract entities:

> The extreme demand for a simple prohibition of abstract entities under all circumstances perhaps arises from a desire to maintain the connection between theory and observation. But the preference of (say) *seeing* over *understanding* as a method of observation seems to me capricious. For just as an opaque body may be seen, so a concept may be understood or grasped. And the parallel between the two cases is indeed rather close. In both cases the observation is not direct but through intermediaries – light, lens of eye or optical instrument, and retina in the case of the visible body, linguistic expressions in the case of the concept. (Church 1951: 104)

Platonism would at first blush, however, seem to be difficult to reconcile with philosophical naturalism as we have been understand- ing the latter outlook since chapter 1, and so also with the sort of synoptic vision sought by Sellars and other naturalistically inclined philosophers. Russell, for instance, frankly admits that a separate, changeless 'world of universals' must be posited in addition to nature understood as a system of dynamic spatio-temporal-material processes. The epistemological and metaphysical relations holding between the unchanging abstract entities (if they *are* held to be unchanging) and ordinary changing material entities inevitably remain difficult to characterize, to put it mildly – as Plato himself demonstrated in his *Parmenides* with unrivalled brilliance.

Many contemporary philosophers consequently are of the view that accepting the existence of abstract objects, like accepting classical soul/

body dualism in the philosophy of mind, ought to be thought of as a kind of philosophical last resort. That is, if the positing of such (apparently) non-spatio-temporal entities can be shown in the end to be *indispensable* as part of an adequate theoretical explanation of something that we all agree needs explaining, then so be it. However, if an adequate alternative explanation eschewing such problematic entities is available, then, other things being equal, such an account is to be preferred. On the other hand, it must be admitted that many, perhaps most, contemporary philosophers do continue to hold that a broadly platonist acceptance of or 'ontological commitment' (to use Quine's term) to universals or other abstract entities is not only intuitively plausible but also, despite initial appearances to the contrary, consistent with naturalism when the latter is interpreted as a *methodological* thesis rather than a substantive ontological thesis (more on this below).

It was against the backdrop of these more recent disputes between platonism and nominalism in logic, semantics, and the philosophy of mathematics that Sellars attempted to articulate a thoroughgoing and substantively naturalistic nominalism that would also succeed in preserving the insights, as he saw them, of both traditional platonism and conceptualism. Here I shall present only the rudiments of his account of abstract entities, and show in particular how it is a generalization of his functional role conception of semantics as introduced in the previous section.

Consider the sentence '*a* is triangular.' Earlier in this chapter we saw that according to many classical 'world-relational' semantic theories the meaning of this sentence would typically be explained in terms of its two main components being related to or designating two items (using 'items' in the broadest possible sense): the singular term '*a*' refers to the particular thing or object *a*, and the predicate '___ is triangular,' let us suppose, has the effect of attributing the property or attribute *triangularity* to the object *a*.[11] The abstract singular term 'triangularity' on such a view may be held to designate the universal *triangularity*, and both the English adjective 'triangular' and the German adjective 'dreieckig' will be said to *stand for* that universal.

Sellars' functional role semantics suggested a different model for meaning. Starting with word-meaning sentences of the form, 'word *x* (in language *L*) means *y*,' the analysis of the sentence

'Und' (in German) means *and*

ultimately yielded

'Und's (in German) are •and•s,

where the contrived common noun '•and•' covers any item in any linguistic system that has the same (or a relevantly similar) norm-governed functional role within that system as that of the term illustrated between the dot-quotes, a role upon which one already has a grip, so to speak. We briefly saw how this account is supposed to be extended to non-logical terms (our example was: 'rot's (in German) are •red•s) in terms of the normative functions that characterize the linguistic behavior of a community as governed by language entry, language exit, and intra-linguistic (i.e., inferential) rules.

So taking up our most recent sentence, '*a* is triangular,' how is the meaning of the predicate '___ is triangular' to be understood now on Sellars' non-relational conception of meaning, in such a way as to avoid any commitment to platonism? Beginning as before with the context of meaning and translation, we analyze

'dreieckig' (in German) means *triangular*

as

'dreieckig's (in German) are •triangular•s.

This reflects the (norm-laden) fact that the behavior of 'dreieckig's in German speakers' linguistic entry/inference/exit uniformities roughly parallels the behavior of 'triangular's in our own linguistic behavioral economy. How now should we understand the statements that the classical relational semantic paradigms fix upon, as when it is said that the predicates 'triangular' and 'dreieckig' both *stand for* the abstract entity *triangularity*?

Sellars' basic strategy, worked out in detail in 'Abstract Entities' (1963; and also see GE in particular), is to suggest that the function in natural languages of abstract singular terms such as 'triangularity' is not to name alleged abstract objects, platonic or otherwise. Rather, they are revealed to be *metalinguistic* terms that serve to pick out linguistic types or roles that may be played by or 'realized in' many linguistic materials or 'pieces' (as the •triangular• is realized in German by *dreieckig*s), in roughly the way in which earlier in this chapter we saw that 'the pawn' in 'the pawn captures diagonally' can serve as a *distributive singular term* or DST, equivalent to '*pawns* capture diagonally' (thus 'distributing over' pawns severally). In this way, as Sellars puts it, " 'triangularity' would be the singular term which stands to the role played by •triangular•s as 'the pawn' stands to the role played by pawns" (AE 55).

In this approach to abstract entities Sellars has built upon and modified some important distinctions introduced earlier by Carnap in his

Logical Syntax of Language (1934). 'Triangularity' as it occurs in sentences belonging to what Carnap called the *material mode of speech* looks as if it refers to a non-linguistic abstract entity. In fact, however, sentences incorporating 'triangularity' are typically what Carnap called *quasi-syntactical sentences* or *pseudo-object sentences*: "sentences which are formulated as though they refer [. . .] to objects, while in reality they refer to syntactical forms" (Carnap 1934: 285). In a logically perspicuous language, on Carnap's view, such sentences are to be analyzed or translated into the *formal mode of speech* as sentences that in fact say something about the word 'triangular.' A statement in the material mode of speech such as 'triangularity is a property of objects,' which is a typical example of a statement in philosophical ontology or in formal semantics, would on Carnap's style of analysis have as its proper formal mode syntactical translation (this is not a quote from Carnap): " '___ is triangular' is a one-place predicate of English taking singular terms as its arguments [that is, names are used to fill in the blank]." Corresponding to 'property' is the syntactical-logical term, 'one-place predicate'; to 'object' corresponds 'singular term'; and 'triangularity' gives way to the predicate '___ is triangular.'

Sellars' functional role account introduced above makes clearer than Carnap's purely syntactical account, from which it takes its initial inspiration, that the senses of such terms as 'triangularity' and 'property' are such as to apply *across languages*. This feature is neatly captured by Sellars' functionalist elucidation of 'the •triangular•' as covering any item in *any* representational system that plays the relevant role. Furthermore, Sellars will take some care to spell out the normative dimensions that are involved in specifying how the relevant functional roles are reflected in linguistic rules and embodied in flesh and blood patterns of behavior – a story that will ultimately climax in an account of inner *thoughts* as the realization in brain-processes of such functionally specified, propositionally contentful episodes as the occurrence, in the mind, of a •Socrates is wise• (that is, of a thinking *that Socrates is wise*). The latter gives at least a hint as to how Sellars will extend his analysis to interpret such abstract entities as *propositions* and *facts*, as built up in natural languages compositionally out of such linguistic role-players as a •Socrates• and a •wise•, and in terms of the parallel holistic functioning for English and German speakers of tokenings of such sentences as 'Socrates is wise' and 'Sokrates ist weise.' Most important here will be the truth context, 'that Fa is true,' or '•Fa•s are true,' along with a normative account of truth-claims as having the function, to put it in a nutshell, of licensing the assertion of the mentioned sentence (see chapter 6). In fact it will turn out that "the primary member of the family of abstract entities [. . .] is the proposition, and the key predicate is 'true' " (*SM* 110). We are clearly only at the beginning of a complex story.

In general, then, for Sellars, traditional distinctions in categorial ontology, philosophy of mind, and semantics that make use of the linguistic framework of abstract entities will in this way turn out to be essentially formal or *metalinguistic* classifications that carve *representational systems* at their joints, rather than directly carving up putatively corresponding non-linguistic entities, whether abstract or concrete. Sellars finds the roots of this philosophical insight in Wittgenstein's *Tractatus*, which had influenced Carnap, but also much earlier in Ockham's nominalism, and in an especially robust and sophisticated form in Kant's theory of the categories as second-order conceptual rules.[12]

In light of what we have seen in this chapter we are in a position to understand why Sellars characterizes his own view as a *psychological nominalism* in relation to what is (and what is not) involved in the mind's capacity to 'grasp' conceptual meanings; or again as a *linguistic nominalism* in relation to his theory of semantics and abstract entities, according to which the latter are ultimately linguistic types or roles themselves explained in terms of particular rule-governed linguistic tokenings. Sellars regards the consequences of these clarifications concerning meaning and abstract entities to be "truly revolutionary" in relation to the possibility of finally developing what he calls an adequately "naturalistic-empiricist" account of the nature of the mind:

> The linguistic framework of abstract entities, which is such an indispensable part of human discourse, not only semantical discourse, but mentalistic discourse and scientific discourse generally, as well, does not involve a commitment to Platonism. It is a misinterpretation of semantical sentences, a 'category mistake,' which has generated the contrary supposition. [. . .] Today, for the first time, the naturalistic-empiricist tradition has the fundamentals of an adequate philosophy of mind. To the creation of this truly revolutionary situation, which is just beginning to make itself felt, Carnap's *Logical Syntax of Language* and *Introduction to Semantics* have contributed at least as much as any other single source. (EAE 282)

Abstract entities: problems and prospects for the metalinguistic account

Although we have only taken the first few steps into Sellars' comprehensive theory of abstract entities, we have taken in enough of his view to be in a position to consider three challenges confronting his basic linguistic nominalism. (The theory of meaning on which that nominalism is based will be further examined in the next chapter.) While Sellars' proposal has challenges to overcome, on the whole it represents an ingenious attempt to demystify the classificatory resources of traditional platonistic ontology and formal semantics by explaining them in terms of his own conceptual role semantics, thus clearing the way for a genuinely naturalistic account of the nature of conceptual thinking.

The first objection may already have struck the reader, and it was voiced by Sellars himself as follows: "I have often been asked, what does one gain by abandoning such standard platonic entities as *triangularity* or *that 2 + 2 = 4* only to countenance such exotic abstract entities as *functions, roles, rules* and *pieces*" (*NAO* IV.137). One might ask, that is, what is really achieved in relation to "the debate between platonistic and anti-platonistic philosophers" by Sellars having argued that the abstract entity "Redness [. . .] is the word •red• construed as a linguistic kind or sort which is capable of realization or embodiment in different linguistic materials, e.g., *red*, *rot*, and *rouge*'" (AE 49)? For it might well appear that, far from having achieved a thoroughgoing nominalism, all that Sellars has accomplished is to replace the classical platonist's picture of *redness* as the same one universal quality multiply instantiated in fire engines, stop signs, and apples, with a picture of the universal •red• as the same one *linguistic type* or abstract role multiply instantiated 'in different linguistic materials,' according to the pattern: one abstract role/many concrete 'realizers' of that role.

Sellars' response to the objection is as follows: "The answer is, of course, that the above strategy *abandons nothing but a picture*. Triangularity is not abandoned; rather 'triangularity' is *seen for what it is*, a metalinguistic distributive singular term" (*NAO* IV.137). This is a rather cryptic response to a serious objection (and the "of course" does not make it more clear). What is left particularly unclear is just how this appeal back to Sellars' initial interpretation of 'triangularity' in terms of the metalinguistic distributive singular term (DST) 'the •triangular•' is supposed to assuage the objector's worry. For the objector's worry is that Sellars' subsequent account of what it is to play the role of a •triangular• simply reintroduces 'such exotic abstract entities as functions, roles, rules, and pieces' by the backdoor, saddling us with platonism again. (Loux 1978: 242 expresses a similar puzzlement.)

However, what Sellars was attempting to convey by the cryptic remark is that *neither* triangularity *nor* functions, roles, rules, etc., are abandoned, but rather *both* are 'seen for what they are': metalinguistic distributive singular terms (DSTs). That is, the basic Carnap-inspired metalinguistic strategy for handling abstract entities turns on itself, as it were, consistently applying the same analysis to, for example, *what it is to be a role* or *rolehood*. As Sellars put it in a later correspondence with Loux on the issue, "surely all I am saying in the passage you quote is that abstract singular terms for these entities [that is, functions, roles, rules, and pieces] are to be handled by the same strategy as is used to handle 'triangularity' " (*NAO*, Correspondence with Michael Loux,

¶23). But how then *are* the DSTs 'the •role•' or 'the •function•' to be interpreted, analogously to 'the •red•' or 'the •triangular•'? Sellars' general strategy dictates that we reflect on the patterns-of-use of the word 'role,' for example, which in the pertinent case of *linguistic* roles will quickly bring us back to the idea that we apply the term 'role' to items that are *rule-governed* in the ways captured by Sellars' language entry, exit, and intra-linguistic uniformities.

The problem of the ontological status of abstract entities thus bottoms out for Sellars, I suggest, in the same location as the general problem of the nature of meaning: namely, at the question of how *norm-conforming, rule-governed behavior* is to be understood – or as we saw earlier, in the issue of how the normative is related to the natural order. As we know, this self-conscious shift of focus has been at the center of Sellars' overall strategy, his naturalism with a normative turn, from the very beginning of his career. What Sellars in the end has done is to trade the problem of abstract entities for the problem of the status of *normative rules*; and as we indicated earlier and shall explore in upcoming chapters, Sellars hopes to be able to render the latter compatible with the sort of thoroughgoing ontological naturalism portrayed in the idealized scientific image of man-in-the-world.

A second intuitive objection to Sellars' theory might be that it seems absurd to suggest that when we speak of a universal, shareable quality such as *redness* we are really talking about a certain linguistic role, and not, as it surely seems we are, about a certain color. Likewise, surely *triangularity* has to do with triangles, triangular things, or the essence shared by all triangular things, and not primarily with language.

However, it is open to Sellars to respond to this objection that, first of all, triangularity on his view is not something parochial to some particular natural language, nor is it something identifiable with some particular linguistic item. Rather, triangularity pertains to •triangular•s in *any* language (or any 'language of thought,' for that matter).

Furthermore, and more importantly, Sellars can insist that triangularity *is* a matter of how reality is carved at its joints, but in a more complex and indirect manner than the naïve realist or the platonist supposes. To put it bluntly, and by way of appeal to some notions that will be developed in chapter 6, the function of abstract entities is to *carve at the joints of representational systems*, and the primary (empirical) function of the latter systems is to *picture or map the structure of reality*. English and German speakers use the words 'triangular' and 'dreieckig' in roughly similar overall patterns in their various perceptual and pragmatic dealings with triangular things and in their geometrical reasonings. These ordinary empirical and formal inquiries result in inner or outer tokenings of propositions such as •*a* is triangular•s that aim to represent the way a bit of the world is. More refined and

systematic inquiries might lead to *conceptual change*, as when Euclidean
•triangular•s ("i.e., inscriptions which function as does our word 'triangular' when it is governed by specifically Euclidian principles,"
NAO IV.134) become non-Euclidean, Riemannian •triangular•s, in
which case our conceptual representation of the fundamental nature of
spatial reality has changed. In this sense, *triangularity* has changed:
"abstract entities, *pace* Plato, change," according to Sellars: "Obviously
it is in no ordinary sense that they change, yet it is a legitimate one at
that" (*SM* V.42). By serving to classify conceptual roles and thus elements of representational systems, abstract entities on Sellars' account
are revealed to be culturally evolved, metalinguistic, cross-language
devices the primary function of which in relation to basic empirical
inquiries, I suggest, is to *conceptually track our ongoing attempts to conceptually represent the nature of reality*. Abstract entities, as it were, are
metaconceptual carvings of our attempts to conceptually carve at the
joints of reality. Consequently the realist intuition that such abstract
entities as shareable qualities or multiply instantiated kinds belong to
the 'real order' rather than the 'conceptual order' is thus accommodated through considerations pertaining to how closely and systematically those two orders are structurally connected on Sellars' view,
when his overall conception of linguistic representation and conceptual
change is taken into account.

This is a powerful version of nominalism – one which, if it succeeds,
would enable us to have our cake of traditional abstract entities and
eat it too. On the one hand, Sellars' view preserves the perennial idea
that abstract entities do in some sense exist – misleadingly put, 'triangularity' is the name of one of them – and in a carefully specified sense
they do indeed transcend particular historical languages and individual minds. An abstract singular term such as 'triangularity' is a
culturally evolved metalinguistic device for conveying the perceptual-
inferential-practical role played by •triangular•s in our ongoing
cognitive engagements with physical reality. That is, it indicates
the role played by any item in *any* language or conceptual framework
that behaves in the same or relevantly similar normatively pattern-
governed way as do typical utterances and inscriptions of *triangular*s
in English and *dreieckig*s in German. Yet, on the other hand,
Sellars can thereby capture the realist's intuition without introducing
different 'kinds of existence' or 'modes of being,' and without
admitting platonic abstract entities *as a special kind of object* in addition
to the spatio-temporal-causal framework of physical objects and
events.

Sellars considers abstract entities so conceived to play a vital role in
philosophy's ongoing attempt to synoptically envision "how things
in the broadest possible sense of the term hang together in the
broadest possible sense of the term" (PSIM 1). The ever more refined

development of such metaconceptual classificatory terms is part and parcel of our Socratic endeavor for rational self-awareness, dramatically symbolized by Socrates' own revolutionary advance, in philosophical dialectic, from the critical classificatory engagement with *things* to include the critical classificatory engagement *with our classificatory engagements* with things. This is why Sellars, though he has proposed the most thoroughgoingly naturalistic, anti-platonist nominalism currently on the philosophical map,[13] also avows that he is a "card-carrying member of the Platonic tradition" who "subscribe[s] to the view that Plato wrong is usually closer to the truth than other philosophers right" (KBDW ¶13).

I conclude that the first two sorts of objections we have considered have not shown Sellars' proposal concerning abstract entities to be implausible. To the contrary, we have seen that the payoffs in relation to the task of achieving a thoroughly naturalistic yet compatibilist synoptic vision of mind-and-meaning-in-the-world are certainly significant enough to recommend philosophers' further attention to Sellars' metalinguistic account.

However, there are other important kinds of objection to Sellars' theory of abstract entities, in particular technical ones concerning both the details and execution of his analysis and the question as to whether this or any brand of nominalism is adequate to handle certain well-known phenomena that continue to be thought by many (perhaps most) philosophers to require the positing of some variety of platonist abstract entities.[14] We should not close this chapter without referring to one further difficulty of the latter kind. This objection concerns the widespread view ably defended in particular by Quine since the 1950s that we must in the end, if reluctantly, fall back on platonism in admitting the real existence of *sets* or classes as mathematical abstract objects. Quine in fact discussed Sellars' particular version of nominalism in a 1980 article entitled 'Sellars on Behaviorism, Language and Meaning' (see also BLM), where Quine put the nub of the issue between them as he sees it as follows:

> [W]e seem to need to quantify over [. . .] sets in order to establish the continuity of the real numbers; and without this we do not, perhaps, have a mathematics adequate to the ordinary needs of natural science. This, finally, is what drives me to a realist position, however unwelcome, regarding sets.
>
> [. . .] My attitude toward talk of numbers or classes is of a piece with the attitude toward syncategorematic expressions [such as 'and'] that [Sellars] and I surely share. One difference between us is that I now tend to attach less weight to reification than I once did, and than he does. Even so, it is strange to find myself on the realist's side of a nominalist–realist debate. I would be over there fighting the good fight shoulder to shoulder with Sellars were it not for the difficulties set forth in my earlier

comments. I need no persuading of the attractions of nominalism if it
can be got off the ground. (Quine 1980: 28, 30)

This particular challenge for Sellars' or any other nominalist outlook
raises difficult and important issues in the philosophy of mathematics.
For instance, Sellars' nominalism commits him to a non-platonist view
of mathematical truth in terms of *provability* (see *SM* IV.62, V.55), which
is a respectable but certainly not uncontroversial outlook in the philosophy of mathematics. Sellars did discuss how his theory of abstract
entities might be applied to certain issues concerning the foundations
of mathematical logic (see, e.g., his 1963 article 'Classes as Abstract
Entities and the Russell Paradox,' CAE); and Jeffrey Sicha (1974, 1978)
has attempted to work out the essentials of a Sellars-inspired treatment
of some key concepts in logic and arithmetic. In several places Sellars
also briefly addresses the challenges his nominalism faces from the
direction of platonist philosophy of mathematics (e.g., *NAO* I.15n,
I.32–4). On the whole, however, I think this is an area in which it
is yet to be shown whether Sellars' nominalist, functional role
account of abstract entities can provide an adequate philosophy of
mathematics.[15]

Let us conclude this chapter with one last twist on this problem,
however, for it is arguable that on this last particularly vexed issue
Sellars is no worse off than anyone else. As was argued by Paul Benacerraf in an important article on 'Mathematical Truth' (1973), philosophers of mathematics continue to be confronted by a fundamental
dilemma: while it might be contended, as by Quine, that the most
plausible accounts of mathematical truth seem to require a platonic
reference to abstract entities, nonetheless the most plausible *epistemological* accounts of how we could come to know mathematical truths
– and hence, we might add, the possibility of any genuinely adequate
synoptic vision of 'man-in-the-world' – would seem to entail the denial
of any such reference.

Those familiar with Quine's work will know that he would mobilize
his *methodological* conception of naturalism in order to disagree with the
latter claim. On Quine's version of naturalism, a theorist is in principle
free to admit the existence of *any* type of entity, whether Cantorian Infinite or Platonic Form or Cartesian Soul, provided that it can be shown
to be an indispensable posit on the most plausible interpretation of our
best current scientific theories.[16] In what follows we can see that Sellars
persuasively takes up the offensive against the particular way of using
"the Duhemian [holistic] strategy" that lies behind Quine's version of
naturalism on precisely those epistemological grounds. The relevant
passage is worth quoting in full for its neat summary of Quine's important views on these matters as well as for indicating Sellars' plausible
and significant area of disagreement with Quine:

[S]uppose a [Quinean] platonist with respect to attributes and/or[17] classes to be asked: "Must there not be matter-of-factual relations between abstract entities and human minds by virtue of which abstract singular terms acquire a hook-up with the world?" Might not our platonist reply: "It is our theory as a whole, including its logical apparatus and such sortal predicates as 'molecule', 'positron', 'attribute', 'proposition', 'class', 'class of classes' etc., which confronts the tribunal of experience. Our language hooks up with positrons and classes alike by virtue of the application of the theory to experience. It is only the will-o-the-wisp of the analytic-synthetic distinction which keeps one from recognizing that 'class' and 'proposition' are in a continuum with 'current' and 'positron'. It is simply a matter of degrees of theoreticity, of remoteness from the occasion-sentences elicited by sensory stimulation."

The following consideration, however, should generate a measure of skepticism with respect to this facile gambit. The theory-whole has specific things to say about the causal relations which connect micro-physical objects with the sensory stimulations which bombard the sensory surfaces of experimenters looking at bubble chambers and photographic plates. The theory explains *how* we are in touch with micro-physical objects.

Thus, in addition to the Duhemian point that *expressions* for micro-physical particles acquire a hook-up with micro-physical particles by virtue of belonging to a theory which is applied as a whole, the theory offers a causal account of the *specifics* of the hook-up. This is not the case with such terms as 'number', 'class', 'attribute', and 'proposition'. This fact introduces a radical discontinuity into Quine's Continuum, one which has important consequences for the problem of abstract entities, for ontology and, above all, for the philosophy of mind. (*NAO* I.32–4, Sellars' paragraph numbering omitted)

It seems to me that Sellars here raises an important objection to Quine's view – although pending an adequately elaborated nominalist account of mathematics it only serves to bring us back to the standoff of Benacerraf's dilemma.

In his article on Sellars Quine reports that he had responded to a letter in which Sellars had asked him the same basic question as above, namely: "How does the mind get in touch with sets?" Quine indicates that he replied to Sellars with "another question: 'How does the mind get in touch with neutrinos?' [. . .] Epistemologically, sets differ from neutrinos only in being somewhat less analogous to observable bodies" (Quine 1980: 28). But in response to the more detailed objection raised above by Sellars, Quine in the end grants that

[b]etween numbers or classes on the one hand and the elementary physical particles on the other there is indeed the important difference, as he [Sellars] says, that our senses are causally connected, however indirectly, with the particles and not with the numbers or classes. An

epistemological account of our talk of numbers or classes is to be sought rather in inferential or semantical connections between sentences that contain references to numbers or classes and sentences that are more sensitive to observational evidence. (Quine 1980: 29)

Following this passage Quine adds the remark quoted earlier: "I now tend to attach less weight to reification than I once did."

Much hinges on the resolution of this debate in the philosophy of mathematics. I will leave the matter, however, with the suggestion that, if successful, Sellars' *substantively* naturalistic account of abstract entities, according to which such entities are fully incorporated, ultimately as rule-governed linguistic tokens, into the one spatio-temporal-causal fabric of nature, in this respect perhaps scores one better than a Quinean *methodological* naturalism the content of which reluctantly includes causally inert (and in that respect surely, for naturalists, *prima facie* mysterious) platonic abstract entities. Overall, then, while the key debate between platonists and non-platonists in the philosophy of mathematics certainly remains an open question, Sellars' novel and detailed functional role conception of abstract entities represents one of the more interesting recent approaches to the philosophical problem of universals and abstract objects, laying out the groundwork for a thoroughgoing and substantively naturalistic nominalism that is well worth philosophers' further attention.

It is time for us now to return, however, to the basic functional role conception of meaning itself, upon which Sellars' unique account of the nature of abstract entities has been based. As anticipated, the question that now confronts us is whether or not Sellars can succeed in putting the hard-earned results of the present chapter to use in accounting for the nature of *inner* conceptual thinking, and in particular whether he can do so in a way that will finally 'stereoscopically' integrate that uniquely human aspect of our manifest mental life into the comprehensive scientific image of our ultimately physical nature.

4

Thought, Language, and the Myth of Genius Jones

In the previous chapter we saw Sellars put forward a 'non-relational' account of meaning and abstract entities that represents a middle way between broadly platonist and broadly empiricist approaches to those topics. In this chapter our first task will be to explore Sellars' alternative functional role conception of meaning in more detail, for this is both the backbone of his philosophical system and the subject of much recent philosophical discussion. Most importantly, however, that examination of linguistic meaning will set the stage for Sellars' 'myth of genius Jones' in the second half of the chapter. The latter is the centerpiece of the novel *normative functionalist* account of the ontology and epistemology of inner mental acts that Sellars was developing as far back as the early 1950s. The question as to whether Sellars is thus justified in approaching the nature of thought through an initial focus on verbal behavior will also be addressed in the later stages of this chapter.

Meaning and pattern-governed linguistic behavior

Sellars' account as developed so far is that meaning is a unique kind of *functional classification* rather than a uniquely problematic kind of relation-to-entities. The meaning of a linguistic item is a matter of the role that it plays or the job that it does within a given linguistic community or conceptual framework. The job description for something to qualify as an •and•, for instance, would specify the relevant logical and grammatical rules of inference for conjunction with which we are all implicitly familiar, as demonstrated by our generally correct patterns of usage. Standard German 'und's do roughly that same job, and that is why 'und' means *and*, which is to say that German 'und's play the role of our •and•s. We have also seen that according to Sellars there are three types of pattern-governed linguistic behavior that are essential to any functioning language:

1 *Language entry transitions*: The speaker responds, *ceteris paribus*, to objects in perceptual situations, and to certain states of himself, with appropriate linguistic activity.
2 *Intra-linguistic transitions*: The speaker's linguistic conceptual episodes tend to occur in patterns of valid inference (theoretical and practical), and tend not to occur in patterns which violate logical principles.
3 *Language departure transitions*: The speaker responds, *ceteris paribus*, to such linguistic conceptual episodes as 'I will now raise my hand' with an upward motion of the hand, etc. (*NAO* IV.31; cf. SRLG §§22–3; *SM* IV.61–2).[1]

Let us begin by looking more closely at the general idea of a linguistic job specification or a semantical rule.

Sellars presents the three types of behavioral transitions or "uniformities" listed above as an idealized and simplified classification of what he calls the "semantical rules" or the "semantical uniformities and rules of criticism" that characterize any language in use (*SM* IV.61–2). These uniformities are the linguistic 'expression' (in several senses)[2] of our three basic cognitive capacities for (1) sense perception, (2) making inferences, and (3) willing or intentional action, respectively. The meaning of an ordinary empirical term such as 'red,' on Sellars' holistic view, is essentially a matter of its norm-governed functional role in all three types of linguistic uniformity (as opposed to a semantic *atomism* that might attempt to assign the term or concept 'red' a meaning based solely on its association or connection with red things or with the property of redness).[3] Philosophical problems pertaining to meaning, on Sellars' view, thus ultimately concern the nature and status of the *rules* that specify the sorts of holistic functional roles in which meaning consists.

Right away, however, we cannot fail to notice that Sellars has characterized these linguistic functions, on the one hand, as *uniformities* or behavioral transitions, but, on the other hand, as semantical *rules* or rules of criticism. This requires some explanation. On the one hand, 'uniformity' suggests a mere factual regularity of some kind, such as the natural uniformity that thunder always follows lightning. On the other hand, 'rule of criticism' suggests something that may be explicitly obeyed or disobeyed by an intelligent agent, such as the grammatical rule that one ought not to split infinitives. What we need to get a grip on is Sellars' complex conception of verbal behavior as *pattern-governed uniformity* which is at the same time *rule-following normativity*; a mode of habitual or 'second nature' behavior that is also a product of critical rationality. In 'Language as Thought and as Communication' (1969) Sellars provided the required clarification of "the nature and status of linguistic rules" (LTC 506) with a carefully elaborated distinction between what he called *rules of criticism* or *ought-to-be* rules, and *rules of action* or *ought-to-do* rules. This distinction will prove to be a crucial one.

Ought-to-do rules of action specify what some intentional agent ought to do. They are of the schematic form, 'if one is in circumstance C, then one ought to do A.' Such rules apply only to intentional agents who know what they are doing in the sense that they have the relevant recognitional capacities: they have the concepts of *doing A* (for example, of *putting the child to bed*) and of *being in C* (for example, *its being nine o'clock*), so that they can set about doing A when they *believe* the circumstances are C (LTC 508).

Ought-to-be rules of criticism specify how something ought to be. An ought-to-be rule might take the form, 'Xs ought to be in state φ, whenever such and such is the case.' Sellars' example is the ought-to-be rule in a given community that *clock chimes ought to strike on the quarter hour* (LTC 508).

There is a connection between rules of criticism and rules of action, which is "roughly, that ought-to-be's imply ought-to-do's" (LTC 508). In this case the implied ought-to-do rule of action is that (other things being equal and where possible) *one ought to bring it about that clock chimes strike on the quarter hour*, which "requires that the item to which *it* applies (persons rather than chimes) have the appropriate concepts or recognitional capacities" (LTC 508).

Consider next, however, another example used by Sellars: the ought-to-be rule that *one ought to feel sympathy for bereaved people* (LTC 509). This resembles an ought-to-do rule of action in the respect that any subject to whom this rule applies must have acquired (or be in the process of acquiring) the concept of what it is for someone to be bereaved. On the other hand, *feeling sympathy* in response to someone else's bereavement is not normally a *doing* in the sense of an *action* that one intentionally performs – one does not normally *intend* to feel sympathy for someone. Rather, feelings of sympathy of this kind are directly circumstance-evoked responses that people within a given cultural context normally find themselves experiencing in circumstances which they are capable of conceptually recognizing to be of a certain kind.

Sellars now applies these distinctions to the three basic types of linguistic rule listed earlier, which turn out to be semantical 'ought-to-be' rules of criticism. The three types of 'entry/inference/exit' semantical uniformities in our verbal behavior, similar to the example of feeling sympathy for the bereaved, are *learned conceptual responses and inference patterns that are not themselves intentional actions* ("though actions can consist of sequences of pattern-governed behavior" of those kinds[4]). Appropriate perceptual responses or language entry transitions, for instance, are in this respect similar to feeling sympathy for the bereaved: they are conceptual responses but not intentional actions. Such responses and behavioral transitions have simply become, as it is commonly put, 'second nature' to us.[5] I do not *intend* to take there to be a burglar when I open the door, as if I might perform this perceptual recognition as an intentional action. Rather, this is just how the visual and auditory scene immediately strikes me, given that I have learned how to recognize burglars: that is, given that I have already acquired the concept of a burglar. The same point holds for intra-linguistic inference patterns and for language departure transitions as well. "It is the pattern-governed activities of perception, inference and volition, themselves essentially *non-actions*, which underlie and make possible the domain of actions, linguistic and non-linguistic" (*NAO* IV.34, italics added). (This ground-level conception of pattern-governed behavior will be central to Sellars' conception of 'thinking-out-loud' later in this chapter.)

There is of course such a thing as *intentionally using language* as an instrument or tool to perform a wide variety of communicative actions and speech acts, such as saying 'I do' to conclude a wedding ceremony, or even simply intending to communicate information to another person.[6] However, this is a higher-level, relatively sophisticated way in which meaning is conveyed through the 'instrumental use' of language to fulfill an agent's intentions. Sellars' *functionalist* conception of 'meaning as use,' however – in terms of a linguistic item's rule-governed conceptual role or 'use' within a wider inferential network, in a "non-instrumental sense of 'use' " (*NAO* V.48) – lies at a more fundamental level. For it accounts for what it is for any utterance or mental event to have any conceptual content or meaning in the first place, which one might or might not aim to communicate or use to perform some linguistic action. The simple, unreflective muttering to oneself 'This bus is late again' is an episode that has conceptual content in this sense, whether or not one intends to communicate that information. (Note that this is consistent with the view, which Sellars also defends, that a cognitively functioning conceptual system does indeed also require systematic higher-level 'ought-to-do' rule-following by agents, as we shall see.)

This point, which we shall find to be central to Sellars' views on the relationship between linguistic behavior and inner thinking, is reflected in Sellars' careful formulation of his three basic semantical rules. He is careful *not* to say, for instance, that in a language entry transition Smith responds to *her observation* that x is red by *saying* that 'x is red.' Rather:

Smith is disposed to respond to *red objects* in perceptual situations by *uttering* 'x is red' (other things being equal, of course). The former formulations are already at too sophisticated a level of cognition for Sellars' more fundamental explanatory purposes. They would presuppose that Smith already possesses the relevant concepts and executes those conceptual capacities in cases where she conceptually recognizes something to be red. Sellars, however, is explaining what wider patterns or uniformities of behavior and utterance must already be in place in order for any such utterance (and consequently, as we shall see, in order for any inner mental event) to successfully constitute a case of observation, conceptual recognition, or propositional saying in the first place.

Accordingly one must carefully distinguish the correctness or rightness of an intentional *action* – for example, was it a rational, wise, or morally appropriate thing for agent Jones to cross the picket line? – from the more basic *semantic correctness* of the sequence or event that consisted simply of Jones's 'language departure' from his tokening (i.e., uttering or thinking) an •I shall *now* cross the picket line• followed immediately by his moving across the picket line. This 'volition →behavior' uniformity or causal transition is not *itself* an action or piece of controversial conduct to be evaluated, though it may be, as in this case, an essential part of such an action. Put figuratively, volition →behavior transitions are the stuff of which intentional actions are made, but the transition *itself* is not a peculiarly fast little intentional action.[7] The language exit or departure transition is simply an unreflective, habitual exercise of the will, a basic acquired conceptual-cum-causal capacity that is necessary for the possibility of any intentional action at all. In sum, the "basic point to bear in mind is that a piece of pattern-governed behavior is *as such* not an action [. . .] and is correct or incorrect not as *actions* are correct or incorrect, but as events which are not actions are correct or incorrect. An obvious example of the latter," as we saw above, "would be the correctness of *feeling sorrow* for someone who is bereaved" (*NAO* IV.29).

Children come to acquire such conceptual capacities in large part because their elders – let us follow Sellars' (and the later Wittgenstein's) convenient if somewhat artificial terminology and call them the language *trainers*, and the learners the *trainees* – provide the proper normative "ambience" of criticism (LTC 513; PSIM 40) by doing and saying, in accordance with ought-to-do rules of action, the sorts of things that will help shape the child's responses to be as they ought-to-be according to communally accepted standards or norms. As Sellars puts it, the trainers "can be construed as reasoning, 'Patterned behavior of such and such a kind *ought to be* exhibited by trainees, hence we, the trainers, *ought to do* this and that, as likely to bring it about that it *is* exhibited' " (*NAO* IV.28; cf. SRLG §§16–17).

Returning to the analogous case of the acquired capacity to feel sympathy for the bereaved, very young trainees will at first lack the requisite conceptual capacities for recognizing cases of bereavement *as* cases of bereavement. It may not be clear to them, for instance, that the reason everyone at the funeral is so gloomy is that someone has lost a loved one. However, through natural imitation as well as the trainers' encouragement of appropriate behavior and admonishment of inappropriate behavior (no giggling at funerals, etc.), the developing sympathetic feelings and associated behaviors of the trainee will gradually come to be of the right sort and to be channeled in the right directions. That is, they will gradually come to be as they ought-to-be.

The point is that roughly the same account as in the bereavement case is applicable to the case of the child's acquisition of those ought-to-be behavioral patterns that constitute the *semantical* uniformities of a given language or conceptual framework. The child is gradually guided (1) to respond to an object with a •this is red• utterance or thought when and only when (other things being equal) she is in fact in the presence of a red object (i.e., a language entry uniformity); (2) to be habitually disposed to 'move' or 'transition' in the language game from an •*x* is red all over• to an •*x* is not green• (a *material inference*[8] uniformity); and (3) to follow up an •I shall lift the red one *now*• by lifting the red one (a language exit uniformity).

In sum: "Trainees conform to *ought-to-bes* because trainers obey corresponding *ought-to-dos*" (*NAO* IV.30). Or as Sellars encapsulates the point in what I have called his *norm/nature* meta-principle: "espousal of principles is reflected in uniformities of performance" (TC 216). What we have gradually been clarifying by means of the examples above is the simultaneously norm-governed yet causally efficacious basis in language learning for the tight link – which a few pages back seemed puzzling – between the notion of semantical *rules* that are subject to rational criticism, on the one hand, and the resulting *uniformities* or habitual patterns of behavior that correspond to them, on the other. The latter 'semantical uniformities,' as Sellars calls them, are the actual flesh-and-blood causal products of the communal commitment to the corresponding semantical rules. We shall return again to this crucial aspect of Sellars' 'naturalism with a normative turn,' as I have called it, later in this and in subsequent chapters. Before closing this section let us tease out just a few more fundamental conceptions concerning pattern-governed linguistic behavior, again making use of the bereavement example.

At what point – of course there is no exact 'point' – the young trainee may be said to have acquired a given *concept* is consequently a holistic matter and one of degree. (We shall encounter these points again in the next chapter in relation to Sellars' theory of knowledge, which closely reflects his theory of meaning.) For any utterance to express an •*x* is bereaved• thought, for example, it must be functioning in a certain norm-governed way within a wider pattern of language entry/inference/exit uniformities. The child, for instance, must have a minimally adequate grip on what sorts of cases are bereavements, which will itself require a basic grasp of what someone's being bereaved entails, and with what sorts of conditions or behavior it might be inconsistent. It is important to note, however, that the successful, gradual conforming of the trainee's behavior to the relevant ought-to-be rules does not require that the *trainee herself* initially possess the relevant conceptual understanding involved. Thanks to the trainers, the properly raised child confronting situations of bereavement will already begin to exhibit appropriate pattern-governed behavior before, and as the necessary prerequisite for, the stage at which we would be prepared to say that the child has a simple grasp of (or ability to recognize) what a situation of bereavement is.

To characterize the trainee's behavior as 'pattern-governed' rather than explicitly 'rule-obeying' behavior is primarily to emphasize this point that while the trainee's behavior occurs *because it fits the pattern* that ought-to-be (in large part due to the trainers doing what they ought-to-do to bring this about), the trainee herself may as yet have no idea that her behavior conforms to that wider pattern.[9] To echo Kantian terminology, the very young child might as yet merely be behaving *in conformity with* the ought-to-be rule rather than being able to act *under the idea* that this is how things ought-to-be, for the child does not yet have an adequate grasp of the reasons why one behaves in these sorts of ways in these types of situation. (This will constitute the ultimate basis in language learning for Sellars' famous conception of knowledge as a normative standing in the *logical space of reasons*, to be examined in the next chapter.)

Bedrock uniformity and rule-following normativity in the space of meanings

All of the above distinctions have gone toward clarifying Sellars' account of meaning in terms of rule-following or norm-conforming behavior. The latter topic has subsequently become the subject of much controversy in the literature, and although we cannot pursue the matter in detail here, it is of sufficient importance to merit at least a brief encounter.[10] Put roughly, and borrowing a size metaphor from Kant's antinomies, the classical 'rationalist/platonist *too much*' vs. 'empiricist/naturalist *too little*' dilemma that we witnessed earlier in relation to accounts of meaning and abstract entities in general has in recent decades taken a particular shape in relation to conceptions of meaning in terms of *rule-following*. Sellars can in retrospect be seen to have presciently articulated and attempted to resolve the difficulties that are involved in such rule-following accounts (see in particular SRLG and LTC).

Sellars approached the issue in 'Some Reflections on Language Games' (1954) in terms of a paradox that threatens any conception of language learning as learning to obey rules, a simplified version of which is as follows. Suppose that for Jones to know the meaning of any word w Jones has to obey (and hence know) some linguistic rule L concerning the correct usage of w. But for Jones to grasp a rule such as L which mentions 'w,' he will clearly have to understand the words that occur in the statement of the linguistic rule itself (at the very least that 'w' refers to w). And this will presuppose that he already possesses knowledge of prior rules governing the use of *those* words, and so on *ad infinitum*.

One obvious way to block the ensuing vicious regress is to suggest that Jones does not need to *know* the rules that govern his correct uses of w. Rather, it merely has to be true of Jones that he *does in fact* use (or is disposed to use) w in ways that are in fact generally correct. However, this broadly empiricist solution in terms of mere factual conformity to a rule seems to give us 'too little' (using Kant's metaphor) to account for meaning. For one thing, this characterization would equally well apply to imaginable cases in which someone just *happened* to (be disposed to) use word w in correct patterns, fortuitously, and hence while not knowing what w means at all. Others such as Kripke have recently raised further difficulties for such purely 'factualist' or 'dispositionalist' accounts by drawing upon Wittgenstein's famous "paradox [that] no course of action could be determined by a rule, because every course of action can be made out to accord with the rule" (Wittgenstein 1953, §201; Kripke 1982). For instance, alternative interpretations of 'how to go on' in accordance with a given rule can be gerrymandered to fit any given sequence of behaviors or any finite set of dispositions to behave in a certain manner, considered merely as such. The latter facts thus do not seem to capture the normative aspect of meaning. This is further evidenced by the fact that we are also, of course, disposed to use words *incorrectly* on occasion, in such a way that presupposes a prior capacity to recognize norms or rules *as binding* on one's behavior. Mere behavioral conformity to a rule, it would seem, is not enough to account for the grasp of meaning.

Alternatively, the rationalist will typically propose that the regress is to be blocked by proposing that Jones does not need to *learn* the most basic linguistic rules after all. Such knowledge, the rationalist contends, is *innately* possessed by Jones prior to, and as making possible, his learning any particular language. However, if that solution is articulated along the classical dualist lines sketched by Platonists and

Cartesians, then for reasons rehearsed since chapter 1 we are likely to be saddled with 'too much' to integrate into a properly synoptic vision of our place within the spatio-temporal-causal fabric of nature. On the other hand, if such innate linguistic knowledge is interpreted as a causal structure that is 'hardwired' into the human brain, then this threatens to reduce to a rationalist version of the first, non-normative alternative of 'mere factual conformity,' which we have just rejected.[11]

One of Sellars' governing insights since his earliest published articles (e.g., ENWW, 1947) has been the idea that both empiricist and rationalist approaches have in this way ultimately been vitiated by their *"factualist"* (and consequently 'relational') pictures of the nature of cognition, meaning, and knowledge. All of the latter phenomena can be adequately accounted for only in terms of a normative 'pure pragmatics,' as Sellars called it in those early writings, which makes fundamental appeal to the role of community norms and the implicit intersubjective espousal of principles.[12] Sellars' resulting conception of pattern-governed linguistic behavior has offered us a middle way through the 'meaning as rule-following' dilemma. Language entry/inference/exit uniformities, as we have seen, conform to the linguistic *ought-to-be* rules of criticism that are espoused within a given linguistic community. Such patterns are what they are *because* of the trainers' espousal of those normative rules (thus avoiding the empiricist 'too little'), yet without those rules or patterns having to be grasped, envisioned by, or innately 'built into' those trainees who are gradually learning to conform to them (thus avoiding the rationalist 'too much'). That breaks the regress.

But of course it does so only by shifting the locus of the puzzle to questions concerning the *trainers'* community-wide espousal of normative rules or principles. However, at that social level the rule-following puzzles arguably become more tractable. For Sellars the lesson is that, "as Wittgenstein has stressed, it is the linguistic community as a self-perpetuating whole which is the minimum unit in terms of which conceptual activity can be understood" (LTC 512). If one were to ask Sellars: 'But where did the communal principles and linguistic ought-to-be rules espoused by the trainers come from?', then the answer is of course: 'By cultural transmission from previous generations.' If one were then to press further and ask: 'But how did the very *first* hominid community ever acquire its knowledge of normative linguistic rules in the first place?', then this turns the matter over to the ongoing theoretical task of adequately explaining the evolutionary origins of language and of rationality in the species as a whole – a problem that hangs Sellars only if it hangs us all.[13]

The overall result is that the patterns or functional roles encapsulated in Sellars' language entry/inference/exit uniformities may now intelligibly be understood in their character as entirely natural, customary, instinctive, or 'second nature' to us, and so as typically taking place without any explicit higher-order cogitation concerning rules or justifications. Yet at the same time these immediate responses and unreflective associations are linguistic 'ought-to-be's which *by their very nature are subject to normative assessment and rational appraisal.* They are bedrock uniformities due to their having become ensconced within a given 'space of reasons.' As Wittgenstein famously put it:

> 'How am I able to obey a rule?' – if this is not a question about causes, then it is about the justification for my following the rule in the way I do.
>   If I have exhausted the justifications I have reached bedrock, and my spade is turned. Then I am inclined to say: 'This is simply what I do.' (Wittgenstein 1953: §217)

Our pattern-governed linguistic behavior is rule-following in the way that Wittgenstein compares to our following a sign-post: "I have been trained to react to this sign in a particular way, and now I do so react to it" (1953: §198). Wittgenstein has his interlocutor object that this "is only to give a causal connexion; to tell how it has come about that we now go by the sign-post; not what this going-by-the-sign really consists in," to which Wittgenstein's response is: "On the contrary; I have further indicated that a person goes by a sign-post *only in so far as there exists a regular use of sign-posts, a custom*" (1953: §198, italics added). It is the maintenance, transmission, and transformation of the *ought-to-be* norms and customs in a given linguistic community that make possible the sort of pattern-governed, rule-following linguistic behavior in which the 'grasp' or 'possession' of meaning entirely consists.

Let us now see how Sellars attempted to apply this overall conception of meaning in terms of pattern-governed linguistic behavior in approaching perennial problems pertaining to the nature of *inner* conceptual thinking and intentionality.

Our Rylean ancestors and genius Jones's theory of inner thoughts

Many philosophers would be inclined to regard all of this elaborate analysis of our linguistic behavior to be a focus on the mere *effects* of our inner grasp of meaning rather than an account of the nature of meaning itself. Surely all of those patterned noises and inkmarks have meaning or are about anything only in virtue of being produced or interpreted by some *thinking* being. Furthermore, surely I can know directly what I myself am presently thinking – I have a 'privileged access' to my own thoughts, as philosophers put it – without my having to rely upon the sort of external behavioral criteria that others must use in order to suss out what I am thinking. In a well-known debate on the nature of intentionality between Sellars and Roderick Chisholm in 1956, Chisholm employed a vivid analogy as part of his criticism of Sellars' fundamentally behavioral-linguistic methodological starting point with respect to the puzzling or "peculiar" phenomena of meaning and intentionality:

> Should we say that there is a funny characteristic (i.e., a characteristic which would not be labelled by any physicalistic adjective) which belongs to living things – or that there is one which belongs to certain noises and marks?
>
> When the question is put this way, I should think, the plausible answer is that it's the living things that are peculiar, not the noises and marks. I believe it was your colleague [John] Hospers who proposed this useful figure: that whereas both thoughts and words have meaning, just as both the sun and the moon send light to us, the meaning of the words is related to the meaning of the thoughts just as the light of the moon is related to that of the sun. Extinguish the living things and the noises and marks wouldn't shine any more. But if you extinguish the noises and marks, people can still think about things (but not so well, of course). Surely it would be unfounded psychological dogma to say that infants, mutes, and animals cannot have beliefs and desires until they are able to use language. (Chisholm in Sellars ITM 524)

On Chisholm's account, intentionality pertains primarily and intrinsically only to inner mental events or attitudes, and merely secondarily and derivatively to language and all other external signs. If that is so, however, then perhaps Sellars' elaborate 'non-relational' analysis of meaning in terms of pattern-governed linguistic behavior must all along simply have presupposed and relied upon the "peculiar" mental power of intrinsic intentionality – a kind of basic 'relational directedness toward objects' that would be possessed by thoughts as such. This, however, threatens to saddle us with an updated version of the Platonic or Cartesian *cognitive dualism* that was discussed in chapters 1 and 3. If Chisholm is right, then from Sellars' perspective we would really have made no progress at all with regard to our central task of achieving a synoptic vision of the thinking human being within the natural world as ideally characterized in the scientific image.

What Sellars will now attempt to show is in effect that we can have it both ways, in senses that will be clarified presently. The heart of his account was put forward most famously in 'Empiricism and the Philosophy of Mind' in 1956 in terms of his "myth" or "piece of [. . .] anthropological science fiction" concerning the appearance of "genius Jones" among our prehistoric "Rylean ancestors" (EPM XIIff.). In what follows I will freely supplement that story with certain expository devices and terminology that Sellars developed in later writings to fill out what remained essentially the same seminal philosophical account of the nature of the mind and our knowledge of it. Let us take some time and attempt to get a grip on Sellars' overall big picture first, and then circle back to lay out and evaluate the myth of genius Jones in more detail.

First, then, what are the 'both ways' that I have indicated Sellars thinks we can have it?

On the one hand, (a) Sellars wants to hold on firmly to his non-relational 'language game' account of semantics understood exclusively in terms of pattern-governed linguistic behavior as detailed above. Meaning, 'aboutness,' and so-called ('intrinsic') intentionality are thus in the first instance public, intersubjective phenomena pertaining to our rule-following linguistic behavior, according to Sellars (for 'intrinsic,' see *NAO* V.23). However, at mid-century Ryle's philosophical behaviorism in *The Concept of Mind* (1949), as well as in certain respects Wittgenstein's language game account of meaning and understanding in *Philosophical Investigations* (1953), had essentially proposed that we should stop right there. *All there is* to thinking, on Ryle's account at any rate, is to be found in our acquired, multi-track dispositions to verbalize and act in various complex, rule-governed ways. Sellars himself articulated this Rylean outlook in some detail in terms of what he calls the *verbal behaviorist* or 'VB' model of thought as *thinking-out-loud* (see especially MFC, reprinted in *NAO* ch. IV).

Two preliminary points about Sellars' Rylean VB model are worth stressing right away. First, the VB model of thought as overt speech includes, of course, all of our incredibly complex long-term and short-term acquired *propensities* or 'if–then' *dispositions* to think-out-loud (i.e., in speech) in various pattern-governed ways, if and when the appropriate circumstances arise. And secondly, the phrase 'thinking-out-loud' is intended to remind us of the important sense in which Sellars' VB model is to a certain degree "contrived" or simplified (*SM* 158) in that it focuses specifically on that genuine stratum of our thinking which is simply unreflective, candid, spontaneous verbalizing, such as one might quietly mutter all alone by oneself while doing the dishes, without the intention to perform any communicative *action*.[14] (We emphasized this earlier in relation to the discussion of linguistic 'rules of criticism' vs. 'rules of action'.)

On the other hand, (b) while Sellars in this way essentially agrees with the Rylean and Wittgensteinian conceptions of meaning and intentionality as public, broadly linguistic phenomena, Sellars *also* wants to agree with Chisholm and the classical tradition that the Rylean verbal behaviorist account of thinking – which Sellars does believe is correct in certain precisely limited but important respects – is indeed, in the end, explanatorily inadequate. We do have inner thought-episodes or 'mental acts.' And on Sellars' account we have them in a way that goes beyond what Ryle and Wittgenstein would officially allow (on standard readings, at any rate), but which nonetheless fully respects their insights into the social, behavioral-linguistic nature of meaning and intentionality – insights which have been rigorously developed in Sellars' own theory of meaning as detailed since the beginning of chapter 3. Sellars thus indicates that it is his "purpose to defend [. . .] a revised classical analysis of our common-sense conception of thoughts," one which holds that "to each of us belongs a stream of [inner] episodes [. . .] to which we have a privileged, but by no means either invariable or infallible, access. These episodes can occur without being 'expressed' by overt verbal behavior, though verbal behavior is – in an important sense – their natural fruition" (EPM XI.47). So Sellars intends to defend a robust conception of thoughts as propositionally contentful 'inner' mental events or mental acts that are characterized by intentionality, and to which we each have a high degree of privileged access. (The account of privileged access will come toward the end of the story.)

However – and this is the key point – unlike Chisholm and the classical tradition, Sellars believes that our conception of the intentionality of these inner thoughts is itself conceived *by analogy with the autonomous intentionality of public, pattern-governed linguistic behavior* as the latter is described on the Rylean VB model. The intentionality of our inner thoughts is thus conceived on the independent model of the (non-relational, normative) functional role conception of public linguistic meaning and intentionality with which we are by now familiar. Our *conception* of the intentionality of inner thoughts is thus derived from our *conception* of the intentionality of rule-governed linguistic behavior, rather than the reverse. Sellars in this way hopes to "reconcile the classical idea of thoughts as inner episodes which are neither overt behavior nor verbal imagery and which are properly referred to in terms of the vocabulary of intentionality [i.e., (b) above], with the idea that the categories of intentionality are, at bottom, semantical categories pertaining to overt verbal performances [i.e., (a) above]" (EPM XII.50). Thinking is thereby conceived by us as a kind of 'dialogue in the soul' (as Plato put it), as *analogous* to the idea of an 'inner speech.' Or to use later terminology, there is (in a sense that needs to be carefully qualified) a 'language of thought' or 'Mentalese' which embodies in its own distinctive way the crucial semantic 'aboutness' and the systematic propositional features possessed by public spoken languages.[15] Of course, the analogy will have to be purged of obvious disanalogies: inner thinking, for example, is "not the wagging of a hidden tongue, nor are any sounds produced by this 'inner speech' " (EPM XV.57).

This overall conception of thought will in the end allow Sellars, unlike Plato or Descartes, to plausibly contend that the normative functional role-players that are our *inner* perceptions, inferences, and intentions may be fully 'realized in' complex patterns of neurophysiological processes in the brain. This is because those inner thoughts will have been understood on a theoretical analogy with how our semantically rule-governed 'entry/inference/exit' linguistic behaviors are entirely embodied in complex pattern-governed "noises and marks," as Chisholm called them above – in the •It is raining•s and •Would that I were home!•s of various publicly spoken, typed, and written languages. We shall finally have achieved, Sellars contends, a properly naturalistic synoptic vision of our *thinking* nature, while also keeping a firm grip on the irreducibly normative and inter-subjective dimensions that are necessary for the possibility of rational, conceptual thinking.

When the appropriate distinctions are made we can also recognize the various senses in which, as the classical account stresses, inner thinking is more fundamental than the outer 'languagings' to which it sometimes but not always gives rise. Sellars frequently made use in this connection of a general distinction that goes back to Aristotle between that which is *prior in the order of being*, or ontological priority, and that which is *prior in the order of our knowledge* and conception, or methodological priority.[16] (The Aristotelian distinction between the 'better known *in itself*' as opposed to the 'better known *to us*' is another way of framing it.) Let us consider two examples of this general distinction, and then apply it to the present case of thought and language.

First to take a classic example: St. Thomas Aquinas argued that our rational knowledge of the existence and nature of God must, in light of our merely finite nature, be built up painstakingly by analogies and inferences based on the independently secure and autonomous knowledge we have of finite material things. However, once Aquinas has thus undertaken to prove that the finite world ultimately depends on the existence of an Infinite Being, and once he has understood God's attributes as best he can based on various 'negative' and 'positive' aspects of analogy with our own finite attributes (God is wise, but *infinitely* so, etc.), then he will conclude that God is ultimately prior *in the order of being* to the entire finite material world, as its First and sustaining Cause. Aquinas can make the latter ontological claim while continuing to stress that our *knowledge* of finite things is inde-pendent, methodologically autonomous, and primary *in the order of our conception.*

As a second example, returning to the sublunary realm, Sellars' stereoscopic synoptic vision of the human-being-in-the-world involves a similar global distinction but within a radically inverted conception of ultimate reality, with modern theoretical science in effect having replaced Aquinas's theological conception. The manifest image of persons, norms, and ordinary colored objects, on Sellars' view, is methodologically and autonomously prior in the order of our conception to the postulated scientific image of the world in terms of unobservable swarms of colorless microphysical particles. Nevertheless, Sellars' scientific realist contention is that the world as conceived in the scientific image is ultimately prior in the order of being to the world as conceived in the manifest image. As we saw in chapter 2, scientific theories reconceive the intrinsic nature of the manifest phenomena in ways that provide demonstrably and increasingly better explanations of how and why the manifest world appears to us precisely in the ways that it does. The manifest image constitutes our methodologically autonomous and conceptually prior understanding of the world, but nonetheless its categories *ultimately* fail to provide adequate explanations for the phenomena that fall within its own domain.

Sellars now applies the same general distinction to the particular case of attempting to synoptically account for our thinking nature. Let us follow him in using the phrase 'inner thinking' for thought and intentionality as classically construed, and 'thinking-out-loud' for thought and intentionality as construed on his Rylean VB model (where the latter is to be understood in the 'semantically rich' sense of the functional role, normative rule-following account we have been detailing). Sellars' contention is that our conception of rule-governed thinking-out-loud is autonomously prior in the order of knowledge to our conception of inner thought-episodes, and that we understand the latter only by analogy with the former. However, our inner thoughts are ultimately prior in the order of being to our thinking-out-loud (and we *do* think-out-loud, on Sellars' view).[17] This is because the postulation of such "unobserved" inner thoughts – and at a deeper level, the postulation of what Sellars in his last writings called *animal representational systems* in general (MEV 326) – provides a more adequate explanation of the phenomena that fall within the purview of our original Rylean VB model itself. So while Sellars disagrees with the classical view insofar as he construes "*concepts* pertaining to the intentionality of thoughts as derivative from *concepts* pertaining to meaningful speech" (MEV 326), ultimately he takes the intentionality of thoughts to be ontologically and causally prior to the intentionality of meaningful speech that is its natural 'expression.' It is important to bear in mind that according to Sellars our Rylean "verbal behavior as thinking-out-loud has *intrinsic* intentionality" (*NAO* IV.23). This remains true despite the fact that *not all* our thinking is thinking-out-loud; despite the fact that *not all* thinking, in ourselves and of course in other animals, is *linguistic* (as Sellars clarifies in MEV); and despite the fact that the best explanation even of our thinking-out-loud conceives it to be the causal 'expression' of inner conceptual thought-episodes taking place in inner representational systems (e.g., in the cerebral cortex).

That is Sellars' big picture of the nature of thought. Let us now briefly tease out some of the important details of the story as told in the myth of genius Jones itself, in both EPM and later writings.

Sellars' myth of Jones is designed to reveal something about the nature and status of our concept of mind through the telling of a rationally coherent hypothetical story as to how that concept might have arisen on the basis of non-controversial sources of evidence that everyone can now accept on reflection.[18] He compares his myth "to the role of contract theories in political philosophy" (*SM* VI.10). No one believes that at some point in history there was 'an original social contract' that was actually agreed between sovereign and citizens by which the inalienable political rights of all citizens were forever secured. Yet Locke and others shed much light on the source of our rights by telling a pseudo-historical story of that kind which appeals only to general principles that are reflectively sanctioned by *our own* practical rationality.

Sellars' myth of genius Jones has it that at a certain stage in prehistory our Rylean ancestors – named, of course, after Ryle's own sophisticated account in *The Concept of Mind* – were limited to a concept of mind that construes all thinking as (what *we* post-Joneseans would call merely) *thinking-out-loud* in overt speech and acquired dispositions to such. And then along comes genius Jones:

> Suppose, then, that in the attempt to account for the fact that his fellow men behave intelligently not only when their conduct is threaded on a string of overt verbal episodes – that is to say, as *we* would put it, when they 'think out loud' – but also when no detectable verbal output is present, Jones develops a *theory* according to which overt utterances are but the culmination of a process which begins with certain inner episodes. *And let us suppose that his model for these episodes [. . .] is that of overt verbal behavior itself. In other words, using the language of the model, the theory is to the effect that overt verbal behavior is the culmination of a process which begins with 'inner speech'.* (EPM XV.56)

According to this "Jonesean theory," again in terms of the model, "the true cause of intelligent nonhabitual behavior is 'inner speech' " (EPM XV.56).

Thus, when our silently fidgeting Rylean ancestor Sally, for example, looks around and then suddenly switches to another ticket line, genius Jones posits that something is going on in Sally which is similar to, and which she would naturally have expressed by muttering to herself: 'That line is moving faster than this one.' The cause of her line-switching behavior, Jones now proudly teaches his fellow Ryleans, was the occurrence in her mind of a silent inner *thought* that is language-like in (at least) the sense that it has the same meaning or propositional content as the sentence Sally would have mumbled to herself had she been in a thinking-out-loud frame of mind. That is, Jones theorizes (using what *we* would think of as simply common-sense psychological explanation), that something functionally classifiable as a •That line is moving faster than this line• occurred within the holistic 'entry/inference/exit' logical space of Sally's language of thought as she stood there fidgeting. And this inner thought, in conjunction with the similar covert presence in Sally of a •Would that I enter quickly!• thought (or *desire*), led to Sally's •I shall now switch lines• thought (or *intention*), which was the 'language exit' volition that caused the silent but rational line-switching behavior that genius Jones has now explained.

Why exactly is this Jonesean explanation of our behavior in terms of inner thoughts more adequate than the semantically and normatively rich *pre*-Jonesean Rylean explanation in terms of complex long-term and short-term propensities to think-out-loud? Why not stick with the original Rylean VB account interpreted as the whole truth? Why not endorse Ryle's own behavioristic *analysis* of the concept of mind (as supplemented with Sellars' normative-semantic account, of course), rather than using it as a model for a theoretical account of inner thoughts, as on Sellars' and Jones's merely *methodological* behaviorism? On the former, our thinking is entirely analyzed in terms of complex 'if–then' behavioral-linguistic dispositions and social-normative rules pertaining to such. On the latter, which might also be called the 'outside-in' approach to the mind, the postulation of inner functional role-players in a kind of 'Mentalese' is part of a proposed *causal explanation* as to why those behavioral patterns are the way that they are. Why go for the latter? Sellars in various places suggests several respects in which Jones's explanation counts as an improvement on the complex verbal behaviorist analysis.[19]

First, once the general Jonesean idea is proposed, we can better account for the behavioral evidence which suggests, for example, that we can think much *faster* than we can speak. As Sellars put it in his introductory undergraduate lectures (and likewise see also *NAO* V.13, SK II.50-52, and MFC 465, on the 'speed' of thought):

> [V]erbal behaviorism cannot get off the ground unless you go from what people actually say out loud to their propensities. But then since people act reasonably much more quickly than they can talk, we must suppose that these propensities change and shift very, very quickly. Thus, already at the level of verbal behaviorism, these propensities get characteristics which do not, in any direct way, mirror the clumsiness of sheer verbal expression. It has always traditionally been said that thought moves very quickly; we speak of moving with the speed of thought and so on. Therefore, already at the commonsense level, I think people begin to sketch a richer theory according to which there are episodes that occur in persons which can occur very quickly. The idea is that there are episodes which

are not propensities to say things, but are part of a framework for explaining why these propensities occur as they do, how they are related to one another, and why they change with the speed with which they can change. (*ME* 333)

The final sentence in this passage also points to a second, more fundamental sense in which Jones's explanation is superior to the VB account, as follows.

One general characteristic of many good theoretical explanations, as we saw in chapter 2, is that they explain why and how things are observed to exhibit the propensities to behave in the ways that they do by revealing the 'unobservable' *constituent structures and occurrent processes* that are causally responsible for those behavioral regularities. We observe that a certain pill, for instance, regularly prevents sea-sickness, and this observed uniformity is neatly summarized in various 'iffy' truths concerning its propensity to do so. A good theory, however, will seek to explain how such dispositions are caused by specific postulated events that are occurring throughout the process at the micro-chemical level as the digested ingredients in the pill circulate in the human body. Or again, we explain a magnet's "iffy property of being such that if iron filings are present, then they cling" to it, by means of the postulation of certain 'categorical' or non-iffy constituent "physical processes which are induced by the current" (SK II.51).

In this way too, Sellars suggests, genius Jones's "classical conception of thoughts as pure occurrents is motivated by the familiar attempt to relate changes in *dispositional properties* to changes in *underlying non-dispositional* states" (*NAO* IV.37). We need not rehearse Sellars' various arguments for the virtues of such theoretical explanations over their dispositional counterparts at the observational level, as discussed in chapter 2. The overall emerging picture is clear, however, as Sellars asks:

Can we not regard classical theories of mental acts construed as *pure* occurrents (as contrasted with short-term propensities to think-out-loud) as *theories* in a sense which is analogous to micro-physical theories? Indeed, cannot we regard our common-sense conception of thought processes as such a theory? Such a theory would be designed to *explain* propensities to think-out-loud as micro-physical theory is designed to explain the powers and propensities which we know things to have at the perceptual level, sophisticated by laboratory techniques. (SK II.52)

Note that Sellars is here employing a model or analogy in a wider sense (a 'meta-model,' as it were) in comparison to the way in which VB thinking-out-loud itself serves as a 'concrete' explanatory model for Jones's theory of inner thoughts. That is, Sellars is using his familiar realist account of the scientific theoretical explanation of perceptibles in terms of postulated imperceptibles (which involves the use of specific, contentful theoretical models) as itself "a philosophical model" for reconstructing the closely analogous *inference to the best explanation* that is made by common sense in inferring from people's perceptible rational behavior to their imperceptible inner thought-processes (*SM* VI.7–12). This also constitutes Sellars' seminal solution to the classic problem of our knowledge of 'Other Minds': that is, to the problem of how it is that we are able to know that other people have minds, when our evidence is restricted solely to their observable behavior (linguistic or otherwise). Sellars' solution has attempted to chart a subtle middle way "between the Scylla of logical behaviourism and the Charybdis of Cartesianism" (*SM* VI.36).

Finally, there is a third general reason to follow Jones's theory beyond the Rylean VB account. The reason is that only by doing so can we explain why, as Sellars (EPM XI.46) and many other critics of behaviorism have pointed out, the explanations offered by the verbal behaviorist for our silent stretches of nonhabitual yet rational behavior always threaten to collapse into vicious circularity when pushed. Consider any case of such a silent stretch in which we lack a firm grip on any clearly relevant past or present verbal accompaniments. In such cases the VB theorist has to continually resort to hypotheses attributing incredibly elaborate successions of shifting propensities-to-speak pertaining to what Sally *would have* said and done during an entire hour, for example, during which she was just sitting there scratching her head with her pencil before proceeding to solve some elaborate practical or theoretical problem. All of these hypotheses, it becomes clear, simply reflect the VB theorist's (officially proscribed, Jonesean) background assumptions concerning what Sally is likely to have been *thinking* and *intending* during all that time.[20]

So Sellars' complex attitude toward Ryle and the Ryleans is that while "logical behaviourism does reconstruct a dimension of our concept of mind," in particular correctly articulating the conceptual and hence "epistemic priority" of the *intersubjective* dimensions of meaning and intentionality, it does not in the end provide "an adequate account of the mental *überhaupt* [i.e., overall]"; and so it must ultimately yield to Jones's causal-explanatory enrichment in terms of inner episodic thoughts (*SM* III.26–8, IV.16–17, VI.34–5).

Let us assume, then, that a triumphant genius Jones now teaches his Rylean colleagues to explain one another's verbal and other rational behavior by supposing that such behavior is the causal manifestation of covert inner episodes or states of thinking. What are such thoughts?

Well, Jones starts by doing what *we* do when we seek to describe, narrate, or draw a picture of what someone is or must have been thinking: he *quotes* the relevant sentences in the VB model. The thought Sally had was, for instance: 'This line is moving slowly.' Of course, Jones is more sophisticated than to think that Sally must have literally silently uttered that English sentence to herself. That English sentence is just Jones's theoretical *model* for what Sally's thought must *in certain respects* be like. Sally's thought, whatever it is, is a state of Sally that plays the functional •This line is moving slowly• role within the 'entry/inference/exit' patterns of her so-called 'language of thought.' And like the corresponding English sentence on which it is modelled, this complex thought is presumably built up 'compositionally,' in the sense we briefly encountered in chapter 3, out of its functional role-playing parts in ways that may be further investigated by theoretical linguists, psychologists, and philosophers. (They were so investigated by Sellars himself, for example, in his theories of *predication* and of linguistic *representation*, to be discussed in chapter 6.[21])

These thoughts are not *initially* conceived as inner states of Sally in the literal spatial sense of 'inner,' but only in the sense that they have the status of theoretically postulated rather than empirically observed states of Sally. What these functionally characterized states of Sally turn out to *be* is a matter for further investigation. Platonists and Cartesians used familiar arguments in support of the inference that such thoughts must be states of a non-physical soul – arguments which Sellars takes Kant to have correctly diagnosed as fallacious (see I and MP). If by contrast we take Jones's sentential VB model seriously, and we attend to the fact that the relevant semantic roles are, in our linguistic behavior, autonomously 'realized in' various concrete material structures consisting of pattern-governed "marks and noises" (i.e., symbol systems), this gives rise to "the idea that there must be inner-linguistic *vehicles* (materials)" for thoughts as well (*NAO* IV.36). And of course our scientific background information has subsequently made it reasonable to hypothesize that the relevant role-playing vehicles or materials of our inner thinking are in fact patterns of neurophysiological activity – although Sellars wisely leaves it as a matter that is open for future scientific and further philosophical investigation just how such a system of representations might be structurally realized in detail in the cerebral cortex (cf. EPM XV.58). As Daniel Dennett has recently observed with regard to all these aspects of Sellars' seminal work: "Thus was contemporary *functionalism* in the philosophy of mind born, and the varieties of functionalism we have subsequently seen are in one way or another enabled, and directly or indirectly inspired, by what was left open in Sellars' initial proposal" (Dennett 1987: 341).

Let us turn now to the final stage, "the *dénouement*," as Sellars calls it (EPM XV.59), of the myth of Jones: the account, on the basis of the above theory of inner thoughts, of our privileged access to our own thoughts. We shall also briefly consider some well-known challenges to Sellars' overall account of the nature of thoughts.

Privileged access and other issues in Sellars' account of thinking

In *Science and Metaphysics* (1968) Sellars summed up in the following way the "two demands" that must be satisfied by his account of thoughts in terms of the myth of genius Jones; so far we have been exploring his account of how the first, more fundamental demand is satisfied:

(a)   the demand that a form of linguistic behaviour be describable which, though rich enough to serve as a basis for the explicit introduction of a theoretical framework of non-Ryleian episodes [i.e., inner thoughts], does not, as thus described, presuppose any reference, however implicit, to such episodes, just as we can give an Austinian [i.e., a common-sense or manifest image] description of physical objects which is genuinely free of reference to micro-physical particles;

(b)   the demand that an account be available (in principle) of how a framework adopted as an *explanatory hypothesis* could come to serve as the vehicle of direct or non-inferential self-knowledge (apperception). (*SM* VI.11; cf. III.26)

Let us turn to this second task, which concerns our privileged access to our own thoughts. After this we shall close with a brief look at one broad source of objections to Sellars' particular approach to thinking, specifically in relation to the first demand.

The second demand, then, is that we be able to explain, 'from the outside in' as it were (i.e., using only our intersubjectively evidenced Jonesean resources), the common-sense idea that people are to a large degree capable of *knowing directly* what are their own conscious thoughts, feelings, and intentions. The sense of 'direct' here is that this knowledge does not depend on their making any *inferences* from their own or anyone else's observable behavior. We are capable of non-inferential introspective knowledge of our own mental states. Sellars argues that satisfying this second demand requires only "a short step" from what we have already seen in relation to satisfying the first demand (EPM XVI.59). He firmly insists that

this second demand is, from a philosophical point of view, the less inter-esting of the two, *for even a logical behaviourist must give some account, in principle, of privileged access*, in other words, of how language pertaining to behavioural dispositions and propensities can acquire the use by which one's possession of such dispositions and propensities is avowed. (*SM* III.26, italics added; similarly *SM* VI.11)

Sellars holds, I believe, that in their stampede away from logical behaviorism since the early 1960s contemporary philosophers of mind have lost certain crucial, if limited, insights that were due to Ryle and Wittgenstein.[22] One of those insights concerns precisely the second demand and our "acquisition of the avowal role" (*SM* III.26). (In the next chapter we shall see Sellars make a similar point with regard to philosophers' stampede away from 'sense-datum' epistemologies.)

The avowal role basically pertains to our ability to avow or *report*, directly and reliably, the contents of our own thoughts and feelings. On Jones's theory, of course, this verbal ability, too, is to be explained as the causal manifestation of an inner thinking process that constitutes, in this case, our introspective awareness of our own thoughts and feelings. Sellars' view is that this particular cognitive ability, as with all our cognitive abilities, can be successfully and autonomously reconstructed – though again, not ultimately adequately explained – in terms of the Rylean verbal behaviorist model.[23]

The general idea is that not only is Sally 'trained' on the VB model (as described above) to perceptually-respond-out-loud (c.p.) to the presence of apples by uttering 'that is an apple'; and to be disposed (c.p.) to follow her utterances of '*x* is red all over' with '*x* is not green,' and so on. On the VB model she also learns the language appropriate to ascribing her own thinkings-out-loud to herself. Let us start with an artificially simple VB example (cf. *SM* VI.11–12; *SK* II.46–7; *ME* 264ff., 331-40; and of course *EPM* XVI.59).

On the Rylean VB model, Sally can clearly be trained to be disposed, if called upon or in appropriate contexts, to reliably follow up her thinking-out-loud:

That line is long

with the (meta-)thinking-out-loud:

I just thought-out-loud 'That line is long.'

The VB model for the *introspection* of our own thoughts thus begins with our capacity to think-out-loud about our own thinkings-out-loud. There is no mystery, in this VB model example, as to why Sally will as a result generally be in the best position to report-out-loud on her own spontaneous thinkings-out-loud (though there are conceivable scenarios in which she might not be). In general, and as things are, who could be in a better position to so report than Sally herself?

The next step is to make the VB model more sophisticated in the usual way. Sally can thus also be trained to respond directly to her own short-term *propensity* to think-out-loud 'That line is long' with the *propensity* to think-out-loud:

I was about to think-out-loud 'That line is long.'

In particular, she is able to do so while remaining silent on this occasion, for she has also been trained to 'hold back' her thinkings-out-loud in appropriate circumstances. By the time our *pre*-Jonesean VB culture is in full swing, Rylean Sally will be able, if called upon, to give highly elaborate and uniquely reliable (but by no means infallible) reports-out-loud on her own recent personal history of thinkings-out-loud and her propensities to such. No one can beat her at it; she can do it with her eyes shut. She avows her own thoughts-out-loud directly or non-inferentially, that is, without any inference in these cases from 'outer' behavioral evidence. She now has a *privileged access*, within the sophisticated VB model, to her own thoughts-out-loud.

It takes only a bit of his usual genius for Jones simply to apply this independently available, conceptually autonomous Rylean account of privileged access within his broader theory concerning our inner episodic thoughts or representations generally, just as he has with the rest of our pattern-governed linguistic behavior. Suppose, then, that Sally has now been trained into Jones's theory of inner thoughts, and she is busily attributing various thought-episodes to all her friends based on their unstudied behavior ('Fidgeting Jane over there is also thinking that this line is long'). She has also learned, of course, to construe her own thinkings-out-loud, including her propensities and responses to such, as just described, as having the same Jonesean source in inner episodes of thinking. We now have all the materials we need in order to understand Sally's capacity for reliable introspection, acquainted as we already are with her impressive *Rylean* reliability regarding her own thinkings-out-loud, combined with her grasp of Jones's theory of inner thoughts in satisfaction of the first demand (a) above. We Joneseans, Sally included, can now see that Sally has become disposed (in appropriate contexts, etc.) *to respond to her own inner thought-episodes* – directly or non-inferentially, and with a reliability no one else can match – by having the second-order introspective thought: 'A moment ago I had the thought that *this line is quite long*.' As Sellars sums up this final application of Jones's theory: "*What began as a language with a purely theoretical use has gained a reporting role*" (EPM XV.59).[24]

The resulting Sellarsian theory of introspective self-awareness, to put it in semi-technical terms, is that introspection is an acquired functional capacity, in an internalized 'logical space' or language of thought, to respond non-inferentially to one's own inner thoughts and feelings with highly reliable (meta-)thoughts as to what those thoughts and feelings are or were.[25] If this Jonesean account of our relatively privileged inner access to our own thoughts is successful, and both of the demands (a) and (b) above have been satisfied, then the upshot is of tremendous philosophical consequence:

> As I see it, this story helps us understand that concepts pertaining to such inner episodes as thoughts are primarily and essentially *intersubjective*, as intersubjective as the concept of a positron, and the reporting role of these concepts – the fact that each of us has a privileged access to his thoughts – constitutes a dimension of the use of these concepts which is *built on* and *presupposes* this intersubjective status. My myth has shown that the fact that language is essentially an *intersubjective* achievement, and is learned in intersubjective contexts [. . .] is compatible with the 'privacy' of 'inner episodes'. It also makes clear that this privacy is not an 'absolute privacy'. For if it recognizes that these concepts have a reporting use in which one is not drawing inferences from behavioral evidence, it nevertheless insists that the fact that overt behavior *is* evidence for these episodes *is built into the very logic of these concepts*, just as the fact that the observable behavior of gases is evidence for molecular episodes is built into the very logic of molecule talk. (EPM XV.59)

Furthermore, we have also seen why it is reasonable to believe that the ultimate 'categorical basis' of these inner thoughts – as normatively characterized functional role-players that must be realized in some appropriate 'vehicles' or materials of thought – in our case consists in patterns of neurophysiological process taking place primarily in the cerebral cortex. A robust conception of our inner mental life and of our privileged epistemic access to it has thus been defended in such a way that in principle our manifest image of ourselves as persons whose thinking is subject to various conceptually irreducible and autonomous norms of rationality can be coherently integrated or 'fused' with our scientific image of ourselves as natural products of evolution consisting entirely of complex systems of microphysical entities.

On the whole Sellars' highly innovative and detailed functional role conception of thoughts, developed already at mid-century over a decade before the 'official' rise of functionalism in modern philosophy of mind, has a prominent place among those of his positions (such as his defense of scientific realism and his critique of the myth of the given) which in retrospect have stood the test of time quite well. Significant numbers of philosophers during the subsequent half-century of philosophy, both independently and by way of direct influence, were to go on to develop outlooks based on similar functionalist insights. Not surprisingly, of course, there are also a wide variety of important objections that would have to be considered in a full evaluation of Sellars' overall account: for example, in relation to the 'conceptual role' or 'inferentialist' theory of meaning on which his account has been based; in relation to his 'Jonesean' account of inner thought-episodes as having a quasi-theoretical status; in relation to his 'outside-in' account of privileged access; and in particular in relation to his broadly functionalist philosophy of mind in general. For our purposes we may restrict ourselves to considering what seems to be the most important general source of criticisms of Sellars' own particular position, rather than attempting to survey the standard objections that must be handled by all such conceptual role or 'use' theories of meaning and by all functionalist philosophies of mind.

The general form of objection I have in mind hearkens back to Chisholm's comments quoted earlier (see Chisholm in Sellars ITM) and was later raised in related ways by Ausonio Marras (1973a, 1973b). It concerns whether or not Sellars has really managed to satisfy what we saw him characterize earlier as the "first demand" (a) on his theory: namely, that he successfully describe a form of pattern-governed linguistic behavior (the rule-governed Rylean VB model) that (i) is genuinely conceptual and hence fully characterized by categories pertaining to meaning, reference, truth, and intentionality, and yet (ii) does not in any way presuppose the concept of *inner* thoughts in genius Jones's sense. As Sellars elsewhere puts the challenge:

> It is clear that one who hopes to explain the conceptuality of 'inner episodes' in terms of the conceptuality of overt linguistic behavior must have a satisfactory account of the latter that does not covertly make use of the idea of inner conceptual episodes. I have attempted such an explanation. Professor Marras argues that I have not succeeded. (RM 485)

Both Marras and Chisholm in their different ways in the end contend either that (1) Sellars succeeds in giving an account of verbal behavior that exhibits genuine conceptuality and intentionality, but only by presupposing the intentionality of inner thoughts (thus rendering his account viciously circular); or else (2) his account of verbal behavior is simply too impoverished to provide a model that is characterized by genuine conceptuality and intentionality (thus revealing Sellars' whole 'outside-in' approach to be a non-starter). On the whole, both Marras and Chisholm think that Sellars cannot make his Rylean VB model of 'thinking-out-loud' *rich enough* to handle the phenomena of meaning and intentionality without thereby sneaking in concepts pertaining to *inner* conceptual thinking. Sellars, however, thinks he has done precisely that. Hence the controversy.

More specifically, Chisholm holds that the context '*x* [linguistic item] means *y*' cannot be analyzed or explicated – in what sense becomes central to the resulting debate – without reliance on the context '*x* expresses [inner] thought *t*, and *t* is about *y*.' The "funny characteristic" or non-physical property of linguistic meaning, for Chisholm, must be seen as derivative from that pertaining to the intentionality of inner thoughts, just as the light of the moon is dependent on that of the sun. Marras can be seen as spelling out one primary way in which this problem arguably manifests itself in Sellars' own position. He argues that Sellars' account of the Ryleans' verbal behavior becomes rich enough to constitute genuine conceptuality only if we take seriously Sellars' various remarks concerning the required "ambience" of norms that results from the explicit *rule-obeying actions* of the adult linguistic *trainers*, who knowingly shape trainees' mere rule-conforming behavior to be as it ought-to-be. As Sellars himself insists, "[E]ven though conceptual activity rests on a foundation of *conforming* to ought-to-be's of *uniformities* in linguistic behavior, these uniformities exist in an ambience of action, epistemic or otherwise. To be a language user is to conceive of oneself as an agent subject to rules" (LTC 513). But surely, Marras argues in some detail, we cannot understand *that* sort of explicitly rule-obeying intentional action without presupposing *inner* conceptual awareness on the part of the trainers, which would render Sellars' account viciously circular.

In considering Sellars' general response to this kind of objection, let us continue to distinguish carefully between thinking as a process involving *inner thought-episodes*, as posited by Jones, and thinking as rule-governed *thinking-out-loud* and propensities to such, as construed on the Rylean VB model. And let us begin with a preliminary point. One serious but common mistake with regard to Sellars' myth of Jones, as was noted earlier, is to think that he has presented his pre-Jonesean Ryleans in such a way that they are supposed *not to have the concepts of thoughts, intentions, perceptions*, and so on. To the contrary, however, the Ryleans with their linguistic role semantics are persons who have a rich conception of our (Rylean) *psychological* lives, all of it interpreted, of course, in terms of complex, rule-governed patterns of thinking-out-loud. This Rylean conception includes Sellars' entire account of meaning as normative functional classification, which was explained earlier in terms of socially maintained ought-to-be rules of criticism and corresponding ought-to-do rules of action. This framework of semantic rules, as we have seen, enables the Ryleans to interpret each other's utterances, including their own utterances, as *meaning* such and such, as being 'about' this or that, as being *true or false*, and so on (EPM XII). What these semantically sophisticated Ryleans are supposed to lack is only our post-Jonesean concept of *inner* thought-episodes. Furthermore – and this is a crucial point that Sellars himself thinks he left unclear in EPM – the original Rylean behaviorist framework in the myth, even prior to its 'enrichment' with the semantic language pertaining to meaning-roles, is assumed by Sellars *already to include the behavioral-linguistic capacity to use and be motivated by the prescriptive language of 'ought's and normative rules.*[26]

This preliminary clarification must be borne in mind in considering the objections of Chisholm and Marras. On Sellars' view the entire normative framework of *oughts* in particular, with all its sophisticated rule-following and 'knowing how to go on' behavior – including the explicit language-shaping activity of the language trainers fulfilling their intentions to do what they ought-to-do – is autonomously conceived *within the pre-Jonesean* verbal behaviorist framework.

It is also important to recall from our earlier discussions in this chapter that Sellars has carefully outlined a conception of our pattern-governed linguistic behavior according to which "certain basic forms of conceptual activity, whether *linguistic* (candid spontaneous thinkings-out-loud and propensities to think out loud) or *thoughts* as 'inner' episodes, are essentially *non-actions*, yet fully *conceptual*" (RM 492). In relation to the sophisticated, knowing activity of the language *trainers* it is now "essential to note that not only are the abilities to engage in these types of conceptual activity [i.e., language 'entry/inference/exit' transitions] *acquired* as pattern governed activity, they *remain* pattern governed activity. The linguistic conceptual activities which are perceptual takings, inferences and volitions *never* become *obeyings* of *ought-to-do* rules" (RM 490; reproduced in MFC and in *NAO* IV.32). On the VB model, what language trainers gradually learned when they were trainees was how to think-out-loud (i.e., to perceptually-classify-out-loud, infer-out-loud, and will-out-loud, in pattern-governed ways) *about thinkings-out-loud* themselves. "The trainee acquires the ability to language about languagings, to criticize languagings, including his own; he can become one who trains himself" (RM 491; *NAO* IV.34). The full-blown semantic classifications and the practical rule-obeying activities of the language trainers are simply such that the particular *objects* of their basic entry/inference/exit pattern-governed linguistic behaviors have come to include such lin-guistic behaviors themselves. And such activities will of course occa-sionally include pieces of explicit 'practical-reasoning-out-loud' leading to 'willings-out-loud' as part of ordinary training behavior. The latter might for instance take the schematic form: 'It ought-to-be the case that *p*. My doing *A* in *C* would contribute to bringing *p* about. Therefore, other things being equal, I ought-to-do *A* in *C*. The circumstances are now *C*. So, I shall do *A now*' (followed by the doing of *A*). Contrary to Marras's objection, there is no special reason that I can see as to why any of this rule-obeying and meta-linguistic classificatory activity on the part of the language trainers must force Sellars in principle to abandon his VB model and to rely upon Jonesean *inner* conceptual episodes from the start.[27] And this is all Sellars needs in order to consistently maintain that "even though conceptual activity rests on a foundation of *conforming* to ought-to-be's of *uniformities* in linguistic behavior, these uniformities exist in an ambience of action, epistemic or otherwise" (LTC 513).

Some critics might agree with me that Sellars' account is not viciously circular as Marras contends, but nonetheless want to insist that Chisholm and Marras must somehow be right in their contention that the intentionality of thought is 'more basic' than the intentionality of language, and that the latter is derivative from the former. I will close with two observations on this understandable reaction. Firstly, if that contention is true in a sense that Sellars' view cannot accommodate, then of course some other story would have to be told as to how the "funny characteristic" or apparently non-physical property of intentionality possessed by thought can be understood compatibly with what science tells us about the make-up of the natural world, and in particular of ourselves. There are, of course, many other such stories actively being pitched in the philosophical marketplace, ranging along an entire spectrum from Cartesian dualism at one end to 'eliminative materialism' on the other. However, before one decides to reject Sellars' account of the relevant priorities and to head back into that bustling marketplace, it will be worth reflecting on the notions of 'more basic' and 'derivative from' that were used above in stating the understandable reaction, which leads to my second observation.

I suggest that a careful reckoning of the account of intentionality which we have seen Sellars offer in this chapter shows that at the end of the day he is able to *agree* with the above reaction as to the priority, in a crucial sense, of thought over language – which is arguably what drives the worries of Chisholm, Marras, and many others as well. And he is able to do so while still retaining all of the synoptic, anti-Cartesian virtues of his methodologically intersubjective or 'outside-in' account of the mind. This is because, in the end, Sellars can agree that all of us, the pre-historic Ryleans included, have all along been *thinking* in Jones's robust inner-episodic sense. He agrees with Chisholm that 'mere marks and noises' do not intentionality make: "I agree, *of course*," Sellars responds, "that marks in books and noises made by phonographs 'have meaning' only by virtue of their relation to 'living' verbal episodes in which language is the direct expression of thought"; furthermore, he adds in turn, "I agree that 'living' verbal episodes are meaningful *because* they express thoughts. Our difference concerns the *analysis* of this 'because' " (ITM 526). What Sellars takes himself to have shown is that there is a crucial sense in which our understanding of the intentionality of thought is based on our *conceptually prior* understanding of the rule-governed meaningfulness of public languages-in-use. What he also takes himself to have shown consistently with that view, however, is that in the order of being, and in appropriately *causal* senses of 'express' and 'because,' our 'living' verbal episodes are indeed meaningful only because they are the expression of genuinely and non-mysteriously *inner* episodes of conceptual thinking.

5

Knowledge, Immediate Experience, and the Myth of the Given

As the title of Sellars' most famous work indicates, 'Empiricism and the Philosophy of Mind' (EPM) interweaves classical epistemological and metaphysical issues pertaining both to the structure of our knowledge and to the nature of the mind. We have just witnessed the subtle connections between those two domains in Sellars' 'myth of genius Jones' account of the nature of inner thoughts and of our 'privileged' epistemic access to them. The two sets of issues concerning mind and knowledge have traditionally been seen to coalesce within what Sellars calls "the framework of givenness," which is the target of his attack in EPM as a whole (EPM I.1), for what has very often been taken to be 'directly given' in conscious experience is precisely the nature and character of our own thoughts and sensations. With Sellars' views on scientific realism, meaning and abstract entities, and inner conceptual thinking now under our belts, we are finally in a position to begin exploring one of the most difficult and fascinating topics in Sellars' philosophy: the metaphysics and epistemology of *sense perception*. In this case, too, Sellars' story will eventually culminate in the myth of genius Jones, this time in a second stage applied to the problematic status of our 'immediate experiences,' as they have traditionally been called.[1] Ultimately Sellars' view will be that the rejection of the myth of the given is essential to the modern philosopher's central task of integrating the manifest and scientific images of man-in-the-world.

The first section below begins with the general idea of the given and its particular application to the case of perceptual knowledge, and still more particularly in relation to Sellars' critique of sense-datum theories. The second and third sections leave sense-data behind and present Sellars' alternative account of perceptual knowledge, along the way developing further grounds for rejecting the general idea of the epistemic given. In the final section we recover some of the mishandled insights of the sense-datum theorists, and thereby begin to grapple with the problem of how Sellars conceives of the intrinsic nature of sensory consciousness and its problematic relationship to the scientific image of the world.

The idea of the given and the case of sense-datum theories

"Many things," Sellars explains, "have been said to be 'given': sense contents,[2] material objects, universals, propositions, real connections, first principles, even givenness itself" (EPM I.1). Put loosely, to begin with, the given is supposed to be something the nature and character of which are known or apprehended simply in being directly experienced or contemplated. As such, knowledge of the given may be said to be *autonomous* or *independent* in the sense of "presupposing no knowledge of other matter of fact, whether particular or general" (EPM VIII.32). As thus independently knowable, the given would be fit to serve as a *datum*: a secure basis or starting point on which to build an account of our knowledge of other things.[3] Let us call the idea that there is any such independently knowable datum the idea of an *epistemic given*.[4] Sellars wants to show that this widespread idea is a myth: we have no such knowledge.

Sellars thus indicates that "the point of the epistemological category of the given is, presumably, to explicate the idea that empirical knowledge rests on a 'foundation' of non-inferential knowledge of matter of fact" (EPM I.3). The latter idea is roughly as follows. When we assert that such and such is the case – that it is raining outside, for instance – we are generally prepared to respond to the question 'How do you know?' by giving reasons for or citing evidence in support of our belief. 'Because I can hear the rain falling on the roof': this serves as a reason to infer that it is indeed raining outside (*inferential* justification), since experience shows this sort of pitter-patter sound to be nearly always produced by rain. If the skeptic persists by citing other possible causes of that sound, we can cut short the potentially endless regress of justifications by taking him to the window: 'See? It's raining. Dispute over.' Directly seeing that it is raining is plausibly regarded as providing one with *non-inferential* knowledge or adequately justified belief that it is raining, in contrast to knowing that fact by inferring it from something else that one knows. I can then treat that 'immediate' or 'direct' knowledge as a datum for inferring or evidentially supporting other beliefs about the world. On this plausible picture, then, some things we know directly or non-inferentially, and some things we know only by sound inference from other things that we know.

One of Sellars' central aims will be to consider the extent to which this broadly foundationalist empiricist picture, that all our factual knowledge is ultimately justified by appeal to direct perceptual observations, might survive a full-scale assault on the myth of the given in any form. It is important to be clear from the start that the idea or myth of the epistemic given is only one way of attempting to defend the plausible idea that there are justified non-inferential beliefs that are direct in the sense of not being arrived at by any process of inference from other justified beliefs. Sellars himself will hold that (relative to a given context of inquiry) there are such regress-stopping, warranted, non-inferential beliefs – most notably our perceptual beliefs have this status. Yet he will emphatically reject the above idea of a 'presuppositionless' epistemic given. Consequently, after Sellars has rejected the myth of the given his task will then be to understand how this sort of evidence-providing, non-inferential perceptual knowledge is possible without the myth.

Historically both rationalists and empiricists have tended to look to the contents of one's own consciousness as primary candidates for the epistemic given. Every beginning student in philosophy is familiar with Descartes' complete assurance that, even if it were true that he is only dreaming that he is at this moment sitting by the fire, or more generally even if he is being entirely deceived about the nature of external reality, nonetheless he takes himself to have an independently clear and distinct idea of the nature and contents of his own mind – a clear instance of the idea of the epistemic given. Even if it were the case that he is being entirely deceived in that way, wrote Descartes in the Second *Meditation*, "Yet I certainly *seem* to see, to hear, and to be warmed. This cannot be false" (Descartes 1641: 9). Descartes' basic contention was that how things appear in his own consciousness – including the grasp of various allegedly self-evident principles of reason – provides him with an indubitable given upon which he can proceed to build an account of his knowledge of everything else. The empiricist strands in the thinking of Locke, Berkeley, and Hume represented a similar view in relation to what they conceived as the givenness of the 'ideas' or 'perceptions of the mind' of which we are immediately aware, whatever their ultimate cause may be. Twentieth-century philosophers in both the phenomenological and the analytic traditions likewise frequently embraced the idea of the given in the form of facts or reports concerning how things immediately appear to the experiencing subject.

In 1956 in EPM Sellars begins by taking up this picture of the epistemic given in the form in which it had dominated analytic philosophy during the first half of the twentieth century: the idea that our knowledge is based on foundational acts of *sensing sense-data*. That is where we ought to begin as well, for despite what one might initially think, it turns out (or so I will suggest) that Sellars regarded the sense-datum theorists as having achieved important insights that must be retrieved from the rubble of their mistaken epistemology of the given and their mistaken ontological conception of the nature of sensory consciousness – insights that had been lost by philosophers in their mid-century "stampede" away from phenomenalism and from sense-data (cf. PH 60). That stampede, of course, was itself in no small part aided by Sellars' own "attack on sense datum theories [. . .] as a first step in a general critique of the entire framework of givenness" (EPM I.1), an attack which we are now to examine.

Perhaps the best example of the sort of sense-datum views Sellars was criticizing is the following famous passage from chapter 1, 'The Given,' of the book *Perception* (1932) by H. H. Price, professor of philosophy at Oxford from 1935 to 1959.[5] The passage from Price merits a substantial sampling:

> My aim in this book is to examine those experiences in the way of seeing and touching upon which our beliefs concerning material things are based, and to inquire in what way and to what extent they justify these beliefs. [. . .]
>
> When I see a tomato there is much that I can doubt. I can doubt whether it is a tomato that I am seeing, and not a cleverly painted piece of wax. I can doubt whether there is any material thing there at all. Perhaps what I took for a tomato was really a reflection; perhaps I am even the victim of some hallucination. One thing however I cannot doubt: that there exists a red patch of a round and somewhat bulgy shape, standing out from a background of other colour-patches, and having a certain visual depth, and that this whole field of colour is directly present to my consciousness. What the red patch is, whether a substance, or a state of a substance, or an event, whether it is physical or psychical or neither, are questions that we may doubt about. But that something is red and round then and there I cannot doubt. And when I say that it is 'directly' present to my consciousness, I mean that my consciousness of it is not reached by inference, nor by any other intellectual process. [. . .] There obviously must be some sort or sorts of presence to consciousness which can be called 'direct' in this sense, else we should have an infinite regress. [. . .]
>
> This peculiar and ultimate manner of being present to consciousness is called *being given*, and that which is thus present is called a *datum*. The corresponding mental attitude is called *acquaintance, intuitive apprehension*, or sometimes *having*. Data of this special sort are called *sense-data*. And the acquaintance with them is conveniently called *sensing*. (Price 1932: 2–3)

For our present purposes this lucid passage may be regarded as capturing many of the essential points that were common to sense-datum and related theories of the given of the sort put forward by William James,

Bertrand Russell, G. E. Moore, C. D. Broad, C. I. Lewis, A. J. Ayer, and many others. A more extended treatment would have to consider important differences among these views, for there were ongoing internecine disputes among defenders of sense-data as to their true nature and status, despite the fact that sense-data were typically put forward as putatively theoretically neutral and indisputable aspects of experience (e.g., Price 1932: 5, 18–19).[6]

Price's passage brings out the following tightly connected classical themes immediately. Out front, of course, is the foundationalist idea that the having or sensing of sense-data is to provide non-inferential or direct knowledge of the given, with further questions as to how this indubitable knowledge is related to our ordinary perceptual knowledge of material objects in space to be subsequently investigated by the theorist. The indubitable aspect of the experience for Price is "that something is red and round then and there," even if the experience is *non-veridical*: that is, even in cases where what the experience presents as being the case is *not true* in reality. About all else besides the given qualities of the sense-datum we may conceivably be mistaken, on this view. Hence the knowledge of sense-data and their properties is taken to be *independent* of any assumptions as to how matters stand – and perhaps even of how we *take* or judge them to stand – in the physical world.

The general idea is that in both the vividly deceptive and the non-deceptive cases in which we ostensibly see a red tomato, we are surely aware of a red bulgy *something*, whatever it may be – call it a 'sense-datum.' Chisholm in 'The Theory of Appearing' (1950: 173) called this the *sense-datum inference*: crudely put, if something phenomenally *appears* F to subject S (say, a red apple appears bright blue to Jones in abnormal circumstances), then S is aware of something which *is* F (i.e., Jones is experiencing *something* blue). Howard Robinson has recently defended the sense-datum inference in the form of what he calls the 'Phenomenal Principle':

> If there sensibly appears to a subject to be something which possesses a particular sensible quality then there is something of which the subject is aware which does possess that sensible quality. (Robinson 1994: 32)

We shall see that Sellars has a nuanced attitude toward the sense-datum inference.[7] While in one sense he will clearly reject it as a form of the myth of the given, in another sense he will argue that it gestures awkwardly toward a "basic phenomenological fact" (FMPP I.69) concerning sensory experience that does indeed need to be explained, but which philosophers in their stampede away from phenomenalist sense-datum theories have failed to satisfactorily accommodate.[8]

Let us now attempt a brief synopsis of certain central strands in Sellars' complex critique in EPM of the sort of sense-datum account Price and others defended. There are many additional objections to sense-data that we shall not consider, as Sellars did not go into them either. Sellars was not inclined to beat dead horses, but rather he tended to focus his criticisms only on those aspects of philosophical theories that in his eyes represented at least near misses on the truth.

In his critique of sense-datum theories and in developing his own view of perceptual knowledge Sellars will explore in detail three closely related distinctions:

- *propositional* knowledge of facts as opposed to (alleged) *non-propositional* knowledge of particulars or occurrences;
- *epistemic* and *conceptual* factors as opposed to *non-epistemic, non-conceptual* factors involved in sense perception; and finally,
- *perceiving* as a non-inferential knowing or judging that something is the case, as opposed to *sensing* or having a (non-conceptual) sensation.

Sellars will argue that sophisticated sense-datum theorists such as Price recognized that all of these dimensions were involved in our perceptual knowledge, but they construed them in a way that makes it impossible to bring them together in an overall coherent explanatory account. In particular, as he put it in 1954 in 'Some Reflections on Language Games,' the sense-datum theorists did not adequately "distinguish the epistemic and non-epistemic senses of 'immediate experience' – roughly *inspection* and *sensation* respectively":[9]

> Sensations are no more epistemic in character than are trees or tables, and are no more ineffable. They are private in the sense that only one person can notice them; but they are public in the sense that, in principle, I can state the same facts about your sensations that you can report, and can state the same facts about your sensations that I can report about my own. (SRLG 40)

Stepping back from the details of the text of EPM, the opening stages in Sellars' critical argument may be presented informally as follows.

Sense-datum theorists were generally concerned to defend the idea of an *epistemic* given, which as we saw requires that the given be the sort of thing that can provide foundational evidence for our claims concerning how matters stand in the world. (For example, see the role of the phrases "upon which [. . .] are based" and "justify these beliefs" in the opening passage from Price.) Such ordinary factual claims have propositional structure, exhibiting the general form 'p' or 'x is F' in 'I know that *p*' or 'I know that *x* is *F*' – they are at the very least, as it were, shots at saying (or thinking) something true about something. But when sense-datum theorists wished to stress the *immediacy* of the given, they tended to construe sense-data as simply particulars or undeniable happenings in consciousness, like having a pain, or having one's visual field occupied by Price's "red patch of a round and some-what bulgy shape." But a particular red patch or sharp pain does not 'say' or judge anything about anything, and as such it is not clear how it could by itself *give a reason* for predicating something of anything at all. (Hence Sellars' remark above: "Sensations are no more epistemic in character than are trees or tables.") Thus it is not clear how sense-data or any other non-propositionally structured item can serve as an 'epistemically efficacious' given in the desired sense.[10]

This first Sellarsian move raises further general issues as to what is required for *x* to provide a reason (or justification or evidence) for *y*, and also concerning the question as to whether the concept of knowl-edge is a normative notion concerning what is *correctly* judged about some matter, in contrast to the non-normative having of a sensation or the sensing of a sense-datum. At the very least, however, what this opening move does is force the sense-datum theorist to clarify the relationship between the sensing of sense-data and the ordinary epis-temic justification of propositional claims or judgments. A comprehen-sive examination of sense-datum theories is outside the scope of our present task, but I think it can now be shown that Sellars has indeed exposed a touchy nerve center at the core of sense-datum and related accounts of the given.[11]

First let us note that Price in 1932 in fact anticipated and offered a response to roughly the sort of initial objection that Sellars has just raised: namely, the objection that, as Price had put it,

> what we apprehend is always a *fact* – something of the form 'that A is B' or 'the B-ness of A'. You cannot apprehend just A. For instance, you cannot apprehend a round red patch without apprehending that it is red and round and has certain spatial relations. But if we apprehend that it has these qualities and relations, we are not passively 'receiving' or (as it were) swallowing; we are actively thinking – judging or classifying – and it is impossible to do less than this.
>
> To this I answer, it is very likely true, but it is irrelevant. The argument only proves that nothing stands *merely* in the relation of givenness to the mind, without also standing in other relations: i.e. that what is given is always also 'thought about' in some sense or other of that ambiguous phrase. But this does not have the slightest tendency to prove that *nothing is given at all*. (Price 1932: 7)

"We must conclude then," Price sums it up, "that the given is still given however much we know about it. *Knowledge-about is the usual, perhaps the inevitable, companion of acquaintance, but it is not its executioner"* (1932: 18, italics added).[12]

Price and other sense-datum theorists in this way inevitably assume that there is a very tight connection, of a sort not clearly specified, between (in Price's terminology) sensing a particular red bulgy sense-datum, and non-inferentially knowing what we might call, taking our cue from Price's remark, the 'usual or inevitable' *companion fact* about the sense-datum *that it is red and bulgy-shaped.* That this red bulgy something is a physical tomato may be doubted or denied, but can the proprietary companion fact about the sense-datum that it is red and bulgy likewise be seen as open to denial by the sense-datum theorist? As Price says in the tomato passage, *"that something is red and round then and there I cannot doubt"* (italics added). If that fact is not indubitably recognized, how can any intelligible story be told as to how it is the given that *"determines* (in part) the interpretation" provided by concepts, as C. I. Lewis puts it (1929: 275, italics added)? This is the raw nerve center mentioned above. Whatever the officially stated view of the theorist, a red bulgy sense-datum or 'presentation' (Lewis's term), if it is to have any hope of playing its intended role in human knowledge, must inevitably carry with it the proprietary companion fact *about* its character that it is a red and bulgy something or other.

This now puts us in a proper position to assess what Sellars presents as the "inconsistent triad" of propositions to which the sense-datum theorist is incoherently committed:

(A) *X senses red sense content s* entails *x non-inferentially knows that s is red.*

(B) The ability to sense sense contents [or sense-data] is unacquired.

(C) The ability to know facts of the form *x is φ* is acquired. (EPM I.6)

This is an inconsistent triad in the sense that "A and B together entail not-C; B and C entail not-A; A and C entail not-B" (EPM I.6). The sense-datum theorist consequently would have to disown one of these commitments.

Sellars' use of 'entailment' in (A) (based on a logical analysis he ascribes to the sense-datum theorist in EPM I.4–5) puts the point more strongly than we have seen Price (or Russell or Lewis) officially wants to put it. However, we have also just seen that such theorists are indeed effectively forced to recognize at least the constant, simultaneous, and systematic (if unexplained) companionship in human knowledge of the particular sense-datum and the allegedly non-inferentially known proprietary fact about it. That is precisely the touchy nerve center that Sellars is pressing his finger on.

Sellars plausibly suggests in support of (B) that all classical sense-datum theorists "without exception" have "taken givenness to be a fact which presupposes no learning" (EPM I.5–6). It takes no training or behavioral learning for animals, infants, and adults to be able to feel a pain or have color sensations when their sensory faculties are appropriately stimulated.[13] In this respect sensing sense-data is assimilated to *being conscious* in the sense of *being awake* (EPM I.6).

So at this point the situation with respect to the inconsistent triad is as follows. If (A) sensing sense-data brings with it the companion knowledge of a "classificatory" fact about that sense-datum (e.g., 'that *s* is red'), and if (B) sensing is an unacquired capacity (infants and animals have it, too), then it looks like sense-datum theorists must regard some classificatory factual knowledge as unacquired – as 'built in' rather than learned (i.e., not-C). That is, if sensing requires no learning, then it seems neither can the companion non-inferential knowing that is entailed by it or which at least 'usually, perhaps inevitably' arises with it (or we would need to be told much more than we are about the latter process).[14]

Finally, however, Sellars now suggests that for good general reasons sense-datum theorists would be loath to abandon commitment (C) as well, for "this brings us face to face with the fact that most empirically minded philosophers are strongly inclined to think that all classificatory consciousness, all knowledge *that something is thus-and-so*, or, in logicians' jargon, all subsumption of particulars under universals, involves learning, concept formation, even the use of symbols" (EPM I.6). For this reason Sellars holds that "to abandon (C) is to do violence to the predominantly nominalistic proclivities of the empiricist tradition" (EPM I.6). To put it in somewhat sweeping historical terms, the empiricist tradition in general defends the view that all factual knowledge derives ultimately from sense experience rather than from pure reason. As a result empiricists (and Sellars, too)[15] attempt to give an account of our knowledge that does not rely upon the direct intellectual or intuitive grasp of essences, universals, or synthetic a priori principles that we find in the Platonic and Aristotelian traditions and in modern rationalism. Consequently what Sellars calls the 'nominalistic proclivity' of the empiricists is their tendency to hold that our *conceptual categorizations* of empirical reality (e.g., '*x* is an apple,' '*y* is a human being') reflect the acquired capacities – in particular the acquired linguistic abilities – of the knower and are not 'directly given' in the way that standard empiricists hold that the impressions of sense are given. The fundamental issue in (C), as we shall see further in the next section, thus has to do with the sorts of conceptual capacities that Sellars contends are required even for the most basic and cautious item of empirical knowledge.

Let us pause and reflect further on (C) before summing up Sellars' diagnosis of classical sense-datum theories. In effect, what Sellars calls the 'nominalistic proclivity' of empiricists has been to reject across *most* domains what I shall call, for reasons to be made clear in a moment, the myth of the *categorial given* (or the myth of the directly 'classified,' 'sorted,' or 'conceptualized' given, as one might also call it). As just indicated, empiricists have nonetheless continually failed to detect the presence of that myth in their own backyard: namely, in relation to the allegedly given nature, sort, or character of our determinate sensory experiences themselves (see, for example, EPM VI on Locke, Berkeley, and Hume[16]). So what exactly is the myth of the categorial given, and how is it related to the myth of the epistemic given?

Categories for Sellars, following Kant, are second-order concepts, or meta-concepts: they are concepts that functionally classify what are the most basic kinds of first-order concepts we possess, and hence what basic kinds or *sorts* of items there are in reality as conceived from within the standpoint of a given conceptual framework or 'logical space.'[17] In speaking of the myth of the categorial given I am drawing in particular on Sellars' clarification in his 1981 Carus Lectures, 'Foundations for a Metaphysics of Pure Process,' that "perhaps *the most basic form* of what I have castigated as 'The Myth of the Given'" is the following "principle" (italics added; the bracketed label below is my own):

> [The *myth of the categorial given*:] If a person is directly aware of an item which has categorial status C, then the person is aware of it *as* having categorial status C. (FMPP I.44)

In accordance with this principle, to reject the myth of the given in its "most basic form" is to hold that there exists no privileged type of direct awareness, whether intellectual insight or sensory receptivity, that has the following revelatory power: simply being directly aware in that way of something *x* which *is in fact* of such and such a kind or sort by itself provides one with the direct awareness of *x as being of* that kind or sort.[18] The idea of the directly apprehended *categorial* given is 'basic' in the sense that, were it not a myth, it is precisely what would provide the mere given with the right cognitive shape to play the foundational evidential role that is envisioned for it in the myth of the *epistemic* given – or indeed to play any other epistemic role at all (whether foundationalist or not).

Sellars will not disagree with the idea that *something*, the nature and hence the categorial status of which is not directly given but is to be discovered by ongoing theoretical inquiry, must be received by the mind from the world (in sensation) in order for empirical knowledge about the world to be possible. This "is a dimension of givenness (or takenness)," says Sellars, "which is not in dispute" (FMPP I.87; more on this topic in the final section of this chapter). To reject the myth, on the other hand, is to hold that there is nothing in our experience or in our intellect which is such that it cannot directly manifest itself to us, so to speak, as being of one sort or kind when in reality it is of another sort or kind. This is so even assuming that we are not misled by perceptual illusions, and that we are fully rational, attentive, critically reflective, and dialectically prepared (within the limits of our particular conceptual framework).[19] As Sellars put it in 1981: "*To reject the Myth of the Given is to reject the idea that the categorial structure of the world – if it has a categorial structure – imposes itself on the mind as a seal imposes an image on melted wax*" (FMPP I.45).

Sellars' view is that, to the contrary, what sorts of items there are in reality and in experience is a matter that must be determined entirely – from top to bottom, inside and out – by reasoned explanatory considerations and fallible but self-correcting scientific inquiry, not by a direct appeal to something the nature of which allegedly manifests itself directly to our receptive faculties, whether intellectual or sensory, once the mind is properly 'opened to reality.' In principle it could therefore turn out, for example, that nothing in reality in fact instantiates the basic conceptual categories that are most fundamental to our common-sense conception of the world, notwithstanding the fact that the manifest image of a system of persisting, colored objects in space strikes us as the very world making itself manifest to us in our receptivity.

We have in fact already seen in previous chapters some of the underlying grounds supporting Sellars' rejection of the idea of the categorial given as a myth. As Sellars sees it, a key step in rejecting this myth is the espousal of what he calls "*psychological nominalism*, according to which *all* awareness of *sorts, resemblances, facts*, etc., in short, all awareness of abstract entities – indeed, all awareness even of particulars – is a linguistic affair" (EPM 29; cf. EAE, and the third section below). The latter thesis, as we have seen, is based upon the holistic functional role theory of meaning, abstract entities, and conceptual thinking that we examined in chapters 3 and 4.

We are now finally in a position to sum up Sellars' overall diagnosis of the ambiguities that cripple the sense-datum theorists' account of the given and lead to the inconsistent triad of commitments. Sellars' diagnosis is that "the classical concept of a sense datum [is] a mongrel resulting from a crossbreeding of two ideas," which we may label the idea that there are (non-conceptual) inner 'episodes' or states of *sensing* and the idea that there are (conceptual, propositional) inner episodes of *perceiving* that something is the case (they are both good ideas in themselves, according to Sellars):

(1) [Non-conceptual *sensing*:] The idea that there are certain episodes – e.g. sensations of red or of $C^{\#}$ which can occur to human beings (and brutes) without any prior process of learning or concept formation; and

without which it would *in some sense* be impossible to *see*, for example, that the facing surface of a physical object is red and triangular, or *hear* that a certain physical sound is C#.

(2) [Propositional *perceiving*:] The idea that there are certain inner episodes which are the non-inferential knowings that certain items are, for example, red or C#; and that these episodes are the necessary conditions of empirical knowledge as providing the evidence for all other empirical propositions. (EPM I.7, bracketed labels added)

It is essentially a good idea, firstly, that there are such sensations as in (1), or 'sense impressions,' as Sellars also calls them. Both science and common sense suggest that having a sensation of red is necessary for either seeing or vividly seeming to see that something is red. This is a causal, "scientific style" explanation (EPM I.7) that seeks to account specifically for the basic phenomenological or "*intrinsic* character" (EPM IV.22) of our veridical and non-veridical perceptual experiences:

How does it happen that people can have the experience which they describe by saying 'It is as though I were seeing a red and triangular object' when either there is no physical object there at all, or, if there is, it is neither red nor triangular? The explanation, roughly, posits that in every case in which a person has an experience of this kind, whether veridical or not, he has what is called a 'sensation' or 'impression' 'of a red triangle'. (EPM I.7)

It will later become important to recognize that this first good idea involves positing sensations not only as necessary causal-mediating factors in perception, but in particular as mediating causal factors that will account for the intrinsic experiential content of the relevant experiences (in a sense that Sellars will carefully qualify) even in the non-veridical case in which there is no literally red and triangular physical object out there to be seen at all, as for example in a vivid hallucination. This is a thorny question in the philosophy of mind that was of far more importance to Sellars than to some of his more recent admirers. We shall encounter it again in the final section of this chapter and in chapter 6.

It is also a good idea, secondly, that there are such non-inferential knowings or propositionally structured perceptual judgments as described in (2), and that these constitute the evidence base or the 'data' that support our empirical knowledge at any given time. In the rest of this chapter we shall see how Sellars attempts to offer an alternative account of perceptual knowledge that will preserve both of these good ideas.

What has been shown *not* to be a good idea, however, is "to suppose that having the sensation of a red triangle is a *cognitive* or *epistemic* fact," and "to attribute to the former [. . .] the 'intentionality' of the latter" (EPM I.7). The passage from Price illustrates how tempting the idea is to treat (non-conceptual) *sensations of red* as if they were basic knowings or indubitable revelations concerning certain contents present to the mind called 'sense-data' or 'presented qualia' (Lewis). 'Sensation *of* a red triangle' looks on the surface like it should go in the same box labelled 'Mental Events with Intentionality' with the (propositionally structured) 'perception *of* a red triangle' or the 'thought *of* a red triangle': are they not all instances of the mind being directed in a certain way toward some object or content (a red triangle), whether such an object in fact exists in reality or not? And we have also seen how tempting the general idea is in epistemology to suppose that our knowledge must be based ultimately on how things *appear* to the experiencing subject, as the common factor in both the veridical and non-veridical cases, since any claim as to how things stand in the world might be mistaken. No wonder the Cartesian 'inward turn' as a starting point in philosophy has proved so difficult to resist. In the form it takes in the sense-datum theory, "the upshot of blending all these ingredients together is the idea that a sensation of a red triangle is the very paradigm of empirical knowledge" (EPM I.7), with the resulting difficulties attending that conception that Sellars has exposed.

Having raised these perplexities, Sellars will now go on to develop an alternative positive account of the apparent intentionality of sensations;[20] of the incorrigibility of appearance judgments; of the causal and phenomenological explanatory role of sensations or sense impressions; and of the foundational evidence-providing role of perceptual judgments. The task is to accomplish all this without any covert appeal to the myth of the given. By developing a coherent alternative account which provides a better explanation of everything that needs to be explained, Sellars also hopes to defuse temptations to import the myth in various other forms as well.

We turn next, then, from the problematic sense-datum particulars and presented qualia-complexes to examine the companion perceptual judgments that inevitably speak on their behalf. Sellars does this in full awareness that certain phenomenological insights of the sense-datum theorists will in the end also have to be retrieved rather than lost in the stampede.

Toward Sellars' account of perception and appearance

There are two main dimensions in Sellars' positive account of perceptual knowledge, corresponding to the two good ideas above concerning non-conceptual sensing and propositional perceiving that the sense-datum theory failed to bring together coherently. In this section and the next we shall primarily explore Sellars' holistic account of perceptual knowing in its propositional dimension. In the final section we examine the non-conceptual sensory core of perceptual experience, developing the early 'Jonesean' stages in Sellars' own positive account of sense impressions, or, as he ultimately characterizes them, 'sensa.'

Consider the following three perceptual experiences, which we may variously refer to as experiences of seeing or seeming to see that something is the case, or as *ostensible* seeings or perceptual *takings* (in the sense of taking-to-be: in perception we unreflectively take something to be the case). They are the sorts of experience that led Price to posit sense-data:

(a)   Seeing that x, over there, is red[21]
(b)   Its looking to one that x, over there, is red
(c)   Its looking to one as though there were a red object over there (EPM IV.22)

Experience (a) is a veridical perceptual knowing: a 'seeing that' in the *factive* or *achievement* sense that involves the truth of the proposition that x over there is red. Experience (b) is called by Sellars (following Price) a non-veridical *qualitative appearance*, if, for example, x over there is in fact a non-red object that merely looks red in the circumstances; and (c) is a non-veridical *existential appearance*, if there is in fact no red physical object over there at all (for example, in cases of seeing double-images, hallucinations, wearing 'virtual reality' goggles, etc.).

Sellars holds that there are two different types of common factor shared across such veridical and non-veridical ostensible seeings: a *common propositional content* and a *common non-propositional content* (again corresponding to the dimensions of perceiving and sensing, respectively).

As to the latter non-conceptual factor, Sellars holds that whether there is in fact, for example, a red triangular physical object out there to be seen or not, "phenomenologically speaking," in cases like (a), (b), and (c), "the descriptive core consists in the fact that *something* in *some* way red and triangular is in *some* way present to the perceiver *other than as thought of*" (SK I.55). This is the central insight mishandled by the sense-datum theorists. Sellars repeatedly insists in this way throughout his writings that there is an intrinsically indistinguishable non-conceptual sensory core or phenomenal content shared as a common factor in such veridical and non-veridical experiences. Figuring out how to account for the 'somehow' red and rectangular 'something' that is in 'some way' present in one's experience when one vividly hallucinates a pink ice cube or a red brick right in front of one

– and doing so without either denying this problematic phenomenological presence altogether or reducing it merely to the content of a
false *belief* – is a serious problem.[22] In fact, it is arguably the most difficult problem of all for the synoptic philosopher, as we saw briefly in
chapter 1 and will see again in the next chapter. This is because in cases
such as (b) and (c) nothing in the (outer or inner) situation is *literally*
red or rectangular in the way that physical objects are red and rectangular; and yet we also want to avoid retreating back to the abandoned
idea that we are aware of Price's red rectangular *sense-data* or C. I.
Lewis's *qualia*. Again, we return to this difficult issue in the final section
and in chapter 6.

As to the common *propositional* content in situations (a), (b), and (c),
what we are ostensibly seeing in each case is *that there is a red object over
there*. Owing to the nature of our social-normative linguistic development and training, as we saw in chapters 3 and 4, the proposition that
x, over there, is red is involved in the manner in which all three cases
are spontaneously and non-inferentially conceptualized, at the most
unreflective responsive level of pattern-governed (and for human
beings, also rule-governed) behavior. In particular Sellars' treatment
of perceptual knowledge will depend upon his account of •this is red•s
as *language entry transitions* or perceptual thoughts the conceptual
meaning of which depends upon the holistic conceptual role of •red•s
in such inferences as 'if *x* is red, then *x* is colored,' as governed
by linguistic 'ought-to-be' rules of criticism. We thus acquire a conceptually structured logical space only by being initiated into a normative network of formal and material inference patterns in which our
conceptual responses to objects are caught up. How we perceptually
take things to be in our immediate responses to the passing scene
depends upon the concepts embedded in those responses as a result
of our having been trained into a particular linguistic-conceptual
framework. (In EPM this crucial 'anti-Augustinian' conceptual role
semantics is developed all too quickly in the short space of part VII,
'The Logic of "Means." '[23]) Our current task is to come to understand
how the propositional content •this is red• that is shared across the
experiences (a), (b), and (c) figures in Sellars' alternative non-Cartesian
and non-sense-datum account of perceptual appearance and perceptual judgment.

Sellars' proposal is that when, in a 'seeming to see' situation such as
(b) or (c) above, something has evoked in S the 'visual thinking' (SK
I.44) that *x looks* red, what is going on is that S is having "an experience
which involves in a unique way the idea *that x is red* and involves it in
such a way that if this idea were true, the experience would correctly
be characterized as a seeing that *x* is red," as in the veridical case (a)
(EPM IV.22). That 'unique way' involves in part, Sellars argues, a
crucial further aspect of epistemic appraisal or *endorsement*: the three

situations "differ primarily in that (a) is so formulated as to involve an endorsement of the idea that *x*, over there, is red, whereas in (b) this idea is only partially endorsed, and in (c) not at all" (EPM IV.22).[24] This fundamental epistemic function of the concept of appearance or the logic of 'looks' is a conceptual capacity that we first acquire in learning the sorts of circumstances (awkward lighting, etc.) in which having an experience that *normally would* be an experience of seeing that something is red is not to be trusted as such in these particular circumstances. A fundamental governing principle that is thus acquired in this process – one which is open to serious misinterpretation, as we shall see – is what we may call the '*is/looks*' conceptual contrast connection, which Sellars formulates in terms of our present example as follows (cf. EPM III.12; bracketed title is my own):

> [The *is/looks* principle:] *x is* red if and only if *x* would *look* red to standard observers in standard conditions.

In EPM Sellars brings out the endorsement dimension of appearance concepts by telling a "historical fiction" about young John in the necktie shop, the gist of which is as follows (EPM III.14–15). Sellars asks us to imagine that John "has never looked at an object in other than standard conditions."[25] Suppose that electric lighting has just recently been invented, but that John has only now installed it in his necktie shop and has not yet become used to it. He shows Jim one of his ties, saying, 'Here is a green one for you,' but Jim says, 'That's not green, it's blue; come outside and look.' Unaccustomed, we are to imagine, to the idea of non-standard lighting conditions, John is at first inclined to say that inside the shop he *saw* that the tie was green, and now outside he sees that it is blue. However, John also knows that objects do not change their colors merely by being moved around. The upshot of Sellars' story is that John needs a concept that both registers the (phenomenological) fact that his experience in the shop is such that it *would normally* be a seeing that this tie *is* green – that is what he ostensibly sees – but which also has the pragmatic effect of holding back from endorsing or epistemically committing to that idea, given the awkward lighting conditions. In short, he needs the concept of *looks*, of *appearances*: he must acquire the '*is/looks*' conceptual contrast.

It is crucial to note that on Sellars' conception of appearance the '*is/looks*' connection entails the priority of the concept of how things objectively *are* over concepts pertaining to how they look or *appear* to the experiencing subject (more on this in the next section). That is, it entails that

> the concept of *looking green*, the ability to recognize that something *looks green*, presupposes the concept of *being green*, and that the latter concept

involves the ability to tell what colors objects have by looking at them
– which, in turn, involves knowing in what circumstances to place an
object if one wishes to ascertain its color. (EPM III.18)

As young children we learn in one scrambling process of acquisition
how to judge in general both that *this is red* and (in other situations)
that *this only looks red*. However, even if one could not intelligibly be
supposed to possess the one concept without the other, nonetheless the
latter 'looks' concept is according to the above account essentially a
holding back from, and thus parasitic upon, the former concept pertaining to the colors possessed by ordinary physical objects.

Sellars' account of the endorsement or epistemic appraisal dimension of the concept of appearance, then, is roughly that, as an element
in a perceptual experience, an •*x looks* red• is a directly object-caused
or stimulus-prompted (i.e., non-inferential) conceptual response that
implicitly functions to withhold commitment to aspects of what would
normally, in standard conditions, give rise to an •*x is* red• conceptual
response.

Before considering in the next section an important difficulty that
confronts this alternative conception of perception and appearance,
what does Sellars take its implications to be in relation to the fundamental epistemological issues we have so far been considering in this
chapter?

Many philosophers who regard 'sense-data' to be a mistake have
sought other ways to interpret the above '*is/looks*' conceptual connection consistently with either a classical empiricist or a broadly Cartesian conception of the given in the form of various theses concerning
the *epistemic priority of appearances*. Without necessarily sharing
Descartes' worries concerning radical skeptical doubts, such a theorist
might nonetheless begin with how things *look* – what could be a safer,
more "directly evident" starting point? – and then attempt to articulate
"the criterion" (Chisholm) for when such appearances to perceivers (in
all probability) amount to knowledge of how things *are*.[26] On this view,
the *is/looks* principle would be interpreted as holding true for the reason
that *is red* is criterially defined in terms of *looking red* in certain standard
conditions. If Sellars is right, however, the *is/looks* connection is "a
necessary truth *not* because the right-hand side [concerning looks] is
the definition of '*x* is red,' but because 'standard conditions' simply
means conditions in which things look as they are" (EPM III.18). This
accounts for the '*is/looks*' conceptual connection while simultaneously
denying the alleged epistemic priority of appearances. If successful,
Sellars' account thus redirects our philosophical attention to questions
concerning the justification for such ordinary perceptual claims as
'Jones sees that the brick is red,' which will occupy us in the next
section.

Furthermore, we can now see why epistemologists have always been tempted to account for our knowledge by beginning with how things appear to the experiencing subject. Descartes' idea was that even if an omnipotent Evil Demon is deceiving me such that all of my claims about reality are mistaken, I can at least never be mistaken that it *seems to me* that such and such is the case – that is directly evident, just *given*.[27] One might read the following remark from Hume in a similar spirit: as "long as we confine our speculations to *the appearances* [. . .] we are safe from all difficulties, and can never be embarrass'd by any question" (Hume 1739: 638). If Sellars is right, however, this safe confinement results from the fact that in thus sticking to appearances *no claim as to how things are has been ventured*; it is *not* because a new realm of foundational facts concerning subjectivity has been gained, as the myth of the given would have it.[28] Sellars is certainly not denying that there is, in a sense later to be determined, an experience of *red* going on in all three cases (a), (b), and (c). However, no awareness of either its intrinsic categorial nature or its epistemic status is 'given' simply by considering it as tucked safely away in an epistemic solitary confinement where all propositional commitments have been withdrawn. Sellars' account thus preserves such *incorrigibility* or invulnerability to correction (no venture, no correction) as there is in our inner thoughts and outer reports as to how things *appear*. And it does so while maintaining a perspective according to which the objective cognitive commitment *x is red* is more basic than the commitment-withdrawing *x looks red*, for the latter functions essentially as an epistemic qualifier, as it were, of aspects of the former experientially elicited and pattern-governed propositional response to the world.

Much more could be said in favor of Sellars' epistemic conception of this dimension of "the logic of 'looks'" (see in particular EPM III.17). We have already seen how it neatly handles the distinction between seeing, qualitative looking, and existential looking in cases (a), (b), and (c). By thus illuminating how it is that concepts of appearing express our varying degrees of propositional commitment and caution as to how things are, Sellars is able to explain, for example, the possibility of merely *generic looks*, which had proven to be such a problematic issue on sense-datum and traditional 'imagistic' views of appearance. If a shirt's looking to be polka-dotted were a matter of some sense-datum's *being* polka-dotted, then if the shirt merely looks generically to have an indeterminate number of polka-dots, does the sense-datum *have* a merely indeterminate number of polka-dots? Does the being/seeming distinction then apply to sense-data as well? It is a relief to be able to avoid these problems. In this propositional dimension Sellars' concept of 'looks' admits of all the conceptual flexibility that is available in our qualifications of our *beliefs* or claims about the nature of things. And it does so without our having to go to the other philosophical extreme of holding that perceiving is *merely* a certain kind of causally reliable, object-elicited intentional thought or belief that is directed toward the world, for on Sellars' view we must also recognize the non-conceptual content that is 'somehow' common to all three experiences (a), (b), and (c).

Sellars sums up all of these aspects of his epistemic endorsement or claim-appraisal account of 'looks' in the potentially misleading but important slogan that "*looks* is not a relation" at all (EPM III.13), whether to a sense-datum or as an alleged irreducible 'relation of appearing' to physical objects.[29] We should not be surprised by this, for we have spent the previous two chapters exploring the sense in which for Sellars *word x means y* is not itself a basic word–world or mind–world relation either. Rather, 'means'-statements assert a meta-conceptual functional role classification, and thereby *convey* the information (without asserting explicitly) that various word–world and other natural relations are in place. Both conceptions are readily open to misunderstanding if one does not bear in mind what in earlier chapters I have called Sellars' *norm/nature* meta-principle and its accompanying presupposition structure, as part of what I have characterized as Sellars' *naturalism with a normative turn*. Accordingly, although "looking red" has been shown to be for Sellars an "*epistemic* fact about objects" rather than a "*natural*" fact about or a basic relation to such objects (EPM III.17), appearance judgments do nonetheless *systematically presuppose* (but are not conceptually reducible to truths concerning) the existence of appropriate natural occurrences, causal relations, and acquired dispositions. These are all instances of Sellars' general contention that "the idea that epistemic facts can be analyzed without remainder – even 'in principle' – into non-epistemic facts" is "a radical mistake – a mistake of a piece with the so-called 'naturalistic fallacy' in ethics" (EPM I.5). The concepts of appearance and of perceptual knowledge, of seeming and seeing, just as was the case in earlier chapters with the concepts of meaning and intentionality, thus have a very different normative role than the classical or perennial 'world-relational' models of our cognitive nature, whether intellectualist or empiricist, would suggest.

Our acquired concepts pertaining to the looks and appearances of things are thus shown to be, in this propositional dimension of their use, rather subtle and flexible but easy to use tools of epistemic appraisal. We use them unreflectively all the time; they have come to be second nature to us as elements of the language we speak. In effect, however, they express our take on the truth-merits of those learned sensory-cum-conceptual non-inferential responses that are "evoked or wrung from the perceiver by the object perceived" (EPM III.16). The claim appraisal or endorsement aspect of perception is not *all* there is to the logic of 'looks,' for we still have to grapple with the problem of the intrinsic phenomenal content of perception and appearance. Yet it is a dimension that is crucial for avoiding both the Cartesian 'inward turn' as well as the more general idea, of which that turn is just one instance, of attempting to account for the structure of our empirical knowledge by basing it on how experiencers are 'appeared to,' where the latter is seen as a fact that is just *given* and thus allegedly epistemically prior to ordinary claims as to how things are in the external world.

If the above account of appearance concepts is correct, however, then with a sense of liberation we can now leave the appearances to the derivative safety of their self-imposed epistemic exile. We can instead turn our philosophical attention outward to examine the daylight structure of our more serious endeavors to *say how things are*, as in our ordinary perceptual claim to see that the tomato on the table is red. But is Sellars' alternative conception of 'looks' and of perceptual knowledge, as so far developed, without its own difficulties? It turns out, as a matter of fact, that an examination of one of the most interesting challenges to the tenability of Sellars' account will also serve to bring out the heart of his own conception of the holistic structure of our knowledge. Let us turn, then, to that account and eventually to that challenge, which will also provide further insight into the grounds for Sellars' critique of the myth of the given in all its various forms.

Epistemic principles and the holistic structure of our knowledge

Supposing we reject the myth of the given in the forms canvassed so far, how is it that such non-inferential observation reports or perceptual judgments as

[P]   This physical object *x* is red

provide us with relatively secure instances of perceptual knowledge, as Sellars agrees with the empiricist that they do? To put it in the usual epistemological jargon: how is it possible on Sellars' account, without the myth of the epistemically independent given, for there to be a non-inferentially warranted stratum of justificatory regress-stopping and evidence-providing claims as to basic observational matters of fact (see EPM VIII.32–3)?

In EPM Sellars used his analysis of the priority of the concept of *being red* over that of *looking red* to embark on his own suggestion as to the warrant for such claims as [P], which in retrospect today can clearly be seen to have broken important new ground. He begins by suggesting (as usual taking linguistic behavior as his model) that perhaps an

overt or covert token of 'This is green' in the presence of a green item
... expresses observational knowledge if and only if it is a manifestation
of a tendency to produce overt or covert tokens of 'This is green' – given
a certain set – if and only if a green object is being looked at in standard
conditions. (EPM VIII.35)

Let us call this the epistemic principle of *perceptual reliability* [PR] and
frame it in terms of our example:[30]

> [PR] S's perceptual judgment [P] that *x, over there, is red* constitutes
> a case of perceptual knowledge if and only if there is a gener-
> ally reliable connection between cases of S's judging that [P]
> and its being in fact true that there is a red physical object over
> there.

The general idea behind [PR] is that a typical candid perceptual judgment [P] that, say, *x is green*, made in standard conditions – for example,
made in broad daylight in clear view of an object by someone with
normal eyesight who knows English – is generally *reliable* in the sense
that one can safely (not infallibly) "infer the presence of a green object
from the fact that someone makes this report" (EPM VIII.35). As we
saw in chapters 3 and 4, S has been so trained in accordance with the
normative ought-to-be rules maintained in her linguistic community
that as a result S, other things being equal, has a stable tendency to
judge that *x is green* if and only if there *is* in fact a green physical object
over there in the external environment in standard conditions of perception. Hence we can rely on S's perceptual judgments to be in all
likelihood true, and this norm-generated causal reliability might be
held to constitute the epistemic authority of S's direct observations.

After all of our hesitant explorations among the appearances in the
previous two sections, the perceptual reliability principle [PR] has a
refreshingly common-sense appeal. Someone has knowledge when
and only when what they judge tends to be a reliable guide to what is
in fact the case. Sellars presciently realized, however, that this opening
move concerning perceptual reliability immediately raises some difficult questions concerning the concept of knowledge – questions which
decades later have since become central to *internalism vs. externalism*
debates in epistemology.[31] Sellars, unlike contemporary externalists,
thinks it is clear that in order for S's judgment [P] that *x* is red to constitute perceptual knowledge for S, not only must the principle of
perceptual reliability [PR] be *true of* S (that is, not only must S's judgments that [P] be *in fact* reliable indicators of the fact that [P]), *but S
must herself know that her judgments are thus reliable*.[32] The externally
reliable causal connection between perceptual responses and the facts
is, according to Sellars, a necessary but not sufficient condition for S to

know that [P]. Sellars thus adds an *internalist requirement* on basic perceptual knowledge that S must herself know, in a sense now to be explored, that the general perceptual reliability principle [PR] covers her own particular judgments that [P].

I will argue that Sellars' unique combination, already in the 1950s, of the requirements of external causal-reliability and internal reason-giving results in a defensible and attractive position in epistemology. Sellars himself saw, however, that his account faces a "steep hurdle":

> [T]o be the expression of knowledge, a report must not only *have* authority, this authority must *in some sense* be recognized by the person whose report it is. And this is a steep hurdle indeed. For if the authority of the report 'This is green' lies in the fact that the existence of green items appropriately related to the perceiver can be inferred from the occurrence of such reports, it follows that only a person who is able to draw this inference, and therefore who has not only the concept *green*, but also the concept of uttering 'This is green' – indeed, the concept of certain conditions of perception, those which would correctly be called 'standard conditions' – could be in a position to token 'This is green' in recognition of its authority. In other words, for [. . .] 'This is green' to 'express observational knowledge', not only must it be a *symptom* or *sign* of the presence of a green object in standard conditions, but the perceiver must know that tokens of 'This is green' *are* symptoms of the presence of green objects in conditions which are standard for visual perception. (EPM VIII.35)

In commenting on this passage Ernest Sosa remarks that in EPM Sellars "highlighted inadequacies not only of traditional givenist foundationalism, but also of a more recent externalist reliabilism – a neat trick since, at the time he wrote, such reliabilism had not yet appeared in print. Nevertheless, Sellars's positive proposal is problematic," Sosa claims, for he argues that Sellars is mistaken to think that he can successfully clear the steep hurdle that he recognizes confronts his strong internalist requirement on our knowledge (Sosa 1997: 280, 281). The remainder of this section will be devoted to a brief examination of the novel conception of knowledge initiated in the above passage from EPM VIII and further elaborated in Sellars' later writings in epistemology.

What is the steep hurdle?[33] Sellars recognized that "it might be thought that there is something obviously absurd" about his strong internalist requirement that "observational knowledge of any particular fact, e.g. that this is green, presupposes that one knows general facts of the form *X is a reliable symptom of Y*" (EPM VIII.36). While this view has the merit of giving us yet further grounds, if we needed any, for rejecting the myth of the foundationalist epistemic *given* in that it "requires an abandonment of the traditional empiricist idea that [particular] observational knowledge 'stands on its own feet'" (EPM VIII.36), the resulting epistemic holism itself raises the following puzzle.

On Sellars' view, S can perceptually know that [P] only if S has knowledge of the general perceptual reliability principle [PR], which is the second-order meta-knowledge that her first-order particular judgments that [P] are in fact generally reliable indicators of (say) red objects in standard conditions. But how could S acquire or warrantedly possess the latter general empirical knowledge [PR] except on the basis of *prior* particular observational knowledge claims of the sort that [P]? A vicious regress or vicious circle clearly threatens. Have we in the end avoided the myth of the given only to be left with an impossible feat of epistemic bootstrapping?

Sellars initially responded to the threatening regress or circularity by suggesting (EPM VIII.37) that adult Jones might "give inductive reasons *today*" to justify his meta-knowledge of his perceptual reliability [PR]. He can do this not by appealing to particular cases of his past successful perceptions [P] (for these are possible only if [PR] is already justified for Jones) but rather by appeal to what we may call the *proto-*perceptions [P*] which he had when, to put it roughly, young child Jones was first being trained by his elders to utter 'red' in response to red objects.[34] Child Jones's proto-perceptions that [P*] are, as Sellars puts it, "superficially like" adult Jones's perceptions that [P] – both are superficially similar verbal or covert responses to having intrinsically similar sensations of red, for example. However, child Jones's proto-perceptions did not at the time qualify as instances of seeing (perceptually knowing) that some physical object *x* is red. At that earlier time the child lacked the knowledge of [PR], since he lacked the capacity to wield the various ordinary *is/looks* conceptual contrasts concerning reliable and unreliable conditions of perception that evince one's knowledge of [PR].[35]

It was in fact in anticipation of just this distinction (i.e., superficial similarity yet different epistemic status) that Sellars one paragraph earlier had made a remark that is now frequently cited by contemporary epistemologists:

> The essential point is that in characterizing an episode or a state as that of *knowing*, we are not giving an empirical description of that episode or state; we are placing it in the logical space of reasons, of justifying and being able to justify what one says. (EPM VIII.36)

The "empirical" description of the verbalizations, natural dispositions, and sensory processes that are manifested and undergone by young child Jones and by adult Jones might be quite similar in any given case. However, adult Jones's linguistic and hence conceptual capacities are slightly different from those of very young child Jones. (Recall our discussion in chapter 2 of the phenomenological distinction between 'what we see *of* an object' as opposed to 'what we see an object *as*.' The former sensible contents are relatively constant, while the latter conceptual contents change with learning.) Adult Jones can, if the situation demands it, say something about the sorts of contexts that are unreliable for 'telling colors,' while toddler Jones does not yet have a minimally adequate grasp of the situations in which his visual reactions are and when they are not safe guides to the colors of objects.

What should we make of this initial response in EPM to the regress or circularity worry? More generally, what should we make of Sellars' conception of the holistic and internalist requirements on basic, non-inferential perceptual knowledge?[36] I believe that Sellars later came to see that the 'inductive' aspect of his response in EPM to the steep hurdle was not satisfactory, and that this forced him to clarify his position along several dimensions. In particular the brief discussion in EPM VIII runs together issues concerning the genetic *acquisition* of various conceptual abilities and questions concerning the *justificatory* relationships that obtain between particular perceptual judgments and general epistemic principles such as [PR], although the two issues are certainly related for Sellars.[37] This led Sellars to clarify both our top-level sophisticated knowledge of epistemic principles and the most bottom level of non-linguistic 'animal representations' and human pre-linguistic 'proto-cognitions.'

To begin with a brief discussion of the latter issue, Sellars offered a complex phenomenological account in his Carus Lectures in 1981 (FMPP I) of the proto-conceptual capacities that are presumably possessed by young child Jones (or "Junior"). The purpose of this account was to show that Sellars' thesis of the conceptual priority of 'is red' over 'looks red' does not lead to a genetic-acquisition vicious regress. In this way Sellars also hoped to defuse various sophisticated arguments for the epistemic priority of *appearances* that had long been defended by Roderick Firth in his qualified defense of C. I. Lewis's conception of the given (Firth 1964, 1981).

The upshot of Sellars' somewhat labyrinthine discussion is roughly this. Suppose young Junior does not yet grasp the basic '*is/looks*' conceptual contrast. Junior is at the stage where he blurts out 'red!' indifferently across both situations that *we adults* would conceptually distinguish as an object's 'merely looking red' as opposed to its 'being red.' As Firth interprets this, we adults can see that Junior is responding to what we adults would classify as a *subjective* (that is, *any* sensory) experience of red. In this sense, Firth concludes, "the subjective is prior to the objective," although our sophisticated '*is* vs. *looks*' conceptual contrasts get in the way of our grasping this epistemic priority (Firth 1981: 100).

Sellars interprets the same situation, however, in a way that preserves both the genetic and the conceptual priority of 'is red' over 'looks red,' yet without implausibly crediting the toddler Junior with a grasp of the *is/looks* contrast, thereby successfully eluding the above genetic circularity worry. What Firth has in effect done, according to Sellars' phenomenological analysis, is to mistake Junior's less sophisticated, less determinate proto-concept of (let us say) moving-red-object *x* for a proto-concept of *something other* than object *x* (which we adults might call a 'subjective experience,' or a 'neutral given'). In this way Sellars holds firmly to his thesis that "with respect to color we have no determinate category prior to that of the physical" (FMPP I.86): "*We, as phenomenologists, can bracket the concept of an expanse of red* [. . .] and construe it merely as a *particular* having *some determinate categorial status or other*. Our phenomenological abstraction no more reveals a new determinate category than the concept of *some color or other* generates the concept of a new shade of red" (FMPP I.84). Here again (and as we shall also see in the next section) it is the myth of the *categorial* given that has played the key role in Sellars' argument.

During the same late period Sellars also sketched in 'Mental Events' (MEV, 1981) a bottom-level account of non-linguistic and pre-linguistic *animal representation systems*. The conclusion of this account, too, credits animals and toddlers with object-directed and quasi-propositionally structured proto-cognitions (thanks in part to evolution by natural selection), while at the same time preserving Sellars' account of the holistic '*logical* space of reasons,' the gradual acquiring of which by language learners is what constitutes them as full-blooded knowers of a law-governed world of objects.[38]

What both of these later accounts together provide is a more plausible picture of the naturally sophisticated, world-directed, proto-cognitive representations that nonetheless fall short of the sort of epistemic recognition of objects and their properties that comes only when such episodes are integrated within "the logical space of reasons, of justifying and being able to justify what one says" (EPM VIII.36). What we have seen Sellars call his *psychological nominalist* thesis – that the ability to recognize, notice, observe, or see that an object is red, for example, requires linguistic classificatory abilities – is thus preserved within a more fleshed-out account of cognition in general. These later distinctions also serve to take the sting out of the genetic regress worry insofar as this pertains to the acquisition of conceptual capacities, and thus also to preserve the coherence of Sellars' thesis of the priority of '(physical object) *x* is red' over '*x* looks red.' What remains to be addressed is the threat of a *justificatory* vicious circle, and the questions raised by Sellars' awkward appeal in EPM to adult Jones's alleged quasi-inductive support for his own perceptual reliability. This question was also clarified in Sellars' writings after EPM,[39] in particular by his highlighting certain broadly Kantian themes[40] concerning *epistemic framework principles*.

Consider again our two problematically interrelated items of empirical knowledge [P] and [PR]:

[P]   Jones ostensibly sees that physical object *x* is red (in standard conditions: i.e. "no countervailing conditions obtain," SK III.33)

[PR]   In general, if Jones ostensibly sees that a physical object is red (in standard conditions), then it is highly likely to be true that there is a red physical object which Jones has seen.

One of the main sources of puzzlement in relation to principle [PR] is that it is itself a general piece of *empirical* knowledge and yet simultaneously it serves as a fundamental epistemic principle or *criterion* for any particular knowledge claim such as [P]. And if we ask how it is that the belief (whether ours or Jones's) in the reliability principle [PR] is itself epistemically justified, one would think that such an account is going to have to rely upon *some* empirical observation or other. But on Sellars' view any such particular perceptual observation of the sort [P] by Jones is warranted for Jones only if the reliability meta-principle [PR] is already warranted for Jones. "Must we not conclude," asked Sellars in the early 1970s of his own view, "that any such account as I give of the principle that perceptual beliefs occurring in perceptual contexts are *likely to be true* is circular? It must, indeed, be granted that principles pertaining to the epistemic authority of perceptual and memory beliefs are not the sort of thing which *could* be arrived at by inductive reasoning from perceptual belief" (SK III.45). Here Sellars explicitly rules out as circular the idea, which he himself had seemed to propose in EPM VIII, of *inductively* supporting [PR] by past instances of [P]-success, and it is not clear how the quasi-success of past instances of proto-perceptions [P*] would help with this justificatory problem either. The justificatory circularity problem, then, is that for all that has been said so far, it seems reasonable to accept epistemic principle [PR] only because it is in some way supported by particular observations [P]; but it is reasonable to accept observations [P] only in virtue of their being known to fall under the perceptual reliability principle [PR].

Sellars' overall response to this problem (see in particular MGEC IV and SK III, as well as KTE on Kant) involves a distinction between:

(A)   possible naturalistic (for example, evolutionary) *explanations* of how we came to be in the sort of epistemic conceptual framework that is constituted by such principles as [PR] and

> (B)   a kind of non-empirical or *transcendental* argument (in a sense
>   to be explained) for the reasonableness of accepting epistemic
>   principles such as [PR] insofar as they are "elements in a con-
>   ceptual framework which defines what it is to be a finite
>   knower in a world one never made" (MGEC IV.73).

On Sellars' view (B) can also be given a corresponding *linguistic* formulation, insofar as principles such as [PR] can be seen to fall out from
"the unpacking of the notion that meaningful language is language
about a world in which it is used" (RNWW ¶53; and SK III.46). Crudely
put, *transcendental arguments* (B) of the sort Sellars develops in the spirit
of Kant are conceptual analyses (rather than explanations or hypotheses based on empirical data, as in (A)) designed to show that some
principle for which we are seeking a justification, such as the principle
of perceptual reliability or the principle of cause and effect, for example,
is in fact *necessary for the possibility* of some other more general principle
that, for one reason or another, is not in dispute. Perhaps, for example,
even the most radical skeptic cannot deny certain truths about their
own experience without falling into incoherence. Sellars' claim in the
present context will be more modest than that claim, but still controversial: namely, that if it is granted that we possess any meaningful
language about a world at all, then it must be granted that the principle
of perceptual reliability [PR] is epistemically justified. Space permits
only a few brief remarks on these important issues to conclude this
section.

Firstly, then, in relation to the explanatory dimension (A), Sellars
suggests that "Presumably the question, 'How did we get into the
framework?' has a causal answer, a special application of evolutionary
theory to the emergence of beings capable of conceptually representing
the world of which they have come to be a part" (MGEC IV.79). For
this explanatory task we must of course rely on particular perceptual
observations [P], which are in this sense "epistemically prior to *explanations* of the likely truth" of such observations (MGEC IV.86). This is the
sense in which it is true to say that our empirical knowledge at any
given time and within specific contexts of inquiry is justified by appeal
to a foundation – though a fallible and revisable one – of non-inferential perceptual knowings or empirical observations, in the usual sort of
ongoing interplay or search for 'reflective equilibrium' (to borrow John
Rawls' term) between provisionally accepted data and proposed
explanatory hypotheses or principles.

As to the 'transcendental' justificatory dimension (B), on the other
hand, the usual priority is reversed: Sellars' claim here is that certain

epistemic framework principles such as [PR] are "epistemically prior to the reasonableness" of accepting *any* particular observational judgments [P] (MGEC IV.86). With regard to the coherent framework of epistemic principles of which [PR] is a part – however that framework was acquired and however it is ultimately best explained in the (A)-dimension – Sellars ultimately defends the following strong Kantian claim:

> [W]e have to be in the framework of these (and other) principles to be thinking, perceiving, and, I now add, acting beings at all. But surely this makes it clear that the exploration of these principles is but part and parcel of the task of explicating the concept of a rational animal or, in *VB* [verbal behaviorist] terms, of a language-using organism whose language is *about* the world in which it is *used*. It is only in the light of this larger task that the problem of the status of epistemic principles reveals its true meaning. (SK III.46)

In 'Some Remarks on Kant's Theory of Experience,' for example, Sellars argues that what Kant sought to show is that there could be no *particular* item of empirical knowledge that was "not implicitly of the form, 'such and such a state of affairs belongs to a coherent system of states of affairs of which my perceptual experiences are a part' " (KTE 46; ¶11).[41] Sellars argues that the conceptual analysis of any such system will entail, for example, that there are lawful causal connections obtaining both in general and in particular between my perceptual judgments made in standard conditions and the objective state of affairs which they report. These substantive (rather than merely formal-logical) *coherence* principles will also include, for example, the fundamental 'being vs. seeming' or '*is/looks*' conceptual contrasts that we have seen to be bound up with the principle [PR] of the general reliability of our perceptual responses in standard conditions. They also include for Sellars as they did for Kant such meta-conceptual rules as the *principle of causality* (cf. RNWW 456), where this is ultimately interpreted by Sellars in terms of the claim that any language or conceptual framework that succeeds in representing an objective, temporally ordered material world must contain *material inference principles* which warrant the inferential move from '*x* is *A*' directly to '*x* is *B*' for some logically independent empirical contents *A* and *B* (for the details, see CDCM, CIL, ITSA, IM, and SRLG; see also chapter 4, n. 8 above).

It is this broadly Kantian or transcendental (B)-dimension, concerning what Sellars argues are the requirements on our possessing *any* cognitive conceptual framework at all, that is supposed to show how such epistemic principles as [PR] and the principle of causality have the puzzling dual status noted earlier. Such principles have substantive *empirical content* (and are therefore naturalistically (A)-explainable);

and yet simultaneously they function as *epistemic norms* or criteria that legislate for any and all such conceptual frameworks.

In KTE Sellars refers to "a linguistic version of Kant's position" (KTE 58; ¶39) that is clearly intended to be Sellars' own position. As the following important passage makes clear, the general form of Sellars' various Kantian arguments of the kind referred to above, the detailed explanation and evaluation of which would require a more extended treatment than is possible here (but see O'Shea 2006a),[42] is based firmly on the conception of meaning as rule-following, pattern-governed behavior which we examined in chapters 3 and 4:

> To construe the concepts of meaning, truth, and knowledge as metalinguistic concepts pertaining to linguistic behavior (and dispositions to behave) involves construing the latter as governed by *ought-to-be's* which are actualized as uniformities by the training that transmits language from generation to generation. Thus, if logical and (more broadly) epistemic categories express general features of the *ought-to-be's* (and corresponding uniformities) which are necessary to the functioning of language as a cognitive instrument, epistemology, in this context, becomes the theory of this functioning – in short *transcendental linguistics*. (KTE 58–9; ¶40)

Transcendental linguistics thus "attempts to delineate the general features that would be common to the epistemic functioning of any language in any possible world," as Kant's own transcendental philosophy sought to establish "the general features any conceptual system must have in order to generate knowledge of a world to which it belongs" (KTE 59; ¶41).[43] In the end, then, the warrant for the perceptual reliability principle would be that [PR] is necessary for the possibility of any linguistic framework functioning as a cognitive instrument – for example, as providing any action-guiding representations of an objective world at all (see MGEC IV).

In this regard Sellars argues, for example, that an "essential requirement of the transmission of a language from generation to generation is that its mature users be able to identify both extra-linguistic items and the utterances that are correct responses to them," where the correctness of a given conceptual response is constituted by the relevant linguistic 'ought-to-be' or *language entry rule*: "(*Ceteris paribus*) one ought to respond to φ items with conceptual acts of kind *C*" (KTE 59; ¶43). Normatively established language entry rules of this kind are necessary for the possible cognitive functioning of any conceptual framework. We have in fact seen this several times already, in relation to what I have characterized as Sellars' *norm/nature* meta-principle. It is the communal *espousal of such principles* as [PR] that *brings it about* that the particular 'flesh and blood' behavioral *uniformities of performance* (TC 216) in that community are such that (to use Sellars' example) a C-kind of perceptual response will be a *reliable indicator* of the presence of a corresponding φ item out there.

In sum, Sellars' contention is that epistemic principles such as [PR] can be given a (B)-dimension, transcendental justification that is independent of the justified status of whatever particular judgments [P] fall under those principles. At any given time, however, the latter particular empirical judgments [P] will serve as the empirical data for our ongoing search for an (A)-dimension *theoretical* (perhaps evolutionary) *explanation* of how it is that such principles as [PR] have come to play the constitutive roles in our cognitive frameworks that they do play.

Obviously we have only been able to scratch the surface of this important updated-Kantian dimension of Sellars' epistemology,[44] and more would also need to be said about his views on the wider topic of the justification of *first principles* in general (see, in particular, 'On Accepting First Principles' (OAFP) and 'Induction as Vindication' (IV)). Ultimately, on Sellars' account, the (B)-dimension transcendental warrant for such principles as [PR] itself derives from the fact that such principles make possible the achievement of a *cognitive end* or goal that is indispensable for us: that of having any epistemically or cognitively functioning language at all.

I hope, however, that some light has been shed in this section on Sellars' continual efforts, spanning four decades, "to formulate, more clearly than I have hitherto been able to do, the complex interplay in empirical knowledge of the two dimensions which epistemologists have sought to capture by the concepts of the given on the one hand, and of coherence on the other" (FMPP I.6). These are the same two dimensions that he had summed up in the following famous passage from EPM VIII (later quoted by Sellars himself in both SK and MGEC):

> There is clearly *some* point to the picture of human knowledge as resting on a level of propositions – observation reports – which do not rest on other propositions in the same way as other propositions rest on them. On the other hand, I do wish to insist that the metaphor of 'foundation' is misleading in that it keeps us from seeing that if there is a logical dimension in which other empirical propositions rest on observation reports, there is another logical dimension in which the latter rest on the former. (EPM VIII.38)

Before moving on, however, we should note that this discussion has also shed light on "the paradox of man's encounter with himself" (PSIM 6) discussed in chapter 1, and the associated deep problems concerning the genesis and status of human rationality and of normative "standards of correctness" generally. There we saw that such rational principles, when considered from inside the manifest image, as it were, appeared to be on a 'higher level' than the physical world as described and explained in the comprehensive scientific image of the world. As we saw Sellars put it, "this difference in level appears as an irreducible discontinuity in the *manifest* image [cf. the (B)-dimension above], but as, in a sense requiring careful analysis, a reducible difference in the *scientific* image [cf. the (A)-dimension above]" (PSIM 6; cf. SSMB *passim* on 'logical irreducibility *cum* causal reducibility'). The examination of the two dimensions concerning epistemic principles just completed helps to render non-paradoxical how it is that such rational principles are both *normatively legislative* for all particular empirical claims, and yet they are also in principle themselves *scientifically explainable* (see also O'Shea 2006b). As we have seen, Sellars takes it that (in the (A)-dimension) "the question 'How did we get into the framework?' has a causal answer, a special application of evolutionary theory to the emergence of beings capable of conceptually representing the world of which they have come to be a part" (MGEC IV.78).

There are many questions and challenges that might be raised in relation to what might well be called Sellars' *Kantian explanatory coherence* account of our empirical knowledge. Having reached this systematic stage, however, let us return to recoup those immediate sensory experiences from which we first departed in this chapter, lest we too, having now fixed our gaze on the role of holistic coherence, succumb to the temptation to stampede away from the insights – mishandled though they were – of those long-forgotten sense-datum theorists.

Genius Jones, Act Two: the intrinsic character of our sensory experiences

We return, then, to the question of the "*intrinsic* character" (EPM IV.22) of the non-conceptual content that Sellars holds is a common factor across the three veridical (a) and non-veridical (b, c) experiences of ostensibly seeing, for example, the facing side of a red brick:

(a) S's seeing that *x*, over there, is red and rectangular.
(b) Its looking to S that *x*, over there, is red and rectangular.
(c) Its appearing to S as though there were a red, rectangular object over there.

If successful, Sellars' detailed accounts of the propositional endorsement aspects of our concepts of 'seeing' and 'looking,' of the conceptual and epistemic priority of '(physical object) x is red' over 'x looks red to S,' and of both the holistic-explanatory and causal dimensions involved in reliable perceptual knowledge have resolved many of the problems that were raised by the sense-datum theorists and by other philosophers of perception. However, on Sellars' view, the most intractable problem concerning our perceptual knowledge has not yet been addressed, for even when our perceptual judgments have been correctly analyzed in all their conceptual and propositional dimensions, Sellars holds that

> the very nature of 'looks talk' is such as to raise questions to which it gives no answer: What is the *intrinsic* character of the common descriptive content of these three experiences? and How are they able to have it in spite of the fact that whereas in the case of (a) the perceiver must be in the presence of a red object over there, in (b) the object over there need not be red, while in (c) there need be no object over there at all? (EPM IV.22)

To take case (c), for example, suppose that Sue's visual center in her brain is being directly stimulated by a piece of scientific equipment with the result that it appears vividly to Sue that there is a red brick lying on the table in front of her, when in fact there is no brick there at all. Sue can describe in detail the shape and color of the rectangular expanse of redness that seems to belong to a brick over there, but in fact does not.

The question Sellars wants to press in EPM and still more emphatically in his later writings is this: what is the nature of the particular rectangular portion of redness that Sue can vividly visually describe for us, and which seems to but does not belong to a brick in the physical space where the table is? As Sellars puts it in his 1981 Carus Lectures in relation to such cases as Sue's, "what is the status of the redness which one sees when it is not the very redness of a physical object? Phenomenologically speaking, the *normal* status of expanses and volumes of color is to be constituents of physical objects" (FMPP I.78). To use Price's term, in Sue's case we seem to be confronted with a 'wild' expanse of redness that is not a part of any physical object, and which Sellars wants to *account for* without returning to sense-data and the myth of the given.

Sellars is well aware that many philosophers will respond to this question by arguing that in cases such as (b) and (c) there is in no sense an *actual case of redness* that needs to be accounted for. Did we not reject the 'sense-datum inference,' such philosophers will reasonably ask – the dubious inference from the fact that something vividly *looks* or appears red to Sue to the alleged conclusion that Sue must be experiencing *something* (call it a 'sense-datum') that *is* red? Why not argue to the contrary that in such cases Sue has simply been caused by certain specifiable physical processes to *believe*, or *think*, or *represent* that there is a red brick on the table, when in fact there is no actual redness in the situation at all? After all, Sue is merely *hallucinating* rather than successfully perceiving a red brick.

However, as we briefly saw earlier in relation to the *common non-conceptual content* that is shared by all three of the ostensible seeings (a), (b), and (c), Sellars takes it to be a "basic phenomenological fact" that, once various irrelevant and non-intrinsic differences are set aside, in cases such as Sue's vividly hallucinating a red brick on the table she "has an experience which is intrinsically like that of seeing the object *to be* red" (FMPP I.69). We also saw Sellars contend that the most accurate phenomenological description of such non-conceptual sensory contents will of necessity be a highly indeterminate description, but even in the case of Sue's hallucination it will be the description of an *actually experienced* content rather than a merely 'believed in' or conceptually represented content:

> If circumstances are not normal, we do not have another category than that of the physical to fall back on. All that is available is such transcendentals as *actual*, *something* and *somehow*. The red is something which is *somehow* a portion of red stuff, *somehow* the sort of item which is suited to be a part of the content of a physical object, but which, though *somehow* that sort of item, is not, in point of fact, a portion of physical stuff. (FMPP I.90)

In sum, then, in *all three* cases (a) to (c) of ostensibly seeing, say, that there is a red, triangular physical object over there, Sellars holds that "*something*, in *some* way red and triangular is in *some* way present to the perceiver *other than as thought of*" (SK I.55; FMPP I.91). Or as Sellars puts the point in connection with the myth of the categorial given: "[W]hatever its 'true' *categorial* status, the expanse of red [. . .] has *actual existence* as contrasted with the *intentional inexistence* of that which is believed in *as believed in*" (FMPP I.88).

This '*something*' is what Sellars, along with his mythic historical figure genius Jones, will begin by calling a *sense impression*. Let us close this chapter with a few words on how genius Jones conceives of these inner sense impressions, recognizing that we shall have to pursue this topic in more detail at a later stage. Anyone who is familiar with recent discussions of the 'hard problems' pertaining to consciousness and 'qualia' knows that this is a deep and difficult issue in the philosophy of mind.[45] I will close this chapter with a brief exposition of genius Jones's 'analogical' theory of sense impressions, setting the stage for further discussions of Sellars' views on sensory consciousness in the final section of chapter 6.

So enter genius Jones, Act Two, as described in the concluding part XVI of EPM (cf. *SM* VI and SK II). Thanks to Act One of the Jonesean myth, as we saw in chapter 4, our mythical neo-Rylean ancestors have already been equipped with the concept of thoughts as inner conceptual episodes. We also saw how the neo-Ryleans acquired on this intersubjective basis the ability to reliably report the contents of their own thoughts *directly*, i.e., non-inferentially, without having to rely on any inferences from behavioral evidence or criteria. These inner thought-episodes, on Jones's proto-theory, were quasi-theoretical explanatory posits understood on the *analogy* or *model* of outer linguistic episodes: that is, the theoretical model used to understand the nature of thoughts as mental events was the idea of a kind of 'inner language' or 'Mentalese.'

Jones now incorporates all of the above results in his proto-theory of the nature of sense perceptions as inner episodes. These perceptions will include such propositional perceptual 'takings' as the thought that 'This red brick on the table is heavy.' In his final creative step before disappearing into the mists of history, genius Jones now proposes a further bit of proto-theorizing to handle such problematic cases as the one represented by Sue's hallucination, and more generally to explain the systematic non-conceptual and propositional features of our perceptual responses to objects. Jones introduces the good idea that would later be badly mishandled by the sense-datum theorists and other defenders of the given: namely, the idea that Sue is being caused by the stimulation of her visual cortex to have a sensation or sense impression of a red rectangle. This is the non-conceptual sensory component of her ostensible seeing that there is a red brick facing her on the table. This sensation, Jones proposes, is the common factor in experiences (a), (b), and (c) in the rich phenomenal sense that can account for the shared intrinsic character of those experiences. The key is to see how Jones conceives these sensations or sense impressions differently from how the sense-datum theorists conceived their sense-data.

Jones's explanatory postulation gives us what Sellars in *Science and Metaphysics* calls the *sense impression inference* (*SM* 17). This differs in important ways from the sense-datum inference, which was roughly: 'if something appears red and rectangular to Sue, then there is a red rectangular something – call it a sense-datum – which Sue is sensing.' By contrast, Jones's posit, in first approximation, is this: if something appears red and rectangular to Sue, then Sue is having an 'of-a-red-rectangle' kind of sensation, where the latter is not *literally* red and rectangular in the way the side of a brick is conceived to be red and rectangular ("a sense impression of a red rectangle is neither red nor rectangular," *SM* 17n). Rather, Sue's state of sensing, Jones proposes, has intrinsic features that are "somehow" *analogous* to the physical rectangular redness of the sort possessed by red bricks (as conceived within the manifest image). Jones's theoretical *model* for his postulation of sense impressions – as overt linguistic utterances were Jones's model for inner conceptual thinkings, and as billiard balls might be a physicist's 'manifest' model for unobservable atoms-in-motion – is a tiny "inner replica" (EPM XVI.61(1)) of the ostensibly and perspectivally seen physical object itself (in this case, the rectangular facing side of a red brick).

The theory thus involves a 'trans-categorial' analogy: while the inner replicas in the model are conceptually categorized as tiny *particulars* (in this case, a tiny red rectangle), the sensing or sense impression thereby modelled is not itself categorized by Jones as a particular but rather as a *state* of that larger, public particular who is Sue herself, the perceiver. With respect to the analogy itself: "The *essential* feature of the analogy is that visual impressions stand to one another in a system of ways of resembling and differing which is structurally similar to the ways in which the colors and shapes of visible objects resemble and differ" (EPM XVI.61(3)). If Sue is hallucinating that there is a red brick next to a yellow banana, for instance, Jones proposes that Sue is in a complex sensory state that is ("somehow") characterized by analogous structural-geometric relationships and differing intrinsic qualities answering to those specific spatial relationships and those different colors. Jones's model for understanding this complex state of sensing will be an 'inner replica' consisting of a tiny red rectangle adjacent to a tiny yellow wafer-sliver. That Sue is in this specific, complex sensory state explains why – despite the absence of any physical bricks or bananas in her environment in this case – she vividly *seems* to see precisely what she does: the red-rectangular and yellow-oblong facing aspects of a brick next to a banana.

Jones is unable to go into any further detail as to how this theoretically posited *isomorphism* between the characters and relations of perceptible physical objects and the analogous characters and relations of our corresponding sense impressions is actually 'realized' in the perceiver. We shall be in a better position to explore Sellars' views on the ontology of sensory consciousness after having discussed issues pertaining to conceptual change, picturing-isomorphism, and ontology in the next chapter. A few more comments on Jones's analogical proto-theory are necessary at this stage, however.

Note that unlike Price with regard to his sense-data, Jones is *not* proposing that Sue has any 'immediate' or 'indubitable' knowledge of the nature of her own sense-impressions. Sue ostensibly sees the red and rectangular facing surface of a brick on the table, and that is all. She does not perceive or apprehend her own sensation of a red brick. The proposal, rather, is that it is only *by having* (not *seeing*) a sensation of a red rectangle – or put adverbially, by her sensing in the 'of-a-red-rectangle' manner or sensing 'red-rectangle-ly' – that she is able either to see or seem to see a red brick (cf. Sellars' ATS (1975), 'The Adverbial Theory of the Objects of Sensation'). By 'going adverbial' in this way, genius Jones eschews the 'act/object' model of sensory cognition that dominates in Price and Russell, and which leads them to think of sense-data as the (problematic) apprehended *objects* of mental *acts* of sensing. The sense impressions of Jones and Sellars are not themselves objects of perceptual cognition; rather, they are the causally mediating non-conceptual contents which explain why our resulting perceptual cognitions have some of the intrinsic and structural features that they do.

In this way the two mishandled good ideas concerning non-conceptual sensing and propositional perceiving are finally brought together in a coherent shape that is untainted by the myth of the cat-egorial or the epistemic given. Or so Sellars argues. Here again we are at the beginning of a longer story, and in this case it will turn out to be one of the most controversial and speculative aspects of Sellars' phi-losophy. To adequately address Sellars' views on sensory conscious-ness, however, we shall need to pass beyond the ontological confines of the manifest image. For all his proto-scientific, postulational genius, the conceptual reach of Sellars' neo-Rylean genius Jones has remained firmly limited to the ontology of *manifest image* particulars and their states (this fact about Sellars' myth of Jones is not always clearly rec-ognized). It is not yet clear what we should make of Jones's postulation of sense impressions. They are supposed to be (somehow) 'analogously' red and rectangular without being *physically* or *literally* red and rectan-gular; and yet they are supposed to provide the common intrinsic perceptible content of our veridical and non-veridical ostensible seeings of red physical objects. And whatever these analogously-red sense impressions turn out to be, how will they fit neatly within the confines of the physicalist ontology of the ideal scientific image of 'man-in-the-world'? Sellars' concern to preserve the phenomenological richness of sensory experience in its qualitative dimensions has left him with some further explaining to do. In the end the key to an ultimately satisfying synoptic vision, as Sellars sees it, will be made available by the explan-atory freedom to challenge the categorial ontology of the manifest image – a freedom that has been opened up only with the complete rejection of the myth of the categorial given.

Compared to those as yet unresolved questions of ultimate ontol-ogy, what Sellars' now calls the "final chapter" of his Jonesean myth (EPM XVI.62) has in effect already been sufficiently accounted for as a result of our discussions in this chapter and at the end of the preceding one. This is due to the fact that, against the background of genius Jones's public, intersubjective proto-theory of sensations, the neo-Ryleans can now also be taught to *reliably introspectively report the presence of their own sensations* whenever they ostensibly perceive the relevant corresponding state of affairs: 'I am having a sensation of a red rectangle,' reports Sue, in what is a highly reliable and 'direct' (in the sense of non-inferential) judgment of introspection or 'inner sense.' The story here is roughly parallel to the one we saw Sellars give in relation to our reliable access to our own thoughts at the end of the previous chapter. The overall epistemological result is that the highly reliable inner awareness of our own so-called 'immediate experiences,' which has perennially impressed foundationalist epistemologists, has been successfully explained without any reliance on the myth of the given, and while also preserving intact the conceptual and epistemic priority of our judgments concerning a shared world of public physical objects and persons.

6

Truth, Picturing, and Ultimate Ontology

In chapter 2 we examined Sellars' contention that the scientific image has earned a certain explanatory and hence ontological primacy over the manifest image of the human-being-in-the-world. In the meantime we have explored his views on the nature of meaning, abstract entities, inner conceptual thinking, and perceptual knowledge. Throughout, the emphasis has been on Sellars' various attempts to show how all of these aspects of human cognition and experience are in principle consistent with the projected ideal scientific image of our nature as complex physical systems. The previous chapter, however, left us with a conceptually transformed version of a fundamental ontological problem that has been with us since chapter 1. How are we to integrate our sensory consciousness of occurrent color and other 'ultimately homogeneous' sensible qualities into the scientific image of a world of swarming, colorless micro-particles? That stubborn problem has not yet been resolved.

It is time for us to take up once again fundamental philosophical questions concerning 'what there really is' in the world. Let us assume for the purposes of this synoptic chapter that Sellars has successfully argued for the positions examined in earlier chapters. I propose now to begin anew with Sellars' multifaceted views on the nature of *truth* as a framework whereby our examination of the global clash between the manifest and scientific images may be brought toward a final conclusion. This will require using a rather broad brush in relation to some intricate technical matters, but with a compensating payoff, I hope, in terms of achieving a clear perspective on the overall landscape.

Truth as semantic assertibility and truth as correspondence

As was the case with his accounts of meaning, thinking, and knowing, truth for Sellars involves both a normative dimension and an underlying naturalistic or causal dimension.

In the normative and most general sense, Sellars contends that the truth of all kinds of propositions, whether they are empirical, mathematical, or moral claims, consists in their being what he calls *correctly semantically assertible*:

> [F]or a proposition to be true is for it to be assertible, where this means not *capable* of being asserted (which it must be to be a proposition at all) but *correctly* assertible; assertible, that is, in accordance with the relevant semantical rules, and on the basis of such additional, though unspecified, information as these rules may require. [. . .] 'True', then, means *semantically* assertible ('S-assertible') and the varieties of truth correspond to the relevant varieties of semantical rule. (*SM* V.26)

We shall return to the general normative conception of truth as assertibility in a moment.

However, Sellars also argues that there is a further 'correspondence' dimension to truth in the specific case of what he calls *basic matter-of-factual* truths, or 'logically atomic' empirical truths (here we use terms which themselves require explication).[1] Sellars contends that propositions of this kind are true, i.e., correctly semantically assertible, if and only if they *correspond*, in a sense to be explained in the next section, to how matters stand in the world. Whereas truth as correct assertibility is clearly a normative notion, Sellars will defend a strictly non-normative, causal-naturalistic understanding of the sense in which basic matter-of-factual truths correspond to the world. His proposal will turn out to be a carefully qualified descendent of Wittgenstein's 'picture theory' in the *Tractatus*: basic matter-of-factual propositions in some sense form *pictures*, or 'cognitive maps,' or 'representations' of how objects or events in the world are related and characterized (see TC and NS).

First, then, what does Sellars mean by his suggestion above that the meaning of 'true' is "semantically assertible," that is, "*correctly* assertible" in accordance with the relevant semantical rules and such "information as these rules may require"? As we know from earlier chapters, Sellars contends that "essential to any language are three types of pattern-governed linguistic behavior" (*NAO* IV.31). These are the *semantical uniformities* that are brought about by the implicit community-wide espousal of corresponding semantical 'ought-to-be' rules:[2]

- language entry transitions (world → language) [perceptual responses]
- intra-linguistic transitions (language → language) [inferences]
- language exit transitions (language → world) [volitions, intentional actions]

For Smith's judgment that 'this apple is red' to be true, on Sellars' account, is for that judgment to be correctly assertible by Smith in a given context in accordance with the relevant language entry rule, which is itself conceptually embedded within a system of formal and material inference rules. From chapters 3 through 5 we know that in this case the relevant language entry rule would be (roughly): it ought-to-be the case that, other things being equal, perceivers respond to red objects in standard conditions by uttering or being disposed to utter '*x* is red.'[3] Further, we know that for Smith to be a concept user who is capable of genuinely following such a semantical rule he must also have at least a minimally adequate implicit grasp of a certain holistic framework of inferential rules pertaining to color concepts, abnormal conditions of perception, and much else besides. So given that Smith has been initiated into a certain conceptual-linguistic framework, for Smith's judgment that *p* in a given context to be *true* is for *p* to be correctly semantically assertible by Smith in that context in accordance with the relevant semantical rules of that conceptual-linguistic framework.

Sellars illustrates his contention above that the different "varieties of truth correspond to the relevant varieties of semantical rule" by contrasting "the case of logical and mathematical propositions, *where S-assertability means provability*" (*SM* IV.62; also V.55),[4] with the case of matter-of-factual truths in the narrower sense (*SM* V.2; cf. TC 198), on which we shall be focusing for the bulk of this chapter. In the broadest and normative sense, Sellars holds, " 'fact' is properly used as a synonym for 'truth' " or assertibility (*SM* V.2). In this sense there are mathematical facts insofar as various mathematical propositions are successfully derivable within various formal axiom systems. Matter-of-factual truths in the narrower sense, however, are basic, logically atomic, singular empirical truths concerning particular objects or patterns of events in the world as revealed in our perceptual judgments in particular.

'Empirical' or 'matter-of-factual' in the latter sense cannot be defined independently of an overall philosophical account of what it takes for any judgment or theory to be a proper candidate for revealing an objective truth about the mind-independent world. We know from chapters 2 and 5, however, that our perceptual responses to the world in the context of the ongoing task of achieving overall explanatory coherence are the keys to the relevant sense of empirical truth involved in Sellars' account. Crucially, as we shall see later on, our perceptual judgments will include those 'theory-contaminated' singular observations within the ideal scientific image that were crucial to his defense of scientific realism in chapter 2 (recall '*O_i,' for example 'there goes an electron'). The overall idea, then, is that at any given stage and context of empirical inquiry our conceptual framework ultimately bottoms out in atomic matter-of-factual propositions that ascribe properties and relations to basic objects and events in the world. These are the propositions which, if true, *correspond to* or *picture* how matters stand with regard to those objects and events.

Central to nearly all work on truth by philosophers and logicians since the mid-twentieth century has been the Polish logician Alfred Tarski's successful formal, recursive definition of 'true sentence of language L' for specified formal languages L (e.g., Tarski 1944).[5] Tarski's famous 'Criterion T' or 'Convention T' requires that any adequate definition of truth for a language entail all the 'T-sentences' or T-biconditionals of that language, which are standardly illustrated using the following natural language example:

(T)   'Snow is white' is a true sentence (of English) if and only if snow is white.[6]

Philosophers remain divided, however, over the implications of Tarski's 'semantic' definition of truth for our understanding of the concept of truth as it occurs in ordinary natural languages, as well as with regard to its implications for the perennial philosophical disputes concerning the nature of truth and its relationship to meaning.

Put in a nutshell, Sellars' view is that Tarski's successful formal definition of truth should not be interpreted as showing that truth itself consists in a *correspondence relation* between language and the world. Rather, Sellars argues that the fact that Tarski's equivalences or biconditionals capture certain formal properties of truth can be seen to *follow from* the real meaning of truth as correct semantic assertibility, which is not itself a language–world relation (*SM* IV.24–6). On Sellars' account of meaning and abstract entities, the left-to-right conditional in Tarski's (T) becomes

if •snow is white•s are true, then snow is white

and Sellars contends that this is "a consequence" of the definition of 'true' as 'semantically assertible.'[7] On his view of truth as assertibility "the assertion of the right-hand side of the implication statement is a *performance of the kind authorized by the truth statement on the left*" (*SM* IV.27). The move here from the truth statement " 'snow is white' is true" to the authorized assertion of 'snow is white' is what Sellars calls the *truth move*. The role and hence the meaning of truth statements is to authorize the performance of asserting the claim that is said to be true, and so in effect to say: Go ahead, remove the quotation marks and assert the sentence (cf. *SM* IV.29).[8]

Much more could be said about Sellars' conception of truth as semantic assertibility, but our primary concerns in this chapter are ontological, and for Sellars it turns out that "the *primary* concept of factual truth" is "truth as correct picture," and that this "makes intelligible all the other modes of factual truth" (*SM* V.9). Let us turn, then, to Sellars' attempt to offer an affirmative answer to the question: "Is there a sense of 'correspond' other than that explicated by [Tarskian] semantic theory, in which empirical truths correspond to objects or events in the world?" (TC 207). The exploration of this topic will gradually lead us deeper into the topics of truth, reference, and ontology across changing conceptual frameworks. It will also bring out further details concerning the subtle relationships between the natural and the normative which, as I have been contending, form the cartilage structure of Sellars' philosophy as a whole.

Picturing, linguistic representation, and reference

One of the most intriguing aspects of Sellars' philosophy is his contention that once proper distinctions have been made between different semantic levels, close relatives both of Wittgenstein's so-called 'picture theory of meaning' in the *Tractatus Logico-Philosophicus* (1922) and of his later 'language game' conception of 'meaning as use' in his *Philosophical Investigations* (1953) are essential to a correct understanding of the nature of meaning and truth. While Wittgenstein famously rejected his earlier picture theory, Sellars argues for its essential truth as part of a naturalistic theory of linguistic and cognitive representation, rather than as a theory of meaning. For our purposes we shall not worry about the correct interpretation of Wittgenstein's own views. Rather, let us plunge straight into the attempt to clarify Sellars' conception of cognitive-linguistic picturing or representation as a certain kind of naturalistic relation of correspondence between language or mind and the world.[9]

It will be instructive to work up gradually to the case of linguistic representation proper by first considering Sellars' account of picturing in relation to three other sorts of examples he mentions or discusses: (1) the sense in which the grooves on a phonograph record may be regarded as a 'picture' of the music it produces when played (BBK §40); (2) the insights and confusions in a classical 'Humean' empiricist conception of our 'ideas' as mirroring or picturing independent reality (TC

217–19); and (3) a thought experiment concerning future 'anthropoid robots' or androids who are engineered to acquire increasingly accurate internal representations or cognitive mappings of their environments (BBK §§31–59; SM V.70).[10]

During his discussion of picturing in the *Tractatus*, Wittgenstein at one point makes the following claims:

> 4.012 It is obvious that we perceive a proposition of the form *aRb* as a picture. Here the sign is obviously a likeness of the signified. [. . .]
>
> 4.014 The gramophone record, the musical thought, the score, the waves of sound, all stand to one another in that pictorial internal relation, which holds between language and the world.
>
> To all of them the logical structure is common. [. . .]
>
> 4.0141 In the fact that there is a general rule by which . . . one could reconstruct the symphony from the line on a gramophone record [. . .] lies the internal similarity between these things which at first sight seem to be entirely different. And the rule is the law of projection which projects the symphony [. . .] into the language of the gramophone record. (Wittgenstein 1922)

(We shall come to '*aRb*' as a propositional picture later on.) Sellars similarly remarks – no doubt echoing Wittgenstein's example, but adding his own naturalistic twist – on "the way in which the wavy groove of a phonograph record pictures the music which it can reproduce. This picturing cannot be abstracted from the procedures involved in making and playing the record" (BBK §40).

The plastic bumps on the groove of a record, of course, do not in any obvious or everyday sense resemble or form a picture of the music that is produced when it is played. This is a healthy reminder that when we come to cognitive picturing proper we should not expect to find any obvious qualitative or structural similarities between representations and their objects. From an engineering standpoint, however, we know that there is a complex causal and structural 'method of projection' that determines, crudely put, which tiny plastic bumps will correspond to which sounds in the music when the record is played. The relationships among the different qualities and durations of sounds in the music are causally correlated, thanks to the specific causal relationships that have been engineered into the system, with a specific relational structure of differently shaped and textured plastic bumps on the record. There is thus a complex structural similarity or *second-order isomorphism* (or perhaps a 'homomorphism')[11] between the two physical systems. Or as Sellars puts the second-order aspect, picturing is "a relation between two relational structures" (SM V.56).

The phonograph example bears only a "distant analogy" (BBK §40) to the picturing that Sellars argues is involved in the cognition of objects. Consider next Sellars' discussion in 'Truth and "Correspondence"' (1962) of "the Hume who believes that our 'perceptions' are 'likenesses' of states of affairs in a public spatiotemporal world" and who thereby, according to Sellars, "put his finger on an essential truth" (TC 217, 218). This naturalistic, representational realist Hume, as Sellars paints him, was mistaken in thinking of the correspondence between our 'ideas' and their objects as a *first-order* similarity in which ideas are image-like "duplicates" of their objects. Sellars views that as a badly mistaken reductive empiricist account of the sense in which, and of the manner in which, our cognitions do indeed succeed in forming a kind of *mirror of nature* (*pace* Rorty). Sellars does, however, want to "preserve the essence of Hume's contention" insofar as it is the general view that "the 'likeness' between elementary thoughts and the objects they picture is definable in matter-of-factual terms as a likeness or correspondence or isomorphism between two systems of objects, each of which belongs in the natural order" (TC 219).

Hume's specific contention, for example, was that human nature is such that uniform sequences of experienced events of the 'thunder followed by lightning' sort will generate corresponding regular sequences in our 'ideas,' themselves also considered as natural occurrences or (internal) 'objects.'[12] The result is that the occurrence of a 'lightning-impression' or representation in a perceiver will (*ceteris paribus*) be followed by the occurrence of a vivacious 'thunder-idea' or representation in that perceiver. As Hume himself summed it up in using a Leibnizian turn of phrase:

> Here, then, is a kind of pre-established harmony between the course of nature and the succession of our ideas; and though the powers and forces, by which the former is governed, be wholly unknown to us; yet our thoughts and conceptions have still, we find, gone on in the same train with the other works of nature. Custom is that principle, by which this correspondence has been effected; so necessary to the subsistence of our species, and the regulation of our conduct, in every circumstance and occurrence of human life. (Hume 1748: section 5, para. 21)

What is right about Hume's contention, put in Sellars' terms, is that our cognitive interactions with nature do indeed generate over time a natural, matter-of-factual isomorphism of a certain kind between the properties and patterns of our mental representations and the properties and patterns of corresponding events in the world. However, Hume was mistaken not only about the nature of this isomorphism, as noted above, but also about the way in which this mind/world 'harmony' is generated and sustained in the crucial case of concept-using beings such as ourselves, whose judgments have *logical* form. A few general remarks on this point will perhaps be helpful at this stage.

As far as meaning, intentionality, and all the other broadly cognitive and epistemic dimensions of human experience are concerned, we have seen that Sellars defends a linguistically sophisticated version of Kant's 'Copernican revolution' (see Kant 1787, 'Preface to the Second Edition'). It is only because we *bring to* experience a holistic framework of formal and material conceptual rules ('top down,' as it were) that it is possible for us to have in the first place the sorts of basic cognitive experiences of sequences of events that Hume's prematurely reductive (or 'bottom-up') empiricist account wants to take for granted. On Sellars' Peircean-Kantian view, we 'attack' nature with rule-governed conceptual systems of reason's own making. We then learn by experience or by testing that either the world as we have conceptually responded to it in our perceptual judgments 'conforms to' our conceptual representations as they stand (the Kantian Copernican insight), or we must modify the latter in our ongoing quest for explanatory coherence through *critically controlled conceptual change* (the Peircean pragmatist insight). The concomitant, underlying *result* of this rational evolution of gradually improving conceptual frameworks, on Sellars' view, is indeed the causal production of increasingly adequate cognitive mappings, representations, or pictures (and as a regulative ideal, an entire *world story*) of the real object-uniformities that characterize the world.[13]

The non-normative level of picturing will thus be the proper place to locate the sort of representational 'mirroring of nature' that Sellars thinks Hume was insightfully but prematurely attempting to analyze in purely naturalistic terms from the outset. Sellars' corrected Kantian empiricism – his 'naturalism with a normative turn,' as I have been characterizing it – is at its heart the attempt to articulate the subtle transcendental or presuppositional relationships that obtain between the normative, conceptual dimensions and the non-normative, naturalistic dimensions of human experience.

Let us turn next to Sellars' remarkable discussion of picturing in the case of possible "anthropoid robots of the future" in 'Being and Being Known' (BBK §36), presented to the American Catholic Philosophical Association in 1960. Sellars characteristically submerged his prescient thought experiment within a highly complex analysis of the insights and limitations of the Thomistic 'immaterial form' account of the mind–object cognitive isomorphism.[14] Sellars' ultimate target in that article, however, is the question: "what is the intellect as belonging to the real order?"; and his contention is that the intellect "as belonging to the real order [. . .] is the central nervous system, and that recent cybernetic theory throws light on the way in which cerebral patterns and dispositions picture the world" (BBK §59). Or as Sellars elsewhere later remarked: "[T]o see human behavior as a *likeness* of the computer simulation (*contrived* likeness) of human behavior is to be in a position to grasp the complex relations between reasons and causes, uniformities and rules" (*NAO* V.51).

In the context of this particular thought experiment Sellars explains his account of the relationship between the normative dimension of *meaning* and the naturalistic dimension of *representation* in terms of how we might engage in two different types of "discourse about" the possible androids he describes: namely, discourse from the normative standpoint of "the framework of intentionality" as opposed to discourse from the causal-naturalistic "standpoint of the electronic engineer" (BBK §40).[15] Without entering into the full details of Sellars' description of the android, the initial stages convey the general idea:

> Suppose such an anthropoid robot to be 'wired' in such a way that it emits high frequency radiation which is reflected back in ways which project the structure of its environment (and its 'body'). Suppose it responds to different patterns of returning radiation by printing such 'sentences' as 'Triangular object at place p, time t' on a tape which it is able to play over and over and to scan. (BBK §37)

These events of 'sentence-printing' in response to objects, and of play-over and scanning, are the android's analogues of our own perceptions (language entries), memories, and introspections.[16] Sellars goes on to fill out the story in terms of the robot's hardwired capacities for making 'inferences,' including inductive 'learning' based on its past 'experiences' in the context of its 'goal-seeking' behaviors. As a result of coming to exhibit all of these analogues of our own language 'entry/ inference/exit' uniformities, the robot over time gradually "achieves an ever more adequate adjustment to its environment" (BBK §39).

Adopting the familiar intentional standpoint toward the robot, Sellars explains, we describe "in human terms" its ongoing adjustment to its environment: "[W]e would say that it *finds out* more and more about the world, that it *knows* more and more *facts* about what took place and where it took place," and so on (BBK §39). On the other hand,

> we can also consider the states of the robot in mechanical and electronic terms; and the point I wish to make is that in these terms it makes perfectly good sense to say that as the robot moves around the world the record on the tape contains an ever more complete and perfect map of its environment. In other words, the robot comes to contain an increasingly adequate and detailed *picture* of its environment in a sense of

'picture' which is to be explicated in terms of the logic of relations. This
picturing cannot be abstracted from the mechanical and electronic processes in which the tape is caught up. (BBK §40)

The representational states of the robot might well be realized in a
'language' other than English that Sellars calls *robotese*. For example,
the actual pattern on the robot's tape which, from the intentional standpoint, we would say *means* 'lightning at place p and time t' might take
the form: ':: , 9, 15.' From an ideal engineering standpoint we could
carefully study the complex causal uniformities that obtain with respect
to the robot's printings of ' :: 's in response to lightning in its environment, in the patterns of its internal processing of ' :: 's in relation to its
other printings, and in relation to the role of ' :: 's in generating the
robot's active maneuvers in its environment. Recognizing in the
android's input–processing–output mechanisms a highly complex
method of projection in relation to events in its environment and in relation to its own internal states, the engineer could explain to us – with
one eye on each 'standpoint,' as it were – that the tiny ' :: 's caught up
in various patterns in robotese *correspond to* or *represent* lightning events
as caught up in various natural sequences in the robot's environment.
"In the framework of physical theory we can say that a subset of the
patterns on the tape constitute a picture of the robot's environment.
Here is an isomorphism between physical realities" (BBK §57).

From the intentional standpoint of our own conceptual framework,
of course, we simply say that " ' :: ' in Robotese means *lightning*," that
is, ' :: 's are •lightning•s. In so doing we *presuppose* that the sorts of
causal uniformities and naturalistic isomorphisms outlined above from
the 'engineering standpoint' have been or are in process of being established or approximated.

This is the sense in which Sellars held that the " 'external' " (*SM*
V.70) or engineering perspective that is provided by considering the
representational states of cybernetic systems, when considered alongside the (for us) ineliminable perspective of our own intentional standpoint, could help us "to grasp the complex relations between reasons
and causes, uniformities and rules" (*NAO* V.51 above) – those relations
which we have seen to be crucial to Sellars' own naturalistic synoptic
vision of 'man-in-the-world.' In short, that the symbols on the anthropoid robot's tape have the meaning that they do from the standpoint
of intentionality depends upon the fact that the appropriate causal
relations and representational isomorphisms have come to obtain in
the real order as conceived from the naturalistic 'engineering' standpoint: "In this sense we can say that isomorphism *in the real order*
between the robot's electronic system and its environment is a presupposition of isomorphism *in the order of signification* [or meaning] between
robotese and the language we speak" (BBK §53). This is a striking

instance of that complex *norm/nature* presuppositional structure which we have found to be a persistent theme throughout Sellars' philosophy.

We are now better prepared to consider picturing, not in relation to phonograph records, Humean perceptions, or possible androids, but as it occurs in the actual patterns of our own conceptual representations proper. Sellars investigates the latter, as we know, by considering the nature of *linguistic* representation.

To understand Sellars' conception of the picturing dimension of actual and possible natural languages, we must go back to Wittgenstein's statement in the *Tractatus* "that we perceive a proposition of the form *aRb* as a picture. Here the sign is obviously a likeness of the signified" (Wittgenstein 1922: 4.012). Sellars' theory of linguistic picturing is connected with his nominalist account of the nature of *predication*, and this constitutes one of the most difficult aspects of his philosophy. Here I will attempt to bring out the bare essentials as briefly as possible.

The basic idea is that we are now to consider human languages themselves from the naturalistic 'engineering' standpoint, but as always with one eye on the conceptually irreducible normative standpoint of intentionality. Sellars explains that although we know that "linguistic objects are subject to rules and principles – are fraught with 'ought' – we abstract from this knowledge in considering them as objects in the natural order," i.e., as what he calls *natural-linguistic objects* (TC 212). Consider the statement that 'Fido is larger than Fifi,' or its formal equivalent '*aRb*' in formal logic ('PMese'). Sellars argues that

> what Wittgenstein established was that whether one does it perspicuously or not, one can only say of two objects that they stand in a certain relation by placing the corresponding referring expressions in a counterpart relation. Thus, whether we say
>
>   *a* is larger than *b*
> or
> ^a_b
>
> in either case what we have done is form an expression which, from the standpoint of its semantical functioning, is a dyadic configuration of the names '*a*' and '*b*'. (*SM* IV.45)

Or more generally, "one says *how* objects are by inscribing or uttering the corresponding referring expressions in a certain manner" (*SM* IV.48). Statements such as '^a_b' occur in the fictitious but coherently conceivable language that Sellars called 'Jumblese.' Wittgenstein's *Tractarian* insight was that one can say that *a* bears the relation R to *b* only by placing the names *'a'* and *'b'* in some counterpart relation (R*) – for example, the relation *being inscribed top-left-and-bottom-right of one another* (in Jumblese), or *being inscribed to the left and right of an 'R'* (in PMese).

Picturing or linguistic representation can then be seen to have two non-normative semantic dimensions which are presuppositions or implications of the two normative semantic dimensions of matter-of-factual *reference* and *characterization*:

> Clearly a theory of linguistic representation would view the connection between either [*'a* is larger than *b'*] or [$^a{}_b$'] and extra-linguistic reality as involving two dimensions: (a) a dimension in which each name is a linguistic counterpart of an object, and can be said to refer to that object; and (b) a dimension in which names, by virtue of having a certain character, constitute statements [. . .] and can be said to characterize the object referred to. (*NAO* III.44, substituting Sellars' numbered examples in brackets)

The various distinctions between the normative (meaning) and non-normative (picturing) dimensions of semantic reference and characterization in Sellars' account are often hard to keep track of, precisely because on his view *they necessarily track one another* (*ceteris paribus*). Once again this is a consequence of the presuppositional relationship that holds between *semantical rules* and *semantical uniformities*, which is epitomized in what I have called Sellars' *'norm/nature* meta-principle': "Espousal of principles is reflected in uniformities of performance" (TC 216).

Consider the concept of *reference*. In accordance with Sellars' conceptual role theory of meaning, the statement " 'Sokrates' (in German) refers to Socrates" has the sense of " 'Sokrates's (in German) are •Socrates•s," where what it is to be a •Socrates• is determined by the normative semantical rules governing the *uses* of that proper name in our language, English. Roughly put, Sellars proposes that the sentence " *'a's* (in L) refer to *a*" unpacks into the idea that the name *'a'* has some rule-governed *sense* that is 'materially equivalent' to the sense or meaning •*a*• with which we are familiar in the base language (see *SM* III.63–4 and V.62, as well as the appendix to *NAO*, correspondence with Loux). For example, unless we are badly mistaken in our current broadly epistemic presuppositions (which, as Kripke emphasized in *Naming and Necessity* [1980], is always a possibility that any theory of reference must accommodate), other things being equal it ought-to-be that one uses a •Socrates• in contexts where it would also be appropriate to use •the teacher of Plato•, that one does not substitute a •Socrates• in the context •*x* never lived in Greece•, and so on.[17]

At the same time, however, Sellars holds that the "fundamental job of first-level matter-of-factual statements is to picture, and hence the fundamental job of referring expressions is to be correlated *as simple linguistic objects* by matter-of-factual relations with single non-linguistic objects": that is, "their sense is, at bottom, their job, and their job is to be linguistic representatives of objects" (*SM* V.26, 27). What is it, then, for names to be 'correlated' in this representational or pictorial way with the objects to which they refer – for example, •Socrates•s with the flesh and blood historical Socrates?

As in the phonograph analogy and the robot case, the picturing relation in the case of linguistic representation will also be a second-order isomorphism or a relation between two relational structures or patterns of objects. Roughly put, as a result of the semantical 'ought-to-be' rules governing the reference of 'Socrates' in English, tokenings of •Socrates•s have come to stand in systematic natural relations to tokenings of other natural-linguistic objects (such as being concatenated to the right with •is mortal•s, etc.);[18] and the patterns exhibited by the properties and relations of these natural-linguistic objects are isomorphic to corresponding patterns exhibited by the properties and relations characterizing the flesh and blood Socrates.

In the case of one-place or monadic predications such as 'Socrates is mortal' (of the form 'Fa' as opposed to 'aRb'), what we have on Sellars' *nominalist* account of predication is a correspondence between two qualified-objects, or two objects of a certain character.[19] The natural-linguistic object or inscription 'Socrates' has in this case been given a certain character: namely, *being joined to the right by an inscription of 'is mortal.'* However, in the non-subject–predicate language Jumblese, Sellars suggests that the same statement could be made *without any predicate* by giving the name a certain monadic character, for example *being boldfaced*: •**Socrates**•s in Jumblese might thus play the same systematic role as 'Socrates is mortal's in English.

This is similar to how '^a_b' in Jumblese says that object a is larger than object b without the occurrence of any relational predicate ('aRb' does the same job with a predicate). Predicates, on Sellars' view, are *in principle dispensable* (see *NAO* ch. III, 'The Importance of Being Dispensable'). Instead of having the character of being concatenated to the right with an •is mortal•, the semantic rules of Jumblese entail that it is in virtue of having the character of being boldfaced that a name refers to (and pictures) corresponding *mortal objects*. It is in this way that •**Socrates**•s or •Socrates is mortal•s as natural-linguistic objects picture "and can be said to refer to" the historical object Socrates and to characterize him as being mortal (see *NAO* III.44 above). Sellars' fictional language Jumblese is thus crucial for helping us see that in the case of our own subject–predicate natural languages, linguistic representation is a relation between *objects* or configurations of objects in a way that requires no reifying ontology of facts (in contrast to Wittgenstein's *Tractatus*) and no platonic universals. Matter-of-factual *statements*, on Sellars' analysis, are at the end of the day seen to be *designators* of objects and configurations of objects.

As Sellars makes clear in one of his last published articles, 'Towards a Theory of Predication' (TTP, 1981), the overall upshot of this account of both the normative and the causal-naturalistic dimensions of reference is that

> even though
>   'Sokrates' (in German) means *Socrates*
> is not a relational statement, it nevertheless implies the truth of a complicated relational statement pertaining to the German expression 'Sokrates' (in a certain usage) and a certain snubnosed Greek philosopher. It is a statement of a kind which would be expressed by a category in a well organized theory of linguistic representation – if such there were. This category would provide the answer to the question: by virtue of what does a singular term (e.g. 'the moon') pick out a certain object and serve as its linguistic representative? This question is as difficult a question as there is – which is not to say that we don't have vague and open-textured ways of coping with it. (TTP 318–19)

Ideally we would be able to investigate questions concerning the naturalistic picturing relation that underwrites our matter-of-factual references to objects in ways that are similar to how the engineers discussed earlier addressed the question: 'In virtue of what methods of projection and what natural-causal relations do "::"s on the robot's tape represent lightning?'

The Sellarsian theory of reference that has emerged is one according to which, at the level of basic matters-of-fact, the normative rule-governed reference of names and other singular terms both presupposes and contributes to bringing about (via the implicit "Espousal of principles . . .") an incredibly complex causal-historical picturing or representational isomorphism. This second-order isomorphism obtains between the patterns, uniformities, and characters of tokenings of designators considered as natural-linguistic objects and the corresponding patterns, uniformities, and characters of the objects to which those designators are normatively classified as referring. In TTP Sellars describes these causal-historical uniformities as the standing of singular terms in "appropriate psycho-sociological-historical (PSH) relations" to objects (TTP 318).[20] According to his overall account of representation and reference as clarified in that article, then, we have the following three interdependent conditions (this is a paraphrase of TTP 318–19, not a quotation):

(1)   'Sokrates' (in German) means or refers to Socrates (i.e., is a •Socrates•)

      if and only if

(2)   'Sokrates' (in German) is the linguistic representative of (i.e., pictures) the historical, flesh and blood Socrates

      if and only if

(3)   'Sokrates's stand in appropriate psycho-sociological-historical (PSH) [causal-uniformity] relations to the historical Socrates.

Finally, this account of the underlying causal-representational dimension in virtue of which a natural-linguistic object such as a sentence or a claim (and thanks to genius Jones, an inner thought) succeeds in referring to and characterizing corresponding objects in the world enables us to tie all of this back to Sellars' views on truth as semantic assertibility in general, and matter-of-factual truth as correspondence in particular. As Sellars put it in a letter to Gilbert Harman in 1970, roughly speaking (at the basic matter-of-factual level),

'Fa' is true (semantically assertible) if and only if 'Fa's picture a.

Sellars adds that "the right-hand side of this equivalence formulates the truth condition for 'Fa' [where this] condition directly involves the relation of picturing which, unlike concepts belonging to the family explored by classical [Tarskian] semantics, [. . .] is definable in naturalistic terms, thus word–word and word–world uniformities."[21] With regard to basic empirical matters-of-fact, then, truth and reference in the normative, rule-governed dimension stand in a complex relation of interdependence and presupposition with linguistic (or mental) representation as a non-normative, naturalistic correspondence or picturing-isomorphism between language (or mind) and the world.

The latter is the mishandled insight that has animated both classical correspondence theories of truth and causal theories of reference, both of which on Sellars' view contain insights if they are tightly constrained, as they typically are not, by an account of the normative-pragmatic epistemology of ongoing inquiry. And this is how rules and uniformities, or "the Janus-faced character of languagings as belonging to both the causal order and the order of reasons" (*NAO* V.64), are ultimately brought together in Sellars' account of the relationship between mind and world, and in his naturalism with a normative turn more generally.

It would be a mistake to dismiss Sellars' theory of picturing as a relic from a bygone *Tractarian* era. There is no doubt that Sellars thought it was fundamental to his entire outlook. As he put it in 'Philosophy and the Scientific Image of Man,' "whatever else conceptual thinking makes possible – and without it there is nothing characteristically human – it does so by virtue of containing a way of representing the world" (PSIM 17). My own view is that Sellars' account of picturing and of empirical truth as correspondence represented a searching if sketchy attempt to argue that the normative aspects of meaning, reference, and truth are not reducible to, yet presuppose for their possibility, various specific underlying causal patterns and representational mappings of the kinds discussed in this section. It is the latter mappings which systematically relate cognitive and linguistic systems to the world which they thereby succeed in being *about* – even though *aboutness* itself is not a further mysterious relation to the world. Investigation of these modes of cognitive representation has since become the cooperative business not only of philosophers of mind, epistemologists, and philosophers of language, but of linguists, cognitive psychologists, and neuroscientists as well. Central to Sellars' philosophical quest was the attempt to envision the overall conceptual space in which those sorts of detailed epistemological and scientific investigations might be seen to make sense.

Truth, conceptual change, and the ideal scientific image

We are now in a position to approach the topics of conceptual change and ultimate ontology in terms of the above account of truth as semantic assertibility and of matter-of-factual truth as picturing. Our eventual goal is to revisit the clash of the images and the problem of sensory consciousness in light of Sellars' conception of a fully adequate scientific image of the human-being-in-the-world, where the latter is to be understood in terms of the 'Peircean' regulative idea of (ultimate) truth as what would be represented in an ideal 'long run' of inquiry (on these topics see also Pitt 1981).

In *Science and Metaphysics* Sellars connects the topic of conceptual change with the concept of truth as semantic assertibility by stressing that the "explication of truth as S-assertibility raises the question: assertible by whom?" (*SM* V.48). We know that Sellars' main interest in relation to the question, 'Truth is assertibility by whom?' will concern those comprehensive *changes* in conceptual framework which, as we saw in relation to his version of scientific realism in chapter 2, are involved in "the evolution of conceptual structures" and their companion ontologies over time (*SM* V.51). Let us briefly reacquaint ourselves with some central features of that story.

In the relevant cases of postulational scientific theorizing we categorially *reconceive* the fundamental nature of the empirical objects we encounter in perceptual experience, and only thereby, we saw Sellars argue, do we succeed in generating adequate explanations of those objects' lawful behavior. Presuming the soundness of that argument for our present purposes, we may distinguish between those 'predecessor' theories or conceptual frameworks which are thus revealed to be *approximately true but strictly speaking false* and their 'successor' theoretical frameworks which in some sense – there is more to be said on this – bring us *closer* to the matter-of-factual truth about the nature of things. A stock example is the predecessor/successor relationship between the conceptual framework of Newton's physics and that of Einstein's relativity physics (*SM* V.45–7; CC; cf. *NAO* IV.133–6 and LRB 311, ¶37).

The particular example of explanation by conceptual change that we examined in chapter 2, however, concerned the nature of gases. The kinetic-molecular theory of gases reconceived or redefined the intrinsic nature of gases by identifying certain macro-level properties of gases covered by the Boyle–Charles gas law (pressure, temperature, volume) with specific micro-molecular goings-on that are unobservable at the manifest-perceptible level. As we saw Sellars argue, "it is because a gas *is* [. . .] a cloud of molecules which are behaving in certain theoretically defined ways" that the gas obeys the empirical laws that it does obey, to the extent that it does (SRT 314; LT 121).

For simplicity's sake, let us suppose that the Boyle–Charles gas law is a rigorous formulation of essential features of our *manifest image* or 'MI' concept of a gas. The ontological consequence of Sellars' main argument was that, strictly speaking, there turns out to be nothing in the world that answers to the MI-concept of a gas. That is, strictly speaking there exist no gases as they are conceived within the manifest image; there exist only gases as reconceived within the scientific or theoretical image of the world. (Parallel considerations hold for predecessor scientific theories in relation to successor theories *within* the ongoing scientific image.) Let us use 'SI' as shorthand for Sellars' regulative ideal of a potentially fully adequate scientific image or postulational theoretical account of 'man-in-the-world.' And let us use 'MI-pressure' and 'SI-pressure', for example, to refer to the two *counterpart concepts* of pressure as that phenomenon is reconceived across those two global conceptual frameworks in the ways discussed in detail in chapter 2 and just briefly recounted here.

It is crucial to bear in mind the explanatory burden that we saw was placed on the concept of an SI-gas or any other such explanatory successor concept on Sellars' scientific realism. The key point (let us stick with the global 'MI vs. SI' contrast) was that the relevant SI successor theory must explain entirely in its own SI-terms how it is that there *appeared* to be MI-objects or MI-phenomena obeying empirical laws to the extent that they did. That is, what Sellars' account of theoretical explanation as identification-by-reconceptualization showed was this: it is because MI-gases *are really* (identical to) SI-gases that they *appear* in the approximately lawful way that they do *as conceived within MI*. Sellars contends that if we attend carefully in this way to the role of *counterpart-related concepts* across changing theories or conceptual frameworks, we can see that one can coherently hold both (1) that strictly speaking there are no MI-gases (that is, as the latter are conceived within MI) – they are 'mere appearances'; and (2) that in another sense it would be true to say that there *are* MI-gases: namely, as the latter are explanatorily reconceived in terms of their counterpart concepts within SI and thereby identified with SI-gases (see *SM* V.95–102, 149–50; and see further below).[22]

The notion of counterpart-related concepts and propositions is one of the most important fruits of Sellars' conceptual role account of meaning and abstract entities, and it is central to his views on truth and conceptual change (for further details see *SM* V and CC).[23] Briefly put, Sellars argues that we are able to make reasonable judgments concerning the *functional role similarities and differences* that are involved in the rule-governed uses of terms across theories or conceptual frameworks. We frequently make judgments of this general kind throughout common life, as for example when we judge that the bowler plays in cricket a role that is generically similar to, yet differs in specific rule-governed ways from, the role that the pitcher plays in baseball. Sellars' proposal is that comparisons of relevant functional similarity are also in play when we consider, for instance, the concept of *mass* as it functions within Newton's physics in comparison with how it functions within Einstein's physics; or the concept of *pressure* within the phenomenological gas law (which we are calling 'MI-pressure') in comparison with its role in the kinetic-molecular theory of gases (SI-pressure); or for an example explicitly using abstract singular terms, in comparing *Euclidean triangularity* with *Riemannian* (non-Euclidean) *triangularity* (see CC 184ff.; *NAO* IV.133ff.; *SM* V.37–47).

Looking to the norm-governed uses of •pressure•s, •mass•s, and •triangular•s within predecessor and successor theories, in such cases we judge, on the one hand, that Euclidean triangularity and Riemannian triangularity, for example, are both *triangularity concepts*. That is, both are •triangular•s insofar as they are correctly applicable to certain geometrical figures which are *generically similar* in being, for example, three-sided closed figures. Yet Euclidean •triangular•s and Riemannian •triangular•s are *specifically different* concepts of triangularity insofar as (again speaking loosely) the rules for Riemannian triangles entail that triangles have various properties that are *impossible* for Euclidean triangles. This 'sameness-with-difference' analysis of conceptual change makes sense of the intuitively plausible idea that in such cases, as it is often put, *the concept of triangularity has changed*. Using '*f*' for predicates such as 'triangular' and '*f*-ness' for abstract singular terms such as 'triangularity,' Sellars has in effect given us an account of how, as he puts it, "abstract entities, *pace* Plato, change" (*SM* V.42):

> To say that the semantic rules governing '*f*'s in our language could change over a period of time, and yet that the '*f*'s could all be •*f*•s, is what is meant by saying that *f*-ness has changed over this period. Just as we have the concept of a developing language or conceptual scheme, from which the concept of a language as studied in current formal semantics is an abstraction, so we have the concept of a developing linguistic or conceptual role from which the usual concept of a 'sense' or 'intension' is also an abstraction. (*SM* V.47)

In relation to improved scientific explanations such as that of pressure, for instance, it will now make "sense to say that a certain concept belonging to the theory at one stage is a development of a concept belonging to the theory at an earlier stage" (*SM* V.52).

This cross-framework conception of generically similar yet specifically different counterpart concepts, when combined with the scientific realist argument of chapter 2 concerning the demonstrable explanatory improvements that are achieved by successor theoretical ontologies within the scientific image, enables Sellars to give corresponding analyses of the notions of *truth, reference,* and *existence* across conceptual frameworks (*SM* V). In keeping with our central aims in this chapter, let us again take as our comparison conceptual frameworks the two idealized, all-comprehensive manifest and scientific images themselves (MI and SI).

Suppose that a certain proposition *p* concerning the pressure and temperature of a gas is semantically assertible, i.e., is true, from within the perspective of the manifest image (as characterized by the Boyle–Charles gas law, let us continue to suppose). From the perspective of our knowledge of the explanatorily more successful kinetic-molecular theory of gases in SI, however, *we* can say that *p* is true *with respect to MI* because in fact there is a counterpart proposition *p** in SI that has proved to be a successor to *p*, and *p** is true (i.e., is semantically assertible in SI). From the same perspective we can also say, given the argument of chapter 2, that *p* is only *approximately* true but strictly speaking false. In parallel fashion, we shall say from this perspective that the MI-gases referred to in *p exist* in the sense that there are counterpart references to and characterizations of SI-gases in the counterpart predication *p**, which is true in SI.[24] Again, however, we shall say that in a more strict sense MI-gases do not exist *as they are conceived within MI*. There are no such gases.

Finally, in light of this historical record of conceptual change and explanatory improvement across successor ontologies, we can now make at least general conceptual sense of "the *regulative ideal*" of a *fully* adequate SI-framework, one "which defines our concepts of ideal truth and reality" (*SM* V.95).[25] In its functional capacity as a regulative ideal, the conception of a fully adequate or 'completed' SI framework is not something to which we can *refer* directly. Rather, the ideal SI is a projection constructed out of the relationships examined above between predecessor theories and improved successor theories, on which we *do* have a grip. In effect we first project as a goal of explanation that the propositions of our own best current yet explanatorily imperfect SI-theories stand in a parallel relationship to potential improved successor SI-theories, as p stood to its counterpart p^* in the example concerning gases above. On this basis we can form the idea, for example, that what is *really true* is that gases are only approximately as characterized by proposition p^* in our current SI framework, which is to say that p^* would have a counterpart proposition, p^{**}, in the *ideal* SI that plays a relevantly similar role to the role that p^* plays in the kinetic-molecular theory of gases as we know it.

Since theoretical science concerns the domain of matter-of-factual truths, all of the above cross-framework distinctions concerning truth as assertibility will simultaneously be reflected in an underlying causal-representationalist dimension of language–world correspondence or picturing, as discussed in the previous section. In *Science and Metaphysics* (V.75–94) Sellars makes it clear that he conceives the ideal scientific image of the world as one in which the world would be pictured or mapped by singular observation statements which are themselves directly conceptualized in the theoretical terms of some future micro-physical theory or unified 'field' theory:

> *Prima facie*, it makes just as much sense to speak of basic singular statements in the framework of micro-physics as pictures, according to a complicated manner of projection, of micro-physical objects, as it does to speak of basic singular statements in the observation framework as pictures of the objects and events of the world of perceptible things and events. (*SM* V.88)

> Thus the Scientific Realist need only argue that a correct account of concepts and concept formation is compatible with the idea that the 'language entry' role could be played by statements in the language of physical theory, i.e. that in principle this language could *replace* the common-sense framework in *all* its roles, with the result that the idea that scientific theory enables a more adequate picturing of the world could be taken at its face value. (*SM* V.90)

Indeed, as discussed in chapter 2, theoretical picturing already occurs in limited contexts thanks to the (*in principle* dispensable) role of correspondence rules in Sellars' scientific realism (SRII 189). The result in the ideal SI, as opposed to in the "foreseeable future" of our developing SI, would finally be the successful overcoming of the methodological "dualism of observational and theoretical frameworks which the instrumentalist transforms into an ontology" (*SM* V.91; cf. TE 155, quoted at the end of chapter 2 above; see also chapter 7 below).[26]

While we cannot know in advance, of course, what the specific categorial ontology of the explanatorily ideal scientific image would look like, Sellars contends that it is incumbent upon the philosopher to attempt to envision what its most general categorial features would have to be like if certain of our own philosophical perplexities are finally to be rendered capable of solution. In addition to the general issues concerning truth and conceptual change that we have discussed so far in this chapter, we must finally come back to the central puzzle concerning sensible qualities and sensory consciousness that has been with us since the start. Genius Jones and his early modern philosophical and scientific successors have bequeathed this problem to us in a conceptually transformed but nonetheless still problematic shape.

The ontology of sensory consciousness and absolute processes

Let us first briefly tie together Sellars' views on the problem of sensory consciousness as we have seen them emerge from genius Jones's protoscientific approach to the nature of perception. Here we shall focus on the actual, occurrent pinkness that Sellars contends (as we saw in relation to the red brick at the end of chapter 5) is "in some sense" undeniably present to a perceiver who is ostensibly seeing, but perhaps merely vividly hallucinating, a pink physical ice cube.[27]

The Jonesean story posited sense impressions as states of the perceiver in order to explain the systematic character of our perceptual judgments in general and in particular across veridical and non-veridical experiences. We also saw in chapter 5 that Jones's *analogical* theory of sensings involved positing an isomorphism in which "sensations [are] the states of persons which correspond, in their similarities and differences to the similarities and differences of the objects which, in standard conditions, bring them about" (PSIM 34). Initially the common-sense Jonesean theory retains the 'naïve' or 'direct realist' view that colors are intrinsic contents or features of physical objects.[28] However, as every undergraduate student of philosophy knows, a "tension inevitably develops" (FMPP I.96) within this account of the 'doubling' of content in the veridical cases as well as in relation to the content's 'merely illusory' status in the non-veridical cases. In light of the evident causal dependence of the character of our perceptual experiences on factors within the perceiver across all cases, which are made increasingly evident (as we saw) in light of broadly scientific-causal considerations, eventually the best explanation put forward by a proto-theory of the Jonesean sort involves categorially *reconceiving* the occurrent sensible qualities and *relocating* them – or, rather, conceptually recognizing their *true* location – within the perceiver:

> A natural move by a proto-theory which is uncontaminated by the Myth of the Given would be to hold that in perception items which are in point of fact, for example, quasi cubes of pink stuff (of-a-cube-of-pink-stuff states of a perceiver) are conceptualized (i.e., responded to perceptually) as cubes of pink stuff *simpliciter* having the causal properties of ice. (FMPP I.97)

The crucial point here is that the sensing is itself now conceived to be the home of the *actual occurrent pink* that is involved in the original perceptual experience:

> The pinkness of a pink sensation is 'analogous' to the pinkness of a manifest pink ice cube, not by being a *different quality* which is in some respect analogous to pinkness (as the quality a Martian experiences in certain magnetic fields might be analogous to pink with respect to its place in a quality space), but by being *the same 'content' in a different categorial 'form.'* (FMPP III.47, second italics added)

In light of this it becomes clear that when Sellars indicates, as we also saw, that a sensory state cannot be *literally* pink or cubical, he is referring to the very different *categorial sort* of thing a state of a perceiver is conceived to be in contrast to colors as conceived as the content-characters of MI-physical objects and their surfaces. But however much ontological recategorization it may undergo in the course of inquiry, Sellars holds (in accordance with his 'principle of reducibility' and the 'grain argument' introduced in chapter 1) that an actual sensed quantum or volume of pink will never be coherently accounted for if one's ontology includes only colorless microphysical particles and their properties and relations. As conceived within the current scientific image account of the basic microphysical particles that make up the physical world, Sellars has argued, such particles cannot coherently be supposed either individually or collectively to constitute an actual case of a *volume of occurrent pink*.

Yet it is rock bottom for Sellars that we have to find a place for the volume of pink: "Obviously there are volumes of pink. No inventory of what there is can meaningfully deny that fact. What is at stake is their status and function in the scheme of things" (FMPP III.46).[29] It is the categorial status, nature, and function of such volumes of pink that is not simply *given* – not even *as* what C. I. Lewis called a simple *quale* (FMPP I.85) – but rather must be settled by philosophical inquiry and scientific theorizing. All of this hangs together neatly with the priority we placed on Sellars' account of the *myth of the categorial given* in chapter 5. And finally, the background concerning truth and conceptual change explored earlier should be kept in mind as we now explore Sellars' views on the ultimate status of such manifest image claims as that a certain physical object, O, is red:

> Thus the fact that, using the conceptual framework of common sense, we quite properly say,
>   Jones saw that O was red
> does not commit us to the idea that there is such a thing as O *as conceived in the framework of common sense*, nor that O is red *as redness is conceived in this framework*. [. . .] That there is no such thing as O as conceived in the framework of common sense, is compatible with the idea that there is such a thing as O as conceived in another framework, thus that of physical theory. (*SM* V.64)

The above discussion, then, represents the advanced stage of the Jonesean proto-scientific account where we are now to re-enter the dialectic and attempt to convey the final stages in Sellars' speculative account of the ultimate nature of sensory consciousness.[30]

In chapter 1 we introduced the general ontological problem we are now confronting in terms of what Sellars in PSIM called the *ultimate homogeneity* of color and other sensible qualities. We anticipated that this aspect of the clash of the manifest and scientific images would reassert itself in a new categorial guise within the post-Jonesean, post-Cartesian, and modern scientific context within which we are now operating. On the idealized scientific image of the world *as currently projected*, human beings, like everything else in nature, are conceived to be complex physical systems of swarming, colorless microphysical particles. When we bring this exhaustively 'particulate' SI-ontology to bear on the problem of our ("in some sense") homogeneously colored states of sensing, it becomes clear, for the following reasons, that genius Jones's mature account of our 'quasi cubical pink' sensings as *states of persons* cannot be the final ontological assay of the matter.

Within the manifest image, as correctly articulated in the line of the perennial philosophy from Aristotle to Kant and Strawson, a person is a unified, persisting 'substance': a single logical subject of various mental and physical attributes and abilities. MI-persons, as organic wholes and unified conscious selves, are conceived to be ontologically and explanatorily prior to their aggregate material 'parts' and their particular mental states and affections. Our central problem all along has been the question of how this concept of an essentially unified MI-person is to be synoptically integrated with the emerging concept of an SI-person as an *aggregate* of scientifically basic particles and processes. In chapters 3 and 4 we examined the grounds for Sellars' conclusion that meaning, thought, and intentionality can be smoothly integrated within the scientific image.[31] By contrast, the case of MI-persons' states of sensing homogeneous-pink-cube-ly brings us straight back again to the 'grain' problem of chapter 1. That is, in contrast to the smooth 'role/realizer' functionalist identification of (tokenings of) thoughts with neurophysiological states, which has provided a solution in principle to what Sellars calls the 'mind–body problem,' in the case of sensory consciousness the stubborn problem which we are now facing

> is this: can we define, in the framework of neurophysiology, states which are sufficiently analogous in their *intrinsic* character to sensations to make identification plausible?
> The answer seems clearly to be 'no'. (PSIM 35)

This central problem concerning "sensory consciousness, the sort of consciousness we have simply in virtue of feeling a pain or sensing a cube-of-pinkly," Sellars dubbed the "sensorium–body problem." In particular it concerns "the relation between sensations [. . .] and bodily states as in principle describable by the natural sciences" (FMPP III.1–4).

As it reappears within this new framework, then, the original problem concerning the homogeneity of color ultimately becomes the difficulty of reconciling the following three propositions, each of which has found support within Sellars' overall account as developed so far:

[1] No aggregate of colorless scientific micro-particles can constitute a volume of occurrent pink. (The 'grain' argument)

[2] Volumes of occurrent pink nonetheless undeniably exist, and the best explanation of their nature and status is that they are sensory states of perceivers. (The Jonesean proto-theory of perceptual experience)
Yet:

[3] Persons as conceived within the scientific image are complex aggregates of colorless microphysical particles. (The scientific realist account of the scientific image of 'man-in-the-world' as construed up to this point)

Something has to give. The denial of [1] runs up against the 'principle of reducibility' discussed in chapter 1, and thus the whole set of complex problems which for present purposes we may recall to mind using Sellars' rhetorical remark: "How, we would surely expostulate, can an object's having occurrent pinkness consist in facts about its parts, none of which facts involves occurrent color?" (FMPP III.25). The fact that this volume of pink has now been reconceived to be the content of a *sensing* has not resolved this problem, given [3]. And we have seen that Sellars rejects 'intentionalist' and functionalist accounts of perception that would attempt to lessen the impact of [2]. For these reasons, Sellars argues that the sensorium–body problem must ultimately be addressed by further speculation concerning [3], thus reopening the question of the ultimate nature of persons as projected in the ideal scientific image.

To advance the argument at this stage we need to appeal to a distinction that was originally introduced by Sellars and Paul Meehl in their co-authored 1956 article, 'The Concept of Emergence':

> Physical$_1$: an event or entity is *physical$_1$* if it belongs in the space-time network. [Physical$_1$ features are any which belong "in the causal order."[32]]
>
> Physical$_2$: an event or entity is *physical$_2$* if it is definable in terms of theoretical primitives adequate to describe completely the actual states though not necessarily the potentialities of the universe before the appearance of life. (CE 252)

Using 'item' as our categorially neutral term, the 'physical$_1$' includes all and only those items that are denizens of the spatio-temporal-causal universe – or roughly, the 'natural' as opposed to the 'supernatural' (SSIS 439). The 'physical$_2$' covers all and only those items that science must ultimately posit in order to explain all inanimate, insensate phenomena in nature.

Sellars' most detailed reflections on the nature of persons and of sensory consciousness as projected within the ideal scientific image occur in his 1971 article, 'Science, Sense Impressions, and Sensa: A Reply to Cornman' (SSIS), and in his third Carus Lecture in 1981, 'Is Consciousness Physical?' (FMPP III).[33] His main contentions may be very briefly summarized as follows. Persons have been conceived within the scientific image as complex systems of physical$_2$ entities. However, given [1] and [2] above, Sellars holds that any "Reductive Materialist" attempt to account for the occurrent volume of pink, i.e., the "state of sensing a-cube-of-pinkly," by appealing solely to physical$_2$ entities and processes – or, crudely put, to "complex motions of atoms in the void" – is doomed to failure (FMPP III.79–80, 40–2; however, one must bear in mind the controversies mentioned in the notes to this chapter). Sellars then considers and rejects three traditional proposals for modifying the ontology of persons in [3] in order to accommodate the sensing a-cube-of-pink-ly (FMPP III.73–110). "Substantial Dualism" posits a nonmaterial, non-physical$_1$ soul, mind, or sensorium. At this stage we may perhaps be spared the task of rehearsing why most philosophers since the nineteenth century have regarded the posit of a non-spatial spiritual soul to be an explanatory disaster. "Epiphenomenalism" does not posit a non-physical$_1$ substantial entity but only nonmaterial "sense-particulars" traditionally called 'sense-data' or "*sensa*" (FMPP III.88). These particulars are 'epiphenomenal' insofar as they are conceived to be caused by physical$_2$ brain processes but to cause nothing themselves. Finally, "Emergent (or Wholistic) Materialism" holds that sensing is a *state* (rather than a particular or an object) that "is correlated with, but not reducible to, a complex physical$_2$ state [. . .] of the system" (FMPP III.84–5).

Sellars argues that all three of these positions can ultimately be seen to share a weakness concerning *causality*, "a theme which, though it stands out most clearly in the case of Epiphenomenalism, is also lurking in classical forms of Substantive Dualism and Wholistic Materialism" (FMPP III.95). He diagrams the familiar "epiphenomenalist form" of "psycho-physical laws" as follows, where 'φ' represents physical$_2$ brain states, 'ψ' non-physical$_2$ sensory items, '$\Rightarrow$' physical$_2$ causal relations, and '$\rightarrow$' correlation or perhaps some stronger relation of 'upward causation,' 'emergence,' etc. (FMPP III.109):

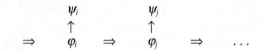

Many of those philosophers who posited (non-physical$_2$) sense-data, sensa, phantasms, sense impressions, qualia, phantasms, etc., have in effect taken them to be epiphenomenal or perhaps 'emergent' properties or states in ways that roughly conform to the above pattern.

Sellars' diagnostic suggestion is that this broadly epiphenomenalist "idea that sensory items do not play an essential causal role in the behavior of the bodies of sentient beings was not a direct empirical finding by psycho-physicists, but rather a consequence of the dualistic picture of man characteristic of the early modern period" (FMPP III.100). What in the 1981 Carus Lectures he now calls "*the scientific ideology of the autonomy of the mechanical*" (FMPP III.109, italics added) is essentially the widespread assumption that the mechanistic causal laws that govern all physical$_2$ entities and processes constitute a *closed system* in (roughly) the sense that physical$_2$ effects have necessary and sufficient physical$_2$ causes. Sellars' own key assessment of the situation is then as follows:

102. This sufficiency of mechanistic variables, combined with the almost tangible *thingishness* of physical objects and with an impact paradigm of causation made it difficult to conceive of a mode of causation in which the development of a system of material particles might be influenced by nonmaterial items, whether *states* of a 'mind' or Hobbesian *objects*.

103. This difficulty made it only too tempting to extend the autonomy of mechanical explanation to the bodies of sentient beings. As bodies they are merely extremely complex systems of material particles.

104. That the proper sensibles – e.g., shades of color – could function alongside of mechanistic variables in psycho-physical laws in such a way that the mechanical variables by themselves did not constitute a closed system with respect to necessary and sufficient conditions (as they do for Epiphenomenalism) made no more scientific sense, given the paradigms of the day, than would a Compatibilist attempt to involve the proper sensibles in the laws of motion. (FMPP III.102–4)

Sellars will now offer an account of 'sensa' or 'sensings' according to which they function in accordance with just such 'a mode of causation' as is thought to be impossible according to the above 'ideology of the autonomy of the mechanical.' He wants his ontology of sensing to "conform to a basic metaphysical intuition: to be is to make a difference," that is, a *causal* difference (FMPP III.126). So he argues that this requires that we *reject* the widespread assumption that the physical$_2$ domain constitutes a causally closed system, i.e., we must reject the ideology of the autonomy of the mechanical.

But how will it be possible to postulate that non-physical$_2$ sensings affect the course of surrounding physical$_2$ processes in central nervous systems without absurdly suggesting that there are no universal laws governing physical$_2$ phenomena themselves, as physics assures us that there *are*? When this problem concerning causal efficacy is combined with the earlier intractable difficulty as to how it is possible *at all* for homogeneous 'volumes of pink' to be conceived to be proper denizens of a world that is entirely composed of colorless physical$_2$ particles (the 'grain' argument in [1]), it is easy to understand why philosophers "of the early modern period" modified [3] by embracing problematic versions of dualism, epiphenomenalism, and emergentism, all of which arguably fail to successfully integrate our states of sensing color into the spatio-temporal-causal fabric of nature. How can *both* the causal efficacy *and* the homogeneity of our states of sensing a-cube-of-pink-ly be preserved, as an ultimately adequate solution seems to require as a result of Sellars' arguments up to this point?

Sellars' final suggestion is that these joint requirements can and will be adequately satisfied only within a comprehensive ontological recategorization according to which both the physical$_2$ phenomena that occur everywhere in nature and the non-physical$_2$ sensings that take place only in complex neurophysiological physical$_2$ contexts are recognized to be equally basic and mutually affecting *absolute processes* in nature. Sellars labels these absolute processes 'φ_2-ings' (physical$_2$-ings) and 'σ-ings' (sensings) respectively. A future micro-theoretical neurophysiology or "*micro*-theory of sentient organisms" (EPM XVI.61) will have to conceive pink-cubical sensa to be non-physical$_2$ items that are as ontologically basic as, and have real (physical$_1$) effects upon, the physical$_2$ microphysical items with which they are correlated.

In the traditionally 'mechanistic' conception of the scientific image, the physical$_2$ processes occurring in the central nervous system are conceived to be states, properties, processes, or changes of such *objects* as "neurons, which consist of molecules, which consist of quarks" and other micro-physical$_2$ particles (FMPP III.124). On that picture (1) the modern metaphysical and scientific prejudice in favor of 'the autonomy of the mechanical' and the 'impact' model of causation inevitably leads theorists to conceive the physical$_2$ domain to be ontologically basic and causally closed in relation to the merely emergent states, supervenient properties, or epiphenomena of sensing that depend on them; and (2) this ultimately particulate or 'granular' ontological picture also leaves the problem of the ultimate homogeneity of sensory qualities as intractable as it ever was.

Suppose, however, Sellars now suggests, that all objects and "object-bound processes" could be conceived as "'logical constructions' out of, i.e., patterns of, absolute processes" (FMPP III.112). In his second Carus Lecture, entitled 'Naturalism and Process,' Sellars had distinguished between *object-bound processes* and *absolute processes*. Roughly speaking, within the manifest image Sellars defends a 'substance ontology' of enduring things according to which "talk about *events*" such as '*a running* by Socrates' is analyzed as "a way of talking about things changing," i.e., '*Socrates* runs' (FMPP II.43, 47). However, initially within these confines of the manifest image Sellars follows the lead of C. D. Broad in his *Examination of McTaggart's Philosophy* (1933) and introduces the concept of 'absolute processes,' "which might also be called subjectless (or objectless) events. These are processes, the occurrence of which is, in the first instance, expressed by sentences [...] which either do not have logical subjects or which have dummy logical subjects" (FMPP II.50). Examples of the latter dummy subjects are 'It lightnings,' or noun expressions such as 'a buzzing' or 'a C$^{\#}$-ing' (FMPP II.48). Although the typical cause of a buzzing might be a certain buzzing *object*, a buzzing sound is primarily "the intrinsic character of a certain kind of process," and we can "say that a buzzing is going on without implying that some object, e.g., a bee, is buzzing" (FMPP II.65–6).

Suppose now that we set aside the substance ontology of the manifest image and consider as a "regulative ideal" an *alternative* ontological framework: in first approximation we may think of it in terms of the sort of *logical atomist* and *neutral monist* ontology put forward by Bertrand Russell, "who sought to eliminate metaphysical and epistemological puzzles by reducing all objects to patterns or complexes of sensibilia" (FMPP II.84–5). On the Russellian logical atomist strategy, which Sellars now wants to put to use in his own way, counterfactual statements concerning the 'iffy' or dispositional properties of persisting objects as conceived within the manifest framework should be viewed not as synonymous with, but rather as in principle *"replaceable by"* or *"eliminable in favor"* of statements concerning the uniformities and co-occurrences of patterns of the truly basic items or 'logical atoms' within this ideal framework.[34] "The replacement would be justified by the greater explanatory power of the new framework" (FMPP II.95, 88ff.). On this ideal Humean and Russellian ontological framework, there "would, so to speak, be no potentialities *in* basic objects" (FMPP II.91), and ordinary things and minds and their powers would be *logical constructions* out of the logically basic or 'atomic' entities.

The pre-Socratic philosopher Heraclitus held that nature is in some sense a scene of continual but lawful *flux* or change. Sellars' own Heraclitean ontological proposal is to construe *"all* the 'atoms' of our neutral monist model as absolute processes" (FMPP II.99) – which brings us back, finally, to our main topic: 'is [sensory] consciousness physical?' Sellars' proposal is that these ultimately 'logically atomic' absolute processes will include among them whatever ultimately homogeneous *sensings* (σ-ings), such as C#-ings, *"reddings"* (FMPP II.100), pinkings, stinkings, and so on, take place as constituting the sensory experiences of various sentient beings. This represents the final categorial "transposition of sensa into the framework of absolute processes" (FMPP III.115). Side by side with these sensings there will also be certain complex patterns of whatever "physical$_2$ absolute processes" or φ_2-ings "suffice to constitute what goes on in non-living things and insensate organisms"; in "a humorous vein we might refer to them as electronings and quarkings" (FMPP III.113–14).

The idea, then, is that in the Peircean ideal scientific image of 'man-in-the-world,' the universe will be conceived as "an ongoing tissue of goings on" or absolute processes, the vast majority of which are physical$_2$ happenings or φ_2-ings ('electronings and quarkings') that do not involve any *sensory* qualities at all. We have seen Sellars suggest above, however, that philosophers "who ponder the sensorium–body problem from the perspective of Scientific Realism" and yet who also take on the challenge of accommodating the real actuality of 'volumes of pink' (unlike the Reductive [physical$_2$] Materialists), have unfortunately been led by the myth of the autonomy of the physical$_2$-mechanical to take some "form of ontological epiphenomenalism for granted," whether explicitly or implicitly (FMPP III.116–17). Now we get Sellars' own final take on the matter:

> 119. But if [these philosophers] were to accept (programmatically, of course) an ontology of absolute process, they would immediately be freed from this last refuge of metaphysical dualism. If the particles of microphysics are patterns of actual and counterfactual φ_2-ings, then the categorial (indeed, transcendental) dualism which gives aid and comfort to epiphenomenalism simply *vanishes*. [. . .]
> 121. Psycho-physical theory, to the extent that it is well confirmed, does, indeed, entail that uniformities pertaining to the occurrence of σ-ings specify that they occur in the context of φ_2-ings which belong to patterns of absolute processes which constitute specific kinds of neurophysiologic process.
> 122. What it does *not* require is that these φ_2-ings be nomologically autonomous.
> 123. Nor does it require that neuro-physiological objects which have φ_2-ings as constituents, have *only* φ_2-ings as constituents. σ-ings could in a legitimate sense be constituents of neurophysiological objects. [. . .]
> 125. The way would be open to a bundle theory of persons. A person would be a bundle of absolute processes, both σ-ings and φ_2-ings. (FMPP III.119, 121–3, 125)[35]

The suggestion is that when quasi-cubical pink σ-ings occur in that 'bundle' or pattern of absolute processes which is Mary's visual cortex, they stand in causal relations with certain highly complex φ_2-ings occurring there as well. Let the latter φ_2-ings be P6 and P7, and let them be members of a wider causal sequence of physical$_2$ processes which ultimately extends outside the neurophysiological context of Mary's pink σ-ings (the latter context is represented by boldfaced characters below). We might hazard a very crude diagram of Sellars' proposal as follows:

$$\textbf{P6} \Rightarrow \textbf{P7}$$

φ_2-ings: . . . P4 → P5   P8 → P9 . . .

$$\textbf{pink σ-ings}$$

The idea is that the simple or homogeneous σ-ings or 'sensing a-cube-of-pink-ly' absolute processes that are occurring 'in' (i.e., partly constituting) Mary's visual cortex *make their presence felt causally*, rather than being merely epiphenomenal, by systematically affecting the course of the requisite physical$_2$ processes also occurring in her visual cortex.

This proposal has the direct consequence that patterns of φ_2-ings such as P4 → P5 which occur outside sensing contexts will be governed by *different laws* than patterns of φ_2-ings such as **P6 ⇨ P7** that are affected by sensings.

Sellars embraces this consequence, which is precisely to reject the ideology of the autonomy or global closure of 'purely mechanical' physical$_2$ laws across all contexts indifferently. In fact it was the burden of Sellars' and Meehl's original 1956 article on the 'Concept of Emergence' to show that the general idea of such context specific and emergent *functional laws* – rather than the posit of emergent or supervening properties, states, or entities – is perfectly consistent with the idea that any and all processes in nature are fully law-governed phenomena relative to the contexts in which they occur. Sellars and Meehl remark in passing that in the context of "living brains" we might discover, for example, that the "flow of electrons at the synaptic interface 'breaks the laws'" that govern such φ_2-ings outside such contexts (CE, section IV). It is only an entirely optional mechanistic 'impact' or 'billiard ball' model of causation that leads us to think that there is something *absurd* in the idea that nature's physical$_2$ patterns or uniformities might be captured by different basic functional relationships or laws in different contexts.

Perhaps the most remarkable feature of this robustly anti-epiphenomenalist ontology of our ultimately homogeneous, non-physical$_2$ sensings is how far Sellars is sticking his neck out. A future micro-neurophysiology must discover – but *will* it? – that the laws governing the sorts of micro-physical$_2$ processes that occur in non-sensory contexts (put crudely, outside brains) *will not hold* in relation to those same sorts of micro-physical$_2$ processes as they occur in those highly complex patterns that are correlated with sensings or sensa (i.e., within brains). It is only on an overall categorial ontology of this kind, Sellars has argued, that the undeniable actuality, as he sees it, of the 'volumes of homogeneous color' that we find in our sensory experience could both be realistically accounted for as the intrinsic contents that they are *and* be construable as causally efficacious and hence explanatorily relevant in relation to the complex non-sensory physical processes with which such sensings are correlated.

The problem of the *ultimate homogeneity* of sensory contents, the non-granular continuity of the volume of pink, is also supposed to have disappeared, for the granular micro-physical particles with which such homogeneity was argued to be incompatible in [1] have *themselves* disappeared from the list of basic entities. Such particles are now conceived to be 'logical constructions' and 'one dimension of' the absolute processes (σ-ings and φ_2-ings) that finally constitute the unified mono-categorial structure of the world. As Sellars had put this speculative ontological proposal back in 'Philosophy and the Scientific Image of Man':

> [A]lthough for many purposes the central nervous system can be construed without loss as a complex system of physical particles, *when it comes to an adequate understanding of the relation of sensory consciousness to* neurophysiological process, we must penetrate to the non-particulate foundation of the particulate image, and recognize that in this non-particulate image the qualities of sense are a dimension of natural process which occurs only in connection with those complex physical processes which, when 'cut-up' into particles in terms of those features which are the least common denominators of physical process – present in inorganic as well as organic processes alike – become the complex system of particles which, in the current scientific image, *is* the central nervous system. (PSIM 37)

So Sellars' answer to his question '*Is sensory consciousness physical?*' turns out to be *yes* insofar as pink-cubical sensings or σ-ings are physical$_1$ processes that have real effects on the course of the physical$_2$ processes with which they are associated in the bustling central nervous systems of sentient beings. However, he is not a materialist as that concept has often, and Sellars thinks mistakenly, been characterized in terms of physical$_2$ processes alone.

There is a sizeable group of contemporary philosophers of mind who contend, as Sellars contended along the above lines from the early 1950s, that physicalist models of the mind constructed along functionalist lines, if they appeal only to relations of representational or informational content, will be insufficient to account for the phenomenal character of our conscious qualitative experiences. In very different ways Thomas Nagel, David Chalmers, Frank Jackson, Ned Block, John Searle, Galen Strawson, Colin McGinn, Michael Lockwood, Roger Penrose, and Joe Levine have argued that phenomenal consciousness, if it can be explained at all (which the 'New Mysterians' among them deny), must be investigated in terms of some alternative model or approach. Sellars' view of sensory consciousness is an example of what the functionalist William Lycan has critically examined under the rubric of 'Recent Naturalistic Dualisms' (forthcoming).[36] In the Carus Lectures Sellars in effect classifies his own view as a physicalistic (i.e., physical$_1$) successor to the broadly *Cartesian* approach to sensory consciousness (FMPP III, *passim*), for "in the Cartesian recategorization, the cube of pink which the perceiver takes to be a feature of his environment is in point of fact a state of himself" (FMPP III.50). Or as further recategorized within the projected ideal scientific image, for Sellars the latter turns out to be a non-physical$_2$ sensing – a quasi-cubical-pinking – as a bottom-level absolute process occurring in the perceiver's central nervous system.

The specific speculative ontology of absolute processes put forward by Sellars has not had a wide influence in contemporary philosophy of mind. However, it is remarkable that the first twentieth-century philosopher to outline a detailed functional role account of the mind in relation to intentionality and conceptual content – as we saw Dennett, at any rate, claim of Sellars in chapter 4 – was *also* one of the first philosophers to argue that sensory consciousness will inevitably have to receive a different kind of theoretical treatment along non-functionalist lines while simultaneously seeking to avoid the dead-end of epiphenomenalism. And that general problem space has indeed become one within which more than a few philosophers of mind are currently working.

7

A Synoptic Vision

Sellars' Naturalism with a Normative Turn

The structure of Sellars' normative 'Copernican revolution'

Our investigations have been structured around Sellars' famous formulation of the central problems of modern philosophy in terms of an apparent clash between what he called the manifest image and the scientific image of 'man-in-the-world.' In chapters 2 and 6 we have seen Sellars contend that a regulative ideal of the scientific enterprise is the conception that human beings along with all the other denizens of the universe are complex spatio-temporal physical systems whose nature is in principle entirely explicable in terms of natural causal laws. Furthermore, he has argued that we conceive the manifest perceptible world to be populated with persisting, colored physical objects that the scientific image informs us do not strictly speaking exist as they are conceived within the manifest image. However, the most crucial, indeed paradigmatic, feature of the manifest image is that it is conceived to be populated with *persons* whose very existence, as noted in chapter 1, hangs upon their conception of themselves as (i) consciously experiencing, (ii) conceptually thinking, and (iii) rationally active beings. The central task of philosophy for Sellars has been the difficult one of attempting to achieve a *synoptic vision* in which those two comprehensive conceptions of the world are successfully 'fused' into one coherent conception of the nature of human persons within the natural universe.

To pick up the lead metaphor of chapter 1, we have now examined some of Sellars' most important efforts to eat that apple to the core. We have investigated his quest for a synoptic vision (i) of the nature of our sensory cognition and qualitative consciousness in chapters 5 and 6, and (ii) of the nature of meaning, thinking, and the 'logical space of reasons' in chapters 3 through 5. What we have discovered in each one of those chapters, however, is that what I have called Sellars' *naturalism with a normative turn* involves tracing our deepest philosophical perplexities to questions concerning the complex relationships between the normative and the natural, between reasons and causal uniformities. We saw this in specifically different but closely related ways in relation to his views on the nature of meaning, abstract entities, thought, intentionality, perception, knowledge, truth, and reference, and I shall not attempt to summarize those findings here.

One might recall in particular, however, three tightly connected fundamental themes that I have argued lie at the heart of Sellars' views on each of those topics:

(a) The crucial role throughout Sellars' philosophy of what I have called his 'norm/nature meta-principle': namely, that the *espousal of principles is reflected in uniformities of performance* (TC 216).

(b) Sellars' repeated contention that all of the various normative conceptual principles at the 'higher levels,' so to speak, *convey, imply, or presuppose, but do not directly assert* that various specific natural uniformities, behavioral patterns, reliable causal connections, and structural mappings at the 'lower levels' are either in place or in process. The result is that meaning, truth, intentionality, etc., are shown to systematically presuppose, *but are not themselves*, real 'relations to the world.' This was Sellars' overarching strategy for resolving various perennial epistemological and metaphysical quandaries. And finally, as arising out of both of those:

(c) The resulting conception of the normative phenomena that constitute the form of our cognitive human experience as being both *conceptually irreducible* and yet *causally reducible* to the various physical processes out of which they are constituted. Those normative or 'epistemic' phenomena (in Sellars' broad sense of that term) both presuppose (as in (b)) and themselves partly serve to bring about (via (a)) the complex physical processes and patterns in which they are entirely 'realized' in the natural world (see O'Shea 2006b).

To borrow Kant's lead metaphor, the heart of Sellars' attempted 'Copernican revolution' in philosophy has thus been the attempt to reorient our thinking in relation to fundamental ontological and epistemological questions by systematically recasting them – or, rather, by coming to recognize their true nature – as questions concerning the complex relationships between the natural and the normative. As Kant also saw, the answers to the key questions of metaphysics have turned out to lie much closer to home than both naturalizing empiricists, on the one hand, and broadly platonic, rationalist philosophers, on the other, have been perennially tempted to think.

What all of the above conclusions do turn our attention toward, however, is ultimately the question of normativity itself – which brings us to (iii) the third and concluding piece of the puzzle in Sellars' attempted synoptic vision. As he put it in the title of the last section of his flagship article, 'Philosophy and the Scientific Image of Man,' our final stereoscopic task is in a sense that of "Putting Man into the Scientific Image." In chapter 2 we examined Sellars' "thesis of the primacy of the scientific image," but for the full establishment of that thesis there remains "the task of showing that categories pertaining to man as a *person* who finds himself confronted by standards (ethical, logical, etc.) which often conflict with his desires and impulses, and to which he may or may not conform, can be reconciled with the idea that man is what science says he is" (PSIM 38). Sellars' views on normativity, practical reason, and morality would by themselves form a rich topic for a book-length treatment, but here unfortunately I shall have to skirt the mere edges of those topics.[1] I shall touch upon just one or two key issues that bear directly on questions concerning Sellars' attempted 'fusion' of the manifest and scientific images, which has been our focus throughout. It turns out that, as Sellars sees the matter, the issue of the nature and status of normative 'ought's does not present any *further* ontological barriers to such a stereoscopic fusion – that is, none beyond those we have already addressed in relation to the nature of *thinking* in chapter 4. Nonetheless there remain some crucial matters to be at least briefly addressed.

Intentions, volitions, and the moral point of view

We may begin by asking: what is Sellars' conception of what philosophers and psychologists have traditionally called *the will*? We have in fact already been introduced to the key notion in his theory of human agency: the idea of a *language exit* or *departure* transition, which serves as the behavioral-linguistic model for our understanding of the corresponding inner mental phenomena (as explained in chapter 4).

We saw that language *entry* transitions or perceptual cognitions on Sellars' account are such thoughts or thinkings-out-loud as •This red apple is tasty•s, as reliably caused or systematically evoked in the perceiver by the relevant state of affairs in the environment: *ceteris paribus*, by a tasty red apple. Such 'world → language' entry perceptions are themselves conceptual thinkings due to their place in a wider social-linguistic, normative inferential 'space of reasons.' Sellars argues in parallel fashion that a 'language → world' exit transition or volition (i.e., a willing, or an 'act' of the will) will likewise be a species of conceptual thinking. An example of an exit transition would be an •I shall *now* shut the door• as thought by Smith and as followed immediately (*ceteris paribus*) by Smith's movements toward shutting the door. As with our perceptual cognitions, but in the reverse 'language → world' causal direction, our capacity for *intentional actions* is thus an acquired conceptual ability that is constituted by both an underlying natural-causal reliability dimension and a normative 'space of reasons' dimension.[2] We have already explored in some detail in previous chapters how the two dimensions of norm-governed conceptual thinking in general and the causal uniformities it presupposes are successfully brought together on Sellars' view. What needs to be explored now is the nature of *practical* thinking or reasoning in particular.

As a tidy formal device, Sellars in his various discussions of human agency formulates such 'practical thinkings' or action-generating *volitions* in terms of a 'Shall' operator on first-person propositional thinkings: for example, 'Shall (I will *now* do A).' An *intention*, on Sellars' account, has the more general form: 'Shall (I will do A at time *t*).' An intention to do A is thus a practical thinking which will become a volition to do A (and, *ceteris paribus*, a doing of A) if the time *t* is recognized to be *now*.[3] Since they are conceptual thinkings, both intentions and volitional exit transitions are part and parcel of the inferentially articulated space of reasons.

Sellars and his former student Hector-Neri Castañeda independently devoted considerable attention over the years to exploring the *logic of intentions*. A key principle governing our practical reasoning, according to Sellars (e.g., IIO 174; *SM* VII.13), put in the form of intentions that various states of affairs be the case, is that

If p implies q, then Shall(p) implies Shall(q)

Hence, for example, 'Shall (I do both A and B)' implies 'Shall (I do A),' and so on.[4] "Intentions imply intentions just as beliefs imply beliefs. [...] An ideally rational being would intend the implications of his intentions, just as he would believe the implications of his beliefs" (*SM* VII.15–16).

Sellars takes it to be a significant virtue of his account of our intentions and volitions that they are *reasoned* insofar as they may thus be caught up intelligibly in practical reasonings, and yet at the same time the very nature of such practical thinkings is to be causally productive of the corresponding *actions* (all going well). Crudely put, to have a minimally competent grip on the basic language of intentions and volitions is to be 'trained' or reliably causally disposed such that one's •I shall A•s are followed by movements toward the doing of A, whether proximately or mediately (*SM* VII.9). If a competent speaker of English candidly responds to a ringing phone with an •I'll get it!•, this will normally be followed by her moving to answer the phone, for she has been trained into the relevant linguistic 'ought-to-be' rule or pattern-governed behavioral uniformity, as we saw in chapter 4. (And of course from that chapter we may also recall that *inner* intentions and volitions on Sellars' view will be propositional content-bearing mental events in a 'Mentalese' or representational medium that is conceived to be analogous to the corresponding linguistic utterances and inscriptions that serve as their model.)

Being in this way both subject to reasoning and action-engendering by their nature, Sellars' suggestion is that our 'shall'-intentions and volitions look at least to have the right conceptual shape to gear in with a possible account of the reasonableness and motivational force of normative 'ought's, including the 'ought's of moral obligation.[5] What Sellars aimed to provide from early on in his career was a general account of practical reason according to which normative 'ought's are both 'internally' or essentially *motivating* for the individuals who recognize them (and are thus *ceteris paribus* productive of the appropriate actions in general),[6] and yet such 'ought's are also objectively or impartially binding on all the agents in a moral community. Whether the latter community may justifiably be conceived to include *all rational beings* turns out to be a problematic issue for Sellars, as it has been for other philosophers who have defended similarly motivated *internalist* conceptions of the moral 'ought.'[7]

We can begin to see the outlines of Sellars' account, first, in the case of what Kant called 'hypothetical imperatives,' or 'ought's that are rationally binding on an agent *relative to* that agent's desired or intended ends. If 'Shall P' implies 'Shall Q,' for example, then "it is *unreasonable* to intend that P be the case without intending that Q be the case," i.e. one *ought* to intend Q if one intends P (*SM* VII.18, 40). We can then reason instrumentally, using our knowledge of the ways of things in the world, concerning which specific sorts of action, A, in which sorts of circumstances, C, are *causally necessary for* (and hence 'implied by') the realization of our intended end, E. Such an "instrumental implication" may be formulated as "a general hypothetical imperative" (*SM* VII.51):

'I shall bring about E' implies 'I shall do A if in C.'

Hypothetical imperatives of this kind, as Sellars puts it, "are simply the transposition into practical discourse of empirical instrumental generalizations" (*SM* VII.52).

The first steps into Sellars' account of moral reasonableness may thus be taken in terms of what he calls a classical " 'enlightened' self-interest" theory of the rational bindingness of moral 'ought's (aspects of which he finds in Plato's account of the 'art of living'). Suppose that my intended end, E, is one that such a theory construes as 'valid' or 'reasonable' in the sense of being intended *all things considered* – for example, as my "over-arching valuing" or "life-plan intention" that *I shall lead a satisfying life* (*SM* VII.61–70, *passim*). Further, suppose that my doing A whenever I am in C is instrumentally implied by (i.e., is a necessary means to) that end, as above. Then such a theory is capable of generating what Sellars interestingly suggests may be classified as *categorical* imperatives in Kant's sense, or non-hypothetical ought statements of the form: 'I ought to do A' – on the supposition, of course, that I am in circumstances C. (Sellars thus carefully distinguishes the mere relativity to appropriate circumstances, which he thinks is required for the full statement of any categorical imperative, from the relativity to a further intended end, which renders an 'ought' a hypothetical imperative.) On the above 'rational self-interest' account, then, such embedded categorical imperatives are understood to be •Shall (I do A)• intentions that are implied by my overarching 'all things considered' life-plan intention to live a satisfying life. "Roughly," as Sellars formulates the matter, "categorical imperatives are *derivative general conditional intentions*" (*SM* VII.69). Sellars now proceeds to argue, however, that this whole account can in fact itself be embedded within a more plausible account of the general 'moral point of view,' one that turns out to be closer in spirit to Kant's own moral philosophy.

For Sellars argues in agreement with Kant that imperatives or 'ought's as understood above do not yet fully succeed in capturing the "categorical reasonableness" that is embodied in the moral point of view (*SM* VII.86–8), and that *overall* on the above account they remain hypothetical imperatives. For even if we suppose that my 'overarching valuing' or intended end, E, on the above account is the *benevolent* one of promoting the general welfare or the common good, the reasonableness of my intended actions, A, on that account is still merely *relative to* my antecedent intention to bring about that end, E, and the reasonableness of the latter end itself has not yet been explicated. Again, it is important to note that it is this relativity which threatens the categorical validity of the 'I ought to do A' (depending on the nature of the end E to which it is relative), not the mere (and unavoidable) relativity to appropriate circumstances C (as above). In fact, according to Sellars the crucial point to see is that the *conditional intention*, 'I shall do A, if I am in C,' would be *categorically reasonable*, *if* the intention to which it is relative (such as the benevolent intention of promoting the general welfare) could also be shown to be so. The categorical reasonableness of the latter end would be transmitted down the reasoning, as it were.

Sellars thus argues that it is a mistake, and a misunderstanding of Kant's moral philosophy, to think that genuinely categorical imperatives of the form 'I ought to do A' could not also be conditional upon circumstances as well as being derivative from or relative to a more basic (but likewise categorically reasonable) imperative. Sellars argued in this spirit since the 1950s that "the idea that the prime mover of reflective moral consciousness is benevolence can be reconciled with the idea that moral action is action *on principle*" (IIO 210).

Now we come to the heart of the matter. One of Sellars' early and key insights in relation to practical reason (later developed in fruitful directions by Michael Bratman and others) concerned the role of *community intentions* as constituting the *intersubjective form* of judgments made from the moral point of view (*SM* VII.117ff., IIO, and elsewhere). To put it bluntly, *I* can think in terms of *we*: in conceiving ourselves to be members of various wider collective communities, each person individually is capable of having intentions the content of which may also be shared by other members of the community.[8] Consider the intention, '*we* shall do what we can to end the war'; or as Sellars also formalizes it in relation to the corresponding 'ought-to-be': 'It shall$_{we}$ be the case that the war end' (*SM* VII.118). While my having that particular community intention does not entail the heroic intention that *I* shall end the war all by myself, it does have various logical implications for my own activities (for example, my not intentionally impeding the anti-war effort, other things being equal).

Sellars now argues that the intersubjective intention or end E, 'It shall$_{we}$ be the case that our welfare is maximized' (or expressed as a valuing, 'We would that our common good is promoted'), may indeed be regarded as *categorically* reasonable. He contends that this community intention

> does seem to have an authority which is more than a mere matter of its being generally accepted. It is a conceptual fact that people constitute a community, a *we*, by virtue of thinking of each other as *one of us*, and by willing the common good *not* under the species of benevolence – but by willing it as one of us, or from a moral point of view. (*SM* VII.132)

That is, "it is by virtue of such an intention that a group or community *is* a group or community" (*SM* VII.140). As he sums it up in his letter to David Solomon, the

> fundamental intention characterizing the moral point of view has the form, '*We* shall any of *us* do that which (in his/her circumstances) promotes (maximizes) *our* common good'. I have argued that such an intention can be construed as 'categorically valid' because sharing such an intention defines what it is to be members of a community. (June 28, 1976, §15; available on the Sellars website, listed under Chrucky in the bibliography)

If the community intention to maximize our welfare could thus be shown to be "intrinsically categorically reasonable," then assuming (as above) that 'x does A_i if in C_i' has been judged to be a necessary means to that end, it would follow that the various particular intersubjective intentions, 'It shall$_{we}$ be the case that each of us does A_i in C_i' "would also be categorically reasonable, though derivatively so" (*SM* VII.131). That is, the *impartial* 'ought' in 'If *any* of us is in C_i he ought to do A_i' would have "*categorical* validity" (*SM* VII.219). Such moral judgments thus exhibit "objectivity" in that "there is, in principle, a decision procedure with respect to specific ethical statements"; and Sellars sees "no reason why this objectivity should not be said to legitimate the use of the concepts of truth and falsity with respect to ethical discourse" (*SM* VII.133). (Recall chapter 6 on truth as assertibility in accordance with different semantic rules appropriate to different modes of discourse.[9])

Sellars believes that these "considerations pertaining to the conceptual structure of the moral point of view amount to a thoroughly Kantian metaphysics of morals" (*SM* II.134). One among several Kantian conclusions he draws from the above analysis concerns the "conception of a moral polity – Kant's Kingdom of Ends":

> It is this conceptual feature of the moral point of view which implies the Kantian principle that everyone shall be treated as an end in itself and not as a means only. For to treat someone as a means only is, in effect, to consider his place with respect to our conduct not from the point of view
>
> > We would that . . .
>
> but from a point of view which singles him out, by virtue of some special relation to ourselves, as an exception. It is to consider him from the point of view
>
> > I would that . . .
>
> or, at least, from the point of view of a sub-community to which I belong. (*SM* VII.134)

Sellars concedes that the "ideal knowledge" of the means that would in fact maximize our common welfare, and hence also the "ideal 'consensus' of those who share the moral point of view is only 'in principle' there" (*SM* VII.135), but he holds that this idealized status does not detract from the intersubjectivity and objectivity of the moral point of view as described above.

Sellars recognized that further concerns will arise and distinctions must be made in relation to the putatively "intrinsically categorically reasonable" intersubjective intention central to his account above, namely, that 'It shall$_{we}$ be the case that our welfare is maximized.'

One well-known difficulty, for example, is that even if on this account the implied categorical imperatives of the form, 'If in circumstance C_i, one ought to do A$_i$,' could be shown to hold for *each* rational being, Sellars admits that "it by no means follows," for all that has been said so far, "that the group whose welfare is 'our' welfare consists of rational beings generally," as Kant himself wanted to claim (*SM* VII.138). The moral point of view in the latter sense would be a universally comprehensive one:

> The recognition of each man everywhere as one of *us* was the extension of tribal loyalty which exploded it into something new. It has a precarious toehold in the world, and *we* are usually a far smaller group. Kant's conception of each *rational being* everywhere as one of us is a still more breath-taking point of view which may yet become a live option. (IIO 210)

But it might be argued that this 'may yet' is not enough, for as Sellars himself remarks, "only if the 'we' of 'our welfare' is the 'we' of 'rational beings generally' is an intersubjective intention of this form categorically valid" (*SM* VII.139). How could we be entitled to assume that rational beings in general necessarily constitute a community in the required sense?

Sellars suggests in the end that the latter "*might* [. . .] be true if the welfare in question is what might be called epistemic welfare, but not if we take into account, as we must, needs and desires generally" (*SM* VII.139). That is, *if* we could show that rational beings implicitly think of themselves "as subject to epistemic oughts binding on rational beings generally" (which, given Sellars' Kantian 'transcendental linguistics' account of epistemology discussed in chapter 5, is not implausible), and *if* we could show that promoting our epistemic welfare implies the intention to promote our *general* welfare, then the wider connection with human needs, desires, and rationality generally might be made. Sellars concludes that the latter conceptual connection, however, "despite Peirce's valiant efforts, remains problematic, and without it the reality of an *ethical* community consisting of all rational beings [. . .] remains incomplete" (*SM* VII.145).

One final and revealing concern has to do with how the above Sellarsian account of our obligations in terms of categorically valid intersubjective intentions would handle the following sort of challenge to the entire framework. Sellars imagines someone asking: "Granted that I and my fellow man have been brought up to have such and such impersonal commitments concerning what is to be done in various kinds of circumstances, is there any reason why I should not let these commitments wither away and encourage self-regarding attitudes, attitudes which, in the vernacular, look out for Number One?" (SE 231). This is roughly the question often discussed in recent moral philosophy under the heading, 'Why be moral?' Some philosophers argue that the question is somehow to be ruled out of court as absurd, but Sellars does not take that tack. When pushed from this direction, his moral philosophy arguably shows itself in the end to have a distinctly Humean underpinning. At the end of the day, Sellars suggests, it is our ground-level commitment or *concern for others' well-being* that provides the only *direct* support for the moral point of view when it is put under such pressure. (Once again we see that on Sellars' 'naturalism with a normative turn' a robustly naturalistic Humean picture of reality typically underlies his various Kantian conceptual analyses, as their ultimate causal presupposition.) Hence this commitment is the *sine qua non* for all of the Kantian categorical principles and 'means–end' reasoning that has been embedded within it on the above analysis:

> [T]he only frame of mind which can provide direct support for moral commitment is what [Josiah] Royce called Loyalty, and what Christians call Love of Neighbor (*caritas*). This is a commitment deeper than any commitment to abstract principles. It is a precious thing, the foundation for which is laid in earliest childhood. [. . .] Recent psychological studies make clear what has always, in a sense, been known, that the ability to love others for their own sakes is as essential to a full life as the need to feel ourselves loved and appreciated for our own sakes, unconditionally, and not as something turned on or off depending on what we do. Thus, in a deeper sense, really intelligent and informed self-love supports, and can be an incentive to forming, the love of neighbor which, nevertheless, alone gives *direct* support to the moral point of view when we are alone in that cool hour. (IIO 212; cf. SE 231–2)

Sellars' account of practical reason and the moral 'ought' is rich and suggestive, and well worth the attention of anyone interested in current meta-ethical debates concerning 'internalism,' for instance. One does get a sense of unfinished business in relation to Sellars' discussions of moral philosophy proper, but as in so many other areas there is no doubt that here, too, there are insights that have yet to be mined from his technically detailed and historically informed investigations (see Hurley 2000 for one recent example).

Persons in the synoptic vision

With more of the rich background account of the nature of normative principles and human agency behind us, we can now close with a few final reflections on the place of persons within Sellars' stereoscopic vision, in particular in relation to what we have seen to be the hard-cutting Sellarsian "thesis of the primacy of the scientific image" (PSIM 38).

First, a few words on a classical philosophical problem in this connection to which Sellars devoted careful attention: the problem of free will and determinism (see FD, RD, and for a clear overview, Gutting 1977). Sellars defended a sophisticated version of the classical *compatibilist* approach according to which, very roughly, a free action is one that follows from an intention or volition, as on the account above, and which one was not *compelled* to do in the circumstances. If one had willed to perform an alternative action, one was in a position to have done so. The anti-compatibilist typically objects to this view that, since the compatibilist admits that *everything* that happens – including my action and my willing – is causally determined (physically necessitated) by the antecedent state of the universe, neither my action nor my willing was avoidable in the actual circumstances, and so on the assumption of determinism I was prevented from willing and so acting otherwise than I did. Sellars' novel rebuttal to this classical objection ultimately involves his distinguishing "between deterministic pseudo-circumstances and genuine circumstances," where it "is with reference to 'real' circumstances that abilities and hindrances are defined": "Thus, as I see it, we are often prevented by real circumstances from willing as we did not will. But the 'metaphysical' circumstances implied by determinism do not render us *unable to will to do* what we did not do, and therefore do not, indirectly, render us *unable to do* what we did not do" (FD 174).

Sellars' distinction here between *real* circumstances and deterministic *pseudo*-circumstances of an action or a willing, I suggest, is based upon his wider account of the distinction between, on the one hand, the *manifest image conception* of 'being caused' to do something, or prevented from doing something, by some intervening agent (here the concept of one's *character* as opposed to one's physically determined *nature* is crucial: see PSIM II; MP III), and, on the other, the modern *scientific image conception* of determinism as universal predictability in accordance with physical law. "The distinctive trait of the scientific revolution was the conviction that all events are predictable from relevant information about the context in which they occur, not that they are all, in any ordinary sense, caused" (PSIM 14). It is the latter ordinary sense of 'caused' within the manifest image that would go toward defining those real circumstances in which an action or willing could correctly be said to be prevented. And the key synoptic point seems to be that, given Sellars' smooth functionalist integration of the nature of thoughts (and hence intentions and volitions) into the scientific image, the required manifest image distinctions between real circumstances and pseudo-circumstances, and between one's character and one's scientific nature, are contrasts that find their naturalistic embodiment within the highly complex 'realizations' of these functional distinctions within the scientific image.

This brings us, finally, to the question of how to understand the place of *persons* within the scientific image: not only as *sensing* beings, in which ideal image Sellars has argued they will be revealed to be 'bundles' of φ_2-ings and σ-ings as absolute processes; and not only as *thinking* beings, in relation to which Sellars has argued that their thoughts are rule-governed functional role-players that are realized in complex physical patterns and uniformities; but also as the *intentional, rational agents* who, among other things, *make the rules.* "From this point of view," as Sellars puts it in the closing stages of 'Philosophy and the Scientific Image of Man', "the irreducible core of the framework of persons" is "the irreducibility of the 'ought' to the 'is' " (PSIM 39). This leads Sellars directly into a brief synopsis of his account of the nature of normative principles, which is what we have examined in the preceding section. In the final paragraph of PSIM, however, he then attempts to bring the whole story together as follows:

> Thus the conceptual framework of persons is the framework in which we think of one another as sharing the community intentions which provide the ambience of principles and standards (above all, those which make meaningful discourse and rationality itself possible) within which we live our own individual lives. A person can almost be defined as a being that has intentions. Thus the conceptual framework of persons is not something that needs to be *reconciled with* the scientific image, but rather something to be *joined* to it. Thus, to complete the scientific image we need to enrich it *not* with more ways of saying what is the case, but with the language of community and individual intentions, so that by construing the actions we intend to do and the circumstances in which we intend to do them in scientific terms, we *directly* relate the world as conceived by scientific theory to our purposes, and make it *our* world and no longer an alien appendage to the world in which we do our living. We can, of course, as matters now stand, realize this direct incorporation of the scientific image into our way of life only in imagination. But to do so is, if only in imagination, to transcend the dualism of the manifest and scientific images of man-in-the-world. (PSIM 40)

There are two central points in this remarkable concluding passage. (1) The framework of persons, as the normative framework of individual and community *intentions,* is ontologically innocent or unproblematic as far as the doggedly naturalistic perspective of the scientific image is concerned ("not something that needs to be *reconciled with* the scientific image, but rather something to be *joined* to it"). And (2) it is the *contents* or subject matter of our practical thinkings or intendings, rather than their nature *per se,* that must be reconceived if we are finally to "transcend the dualism of the manifest and scientific images of man-in-the-world," for Sellars is quite explicitly putting forward the radical thesis that in the ideal synoptic integration *we would construe "the actions we intend to do and the circumstances in which we intend to do them in scientific terms"* (PSIM 40 above, italics added).

The first point might strike some contemporary philosophers as overly sanguine, for the philosophical journals are currently bristling with controversies concerning the question as to whether or not, and in what senses, normativity can be naturalized. In one sense this reveals yet another way in which Sellars can be seen in retrospect to have opened up original lines of inquiry that are now at the center of philosophical discussion. More importantly, however, the resources for addressing the question of the status of normativity itself are already at hand. As I have indicated, in my view the single most important strategy in the Sellarsian corpus was the one he initiated in particular in 'A Semantical Solution of the Mind–Body Problem' (1953) but also in other writings from the late forties and early fifties (see O'Shea 2006b). There Sellars effectively articulated the basic conceptual structure of his naturalism with a normative turn that I have encapsulated in (a), (b), and (c) above, and which we have seen Sellars put to use in attempting to unravel the central problems pertaining to the place of mind, meaning, knowledge, and truth within a scientific-naturalist ontology. The strategy has essentially been one of exposing what *seem* on the surface to be certain puzzling 'factualist' or 'ontological' questions, perennially seen as requiring the appeal to various problematic primitive relations and quasi-relations to reality, to be in reality various complex questions concerning how our multifarious and projected *rule-governed practices* are related (via (a), (b), and (c)) to the *natural-causal uniformities* which they both presuppose and partially contribute to bringing about. What Sellars saw early on was that this same strategy must apply also to normative discourse itself (as has in fact already been implicit in his detailed accounts of our pattern-governed 'language departure' transitions and of 'ought's as certain kinds of 'we'-intentions):[10]

> The situation is even clearer with respect to normative discourse. Whatever users of normative discourse may be *conveying* about themselves and their community when they use normative discourse, what they are *saying* cannot be said without using normative discourse [see (b) above]. The task of the philosopher cannot be to show how, in principle, what is said by normative discourse could be said without normative discourse, for the simple reason that this cannot be done. His task is rather to exhibit the complex relationships which exist between normative and other modes of discourse. (SSMB ¶66, p. 82)

Finally, the second point in relation to the concluding passage from PSIM above concerns Sellars' radical proposal, which we have already met both at the end of chapter 2 and in chapter 6, that in the projected ideal scientific image of the world the *contents* of our perceptual responses to the world, of our thinkings, and – as he is now pointing out – of our intentional actions within the world would all be conceptually articulated in the microphysical terms of that ideal scientific ontology itself. As those examinations revealed, in Sellars' projected synoptic integration of the manifest and scientific images there would no longer be any 'theoretical vs. observational' distinction at all – that last vestige of "dualism" would finally be transcended (PSIM 40, above). In principle, as we saw Sellars argue, "the language of physical theory [. . .] could *replace* the common-sense framework in *all* its roles" (SM V.90), and this includes the roles played by our direct perceptual responses and by our active intentional grapplings with the world that directly confronts and interests us.[11]

Is anyone *saying* anything in this ideal, stereoscopically integrated image of persons-in-the-world? If so, then their sayings and doings about and amongst the microphysical phenomena will be normatively governed by whatever shared intentions will have generated the implicit principles that have given them a *knowable world* for their sayings and doings to be about in the first place. This, once again, is Sellars' normative-linguistic version of Kant's Copernican revolution in philosophy.

It is not easy to grasp Sellars' account of the unity of ourselves as persons in this final synoptic vision without illicitly reintroducing the more 'substantial' ontological categories of the manifest image into that ideal synoptic vision. In chapters 2 and 6, however, it was clearly shown that on Sellars' conception of the ideal scientific image of the world our current 'methodological dependence' on the categories of the manifest perceptible world, and the theory–observation dualism itself, would finally be transcended: "[T]he world of theory and the world of observation would be one" (TE 155). On Sellars' ideally integrated synoptic vision we would finally be in a position to "abandon mediation by substantive correspondence rules": those currently indispensable methodological crutches that serve to link our micro-theories to the superseded ontology of the manifest-perceptible world. We would have achieved, in all the dimensions of perceiving, representing, thinking, intending, and acting, "a direct commerce of the conceptual framework of theory with the world" (SRII 189). The scientifically conceived world, on Sellars' Peircean regulative ideal, would finally be *our* world, and the philosophical alienation discussed in chapter 1 would be overcome. (It is already overcome, "if only in imagination.")

What there ultimately *really* is, for Sellars, is what the ontology of the ideal scientific image finally says that there is. So we persons, too, like everything else in nature, are ultimately complex patterns and sequences of 'pure processes.' How is that ontological vision consistent with the irreducible conceptual unity of the person as a self-conscious, deliberative agent? Sellars' contention all along has been that, once again, it was Kant who had the key insight (assuming, of course, that we replace Kant's unknowable 'things in themselves' with the micro-ontology of the ideal scientific image):

> The heart of the matter is the fact that the irreducibility of the 'I' within the framework of first person discourse [. . .] is compatible with the thesis that persons can (in principle) be exhaustively described in terms which involve no reference to such an irreducible subject. For the description will *mention* rather than *use* the framework to which these logical subjects belong. Kant saw that the transcendental unity of apperception is a form of experience rather than a disclosure of ultimate reality. If persons are 'really' multiplicities of logical subjects, then unless these multiplicities used the conceptual framework of persons there would be no persons. But the idea that persons 'really are' such multiplicities does not require that concepts pertaining to persons be *analysable into* concepts pertaining to sets of logical subjects. Persons may 'really be' bundles, but the concept of a person is not the concept of a bundle. (PH 101)

On Sellars' naturalism with a normative turn, then, the normative conceptual framework of persons, too, is 'logically irreducible' yet 'causally reducible' to the categorial ontology of the ideal scientific image. Making sense of the details of that distinction has throughout been central to our attempt to come to terms with Sellars' quest for a synoptic vision of our own ultimate place in the overall scheme of things.

Notes

Introduction

1   The following is an over-simplified account of 'the given'; see chapter
    5 for the details. References to Sellars' works are given by abbrevia-
    tions listed in the bibliography. In 1956 Sellars delivered three lectures
    at the University of London entitled 'The Myth of the Given: Three
    Lectures on Empiricism and the Philosophy of Mind,' published that
    same year as EPM in the first volume of the *Minnesota Studies in the
    Philosophy of Science*. References to EPM in this work will be to its
    sixteen parts and sixty-three sections, for example 'EPM III.17' is part
    III, section 17. (Section numbers 9 and 16 were mistakenly repeated in
    EPM; references to these will simply cover both repeated sections.)
    The same 'chapter.section' format will be used for many of his other
    works as well; otherwise page references are given.
       EPM has recently been reprinted in its entirety with excellent
    section by section introductory commentaries by deVries and Triplett
    (2000) and Brandom (1997). These are highly recommended editions
    for students and scholars alike.

2   Many students of philosophy have recently had their interest awak-
    ened in Sellars through their encounters with the constructive uses
    made of his views on the myth of the given and the 'logical space of
    reasons' in three highly influential books: Richard Rorty's *Philosophy
    and the Mirror of Nature* (1979), Robert Brandom's *Making It Explicit*
    (1994), and John McDowell's *Mind and World* (1994). We shall have
    occasion to refer to these important works in what follows, but the
    aims of this book preclude the sort of detailed engagement with them
    that they deserve. In a paper delivered at a conference in honor of the
    fiftieth anniversary of Sellars' delivery of EPM at University College
    London, entitled 'On the Structure of Sellars' Naturalism with a Nor-
    mative Turn' (O'Shea 2006b), I discuss the relationship between Sellars'

own views and the works of both the above 'left-wing' Sellarsians and other 'right-wing' Sellarsians, as they have been called. (See also O'Shea 2002.)

3 Throughout the text I shall use both 'man-in-the-world' (generally in single quotes) to recall Sellars' own phrase, but also various more explicitly neutral equivalents such as 'human-being-in-the-world,' in keeping with more recent usage.

4 For these brief biographical remarks I have relied primarily upon Sellars' own 'Autobiographical Reflections' (AR). Both that article and several interesting memorials to Sellars by philosophers are available on the 'Problems from Wilfrid Sellars' website (see under Chrucky in the bibliography). I have also consulted the biographical accounts in deVries 2005 and Brandom 2000b. More detailed work on Sellars' life will be made possible as his collected papers at the University of Pittsburgh are currently being made available to scholars.

5 See Wilfrid Sellars' own contribution to a symposium held in honor of his father's philosophy in 1954, entitled 'Physical Realism' (PR), and also 'The Double-Knowledge Approach to the Mind–Body Problem' (DKMB, 1971). Jaegwon Kim has recently remarked, in an incisive historical and conceptual examination of the nature of philosophical naturalism, that to "see that American naturalists held substantive doctrines in metaphysics and epistemology as constitutive of their naturalism, it is useful to go back to earlier naturalists, in particular, Roy Wood Sellars, a philosopher whose work, in my view, has been unjustly neglected" (Kim 2003: 88).

6 For a good recent defense of critical realism from a Sellarsian perspective, see Coates forthcoming.

7 For an overview of the period, which includes a brief comparison of the views of Roy Wood Sellars and Wilfrid Sellars in relation to wider philosophical developments, see O'Shea forthcoming, 'American Philosophy in the Twentieth Century.'

8 Sellars' best-known collection of published articles is his *Science, Perception and Reality* (*SPR*, 1963). His important early essays were usefully collected by Jeffrey Sicha in *Pure Pragmatics and Possible Worlds* (*PPPW*, 1980). *Science and Metaphysics* (*SM*, 1967) and *Naturalism and Ontology* (*NAO*, 1980) were stand-alone books based primarily on the prestigious John Locke and John Dewey lecture series Sellars delivered at Oxford and Chicago, respectively. Two other major collections of his articles are *Philosophical Perspectives* (1967, later in two volumes: *PPHP: History of Philosophy* and *PPME: Metaphysics and Epistemology*), and *Essays in Philosophy and its History* (*EPH*, 1974). Apart from *EPH*, we have Jeffrey Sicha and Ridgeview Publishing Company (Atascadero, CA: *http://www.ridgeviewpublishing.com*) to thank for the currently available editions of all of these and other works by Sellars (e.g., see also *ME*, *KTM*, and *KPT* listed in the bibliography).

Chapter 1   The Philosophical Quest and the Clash of Images

1   The notion of a 'conceptual framework' or 'conceptual scheme' is not philosophically uncontroversial, and has been challenged in different ways by W. V. O. Quine and Donald Davidson in particular. In chapter 3 and elsewhere in what follows we shall see that Sellars attempted to defend a substantive account of the nature of meaning and of conceptual categories which underpins his use of the notion of conceptual frameworks.

2   The 'perennial philosophy' stretches from the Pre-Socratics, Plato, and Aristotle through Descartes, Kant, and Hegel to Husserl, Wittgenstein, and Strawson, to take the leading exemplars. "It should be clear," Sellars remarks in 'The Structure of Knowledge', "that I regard Aristotle as *the* philosopher of the Manifest Image" (SK I.29). However, we shall find in later chapters that both Kant and the later Wittgenstein in particular added crucial insights to the correct conception of the manifest image within the perennial philosophy. We shall also find that on Sellars' view certain naturalistic philosophical renegades such as Hobbes and Hume anticipated crucial aspects of the emerging ideal scientific image of man-in-the-world, but that in the premature form in which they did so they lost some of the enduring insights articulated by the mainstream perennial or 'broadly Platonic' tradition.

3   That is, unless our sense perceptions are themselves conceptually structured by those micro-theoretical concepts that are presupposed in our successful use of scientific instruments, such as electron microscopes and the like – a topic which will be central to Sellars' scientific realism as discussed in chapter 2. As we shall see, all of our adult sense perceptions are *concept*-laden, according to Sellars. However, taking vision as our lead example, the concepts that structure our perceptions within the manifest image are essentially concerned with the properties of color and shape that we 'see of' the facing sides of objects with our unaided vision. Chapter 5 will explore Sellars' views on the nature of sense perception in considerable detail. (The 'proper sensibles' are roughly those perceptible qualities proper to each sense, such as sound to hearing or color to sight, while the 'common sensibles' such as motion and shape are perceptible to several senses in common.)

4   Actually, the scientific ontologies were not always conceived atomistically or in terms of solid, indivisible particles moving in a void. Descartes, for example, held that matter was a continuous fluid-like ether, and Kant devised one of the first complex 'field of force' conceptions of the nature of (Newtonian) matter. The key point, however, is that on all of these scientific conceptions a *prima facie* problem arose from the fact that matter as so conceived is ultimately characterized by properties and relations the appeal to which – to put it very loosely for now – does not seem sufficient to account for the intrinsic properties of the sensuous colors, sounds, tastes, warmth, smells, etc., as we

consciously experience them. (Note that this problem confronts us, according to Sellars, whether or not the latter 'manifest' properties are conceived to be properties of ordinary objects or rather of our own sensations.)

5 Recall Sellars' remark quoted earlier that it is only when we have eaten the apple of philosophical and scientific reflection that we begin to "stumble on the familiar and to feel that haunting sense of alienation" (SK I.3).

6 For philosophical criticism of Eddington's description of the 'two' tables, see Stebbing 1937. Sellars would in one sense agree with Stebbing's charge that Eddington confuses and runs together aspects of the separate conceptual frameworks of the manifest and scientific images. However, Sellars would disagree with the idea, which was popular among so-called 'ordinary language' philosophers, that simply properly *distinguishing* between these frameworks *by itself* resolves the crucial problems that arise when we consider how they are both supposed to succeed in describing the same world. (See also chapter 2 below against 'irenic' approaches to this problem.) There is accordingly a grain of truth in Eddington's witty reply to Stebbing's criticism:

> Some of the pure philosophers deny that the scientific description applies to the objects which in ordinary speech are called physical objects. Their opinion is voiced by Prof. Stebbing: 'He [the physicist] has never been concerned with *chairs*, and it lies beyond his competence to inform us that the chairs we sit upon are abstract.' Physicists are not concerned with chairs! Are we really expected to take this sitting down? (Eddington 1938: 159)

Underlying this disagreement are highly complex issues concerning the relationships between different conceptual schemes, and they will be examined further in chapters 2 and 6.

7 See PSIM V, PH 103–5, SSIS, and FMPP III. References to a small fraction of the resulting secondary literature on this issue will be provided in chapter 6 below.

8 A multi-colored object is ultimately homogeneously colored in the sense Sellars has in mind here. The point is roughly that each colored expanse of the object is *perceived as being* smoothly or 'continuously' colored in all its *perceptible sub-regions*, too, rather than being particulate or 'gappy' in the sense of having non-colored sub-regions.

9 In chapters 2, 5, and 6 we shall note various alternative theories of perception that would reject Sellars' analysis of the status of color and other sensible qualities within the manifest image.

Chapter 2 Scientific Realism and the Scientific Image

1 The *observable/unobservable* (or perceptible/imperceptible) distinction is importantly ambiguous, and will be at the center of our attention throughout this chapter.

2 Further issues pertaining to *conceptual change* and *theory succession* in the scientific image will be taken up again in chapter 6.

3 See PSIM, TE, SRII, and SRT. For a classic treatment of scientific explanation and inter-theoretic reduction as applied to the case of the kinetic theory of gases, see Ernest Nagel's *The Structure of Science* (1961: 342ff.) – a book which, in the judgment of Sellars in 1965, "not only continues the classical tradition on this subject, but is itself already a classic" (SRII 157).

4 The senses in which the molecules and other theoretical entities are, or are not, 'unobservable' will also be at the center of the dispute below.

5 Throughout this chapter I will assume in the background rather than explicitly represent the *initial conditions* that must be specified in any adequate logical reconstruction of explanation by derivation of cases from general laws. For a good introduction to the standard empiricist account of explanation, see Hempel 1966.

6 This standard logical empiricist view of explanation is also variously called the 'nomological-deductive' (from '*nomos*,' *law*, and deductive subsumption), the 'hypothetico-deductive,' or the Hempelian (after Carl Hempel) 'covering law' model of explanation.

7 We shall see that on Sellars' own conception of the 'observable/unobservable' contrast, there will be one *strict* sense of perceptual observation (namely, of *manifest image perceptibles*) according to which molecules are in principle unobservable; but there is also a wider sense of observation as causally reliable non-inferential response classifications, according to which molecules are properly conceived by the appropriately trained physicist to be *observable* (for example, by means of electron microscopes). Again, more on this important contrast later in this chapter.

8 To give an indication of the general sort of difficulties that such strictly reductionist empiricist approaches encountered, the attempts to explicitly define such terms as 'molecule' in terms of actual and possible sense experiences or measurements turned out to be highly implausible. Roughly speaking, this is because the various theoretical concepts that are inter-defined within the kinetic theory, or (to use one technical term) are 'implicitly defined' by the theory's postulates, cannot be pinned down one-to-one to specific operational procedures or other possible experiences. For example, in the kinetic theory the velocity of *individual* molecules cannot be linked by a correspondence rule to observables, while the average value of the velocities of all the molecules can. This led to more holistic approaches in terms of 'partial interpretations' of theoretical terms, as briefly discussed in the text.

9 There were complex debates throughout this period among logical empiricists as to the correct logical form of these more liberal correspondence rules. In particular, our representation of them as biconditionals, '$O_1 \leftrightarrow T_1$,' above was gradually seen to be too strong and was weakened in various ways that we need not explore in detail or represent here. For a clear yet sophisticated discussion, see Carnap 1956.

10 The interested reader who is unfamiliar with these particular issues will find them discussed under such headings in the philosophy of science as 'Craig's theorem,' 'Ramsey sentences,' and 'Hempel's Theoretician's Dilemma.'

11 On the one hand Hempel indicates that theoretical terms may be construed along realist lines as having "factual reference if what the theory says is true" (Hempel 1958). In the same place, however, he suggests along standard empiricist lines that such theories are also capable of construal for other philosophical purposes "not as significant statements, but as intricate devices for inferring" within the empirical domain alone, thereby construing "theoretical terms as meaningless auxiliary marks, which serve as convenient symbolic devices in the transition from one set of experiential statements to another" (Hempel 1958: 221).

12 Without being able to enter into the matter here, I would argue that the irenic approaches discussed in this chapter and criticized by Sellars bear important similarities to more recent *quietist* as well as *pluralist* responses to realism vs. anti-realism controversies. Here I briefly discuss Strawson as just one such example.

13 For a contemporary of Sellars' offering a scientific realist criticism of Nagel's move here, see Maxwell 1962: 20ff.

14 Carnap's distinction between framework 'internal' and cross-framework 'external' questions (Carnap 1950) is another, particularly important example for Sellars of a broadly 'irenic,' pluralist approach to the ostensible conflict between various conceptual frameworks.

15 Sellars agreed with some of the standard criticisms of the logical empiricist account of explanation as the deductive derivation of laws from theories and the subsumption of observations under 'covering laws' (Hempel), as for example in the well-known insightful criticisms of Michael Scriven, whom Sellars cites at LT 120n. As far as I am aware, however, both Sellars' particular way of criticizing the standard empiricist account of explanation and the particular way in which he defends scientific realism as a result of that critique were original arguments unique to him (in some respects they are perhaps also evident in the early articles of Paul Feyerabend), and both are different from the more usual criticisms of empiricism and the standard arguments for scientific realism discussed in the literature.

16 Sellars here adds in a footnote: "The same is true in principle – though in a way which is methodologically more complex – of micro-micro-theories about microtheoretical objects." We shall see the significance

of this remark below in our brief discussion of the distinction between 'theory/theory' and 'theory/empirical' correspondence rules.

17 The relevant sense of 'is' in which a gas 'is' a cloud of molecules has to do with the definitional *identities* that Sellars contends are established by substantive correspondence rules in theoretical explanation (see TE in particular). We shall see a bit more about this in a moment.

18 The empiricist has other potent weapons in her arsenal. For example, she may appeal to the idea (which the scientific realist may dispute) that there are actual or at any rate possible cases in which *alternative incompatible theories* equally well accommodate all the relevant facts to be explained within a given domain (perhaps quantum physics provides such a case). This is an important issue, but Sellars' argument as I reconstruct it undercuts the empiricist account at the more basic level *of the empirical generalizations themselves*, whether or not they might be accommodated by possible alternative incompatible theories.

19 See also on this topic Gary Gutting's helpful dialogue between a Sellarsian scientific realist and a constructive empiricist (1982). On important disputes concerning scientific realism in general, see Jarrett Leplin's edited collection (1984).

20 The 'so to speak' qualification will be clarified in chapter 6 on Sellars' views on *conceptual change*.

21 Of course, an empiricist such as van Fraassen can retrench again at this new level by arguing that the realist's quest for counterfactual-sustaining *laws* is a demand (along with strong requirements on 'explanation') that the empiricist does not find necessary in order to give an accurate account of what needs saving in good scientific practices. For example, perhaps symmetry considerations are arguably more important than laws in quantum physics. I am indebted to Jack Ritchie for discussions as to how van Fraassen might plausibly fend off the considerations advanced by Sellars here, which certainly remains a topic for further investigation than I can pursue in this context.

22 For further insightful discussion of these points, see Lange 2000. In my reconstruction of Sellars' central argument for scientific realism I have benefited from Lange's discussion of Sellars and the *salience* of empirical kinds and laws.

23 On this point see Sellars' argument in SRII against Ernest Nagel's irenic view in particular.

24 In this respect Sellars' strong scientific realism has perhaps in a sense retained the classical logical *structure* of the standard empiricist's emphasis on the decisive role of direct observations, while nonetheless entirely transforming the account of the *conceptual content* of our basic observations of the world. This is why the rejection of the 'myth of the (empiricist) given' is so crucial to Sellars' account of the ultimate resolution of the clash of the images. Our most basic, logically atomic observations will, at the end of the day for Sellars, turn out to be

theory-contaminated observations of scientifically characterized 'pure processes,' as we shall see during the course of chapter 6.

25 See deVries 2005, ch. 10 for an exploration of this important issue in relation to Sellars' overall synoptic vision; and see chapters 6 and 7 below.

26 Thus the following remark of Sellars' on the previous 'theory/empirical' case applies in an analogous manner to the 'theory/theory' case as well: "[. . .] to offer the theory is to claim that the theoretical language could beat the observation language *at its own game* without loss of scientific meaning" (LT 126).

Chapter 3   Meaning and Abstract Entities

1 'Intentionality' in this sense is not to be confused with the more specific notion of *doing* something 'intentionally.' The former is the more basic notion, in that it concerns the possibility of having *any* thoughts, concepts, beliefs, desires, etc., with 'content' at all (hence, 'intentional content'): that is, of having any mental states that are signs of or are *about* something beyond themselves, whether such mental states are mobilized in intentional action or merely in absent-minded contemplation.

2 For more recent semantic theories that are directly inspired by Sellars' functional role account of meaning to be examined in this chapter, see in particular Brandom 1994, or to begin with, 2000a; Lance and O'Leary-Hawthorne 1997; Rosenberg 1974; and more broadly, a variety of other theorists who today may be found working under the broad rubric of *conceptual role semantics*. Also in the philosophy of mind, Daniel Dennett, Ruth Millikan, Gilbert Harman, William Lycan, and Ned Block are just a few among the many well-known philosophers who have explicitly been at least partly influenced by Sellars' functional role semantics.

John McDowell (1994) presents an interesting case of an influential philosopher who is profoundly influenced by Sellars' overall philosophical outlook, but who nonetheless seeks to preserve Sellars' epistemological insights within a steadfastly *relational* (broadly Davidsonian), and hence fundamentally *non*-Sellarsian outlook on mind and meaning. McDowell argues that Sellars had a 'blindspot' in relation to the possibilities for a plausibly holistic, truth-conditional semantics (see, for example, McDowell's 'Woodbridge Lectures', 1998, lecture 3). Unfortunately I shall have to leave exploration of the relationship between the views of Sellars and McDowell to another occasion.

3 Donald Davidson's truth-conditional theory of meaning as well as a host of versions of 'possible worlds semantics' deriving from well-known works by Saul Kripke, Hilary Putnam, and David Lewis have been particularly influential world-relational outlooks on meaning.

4 The question of the nature of Carnap's views and their evolution (for example, in response to Tarski's work on truth) is a matter of considerable complexity. An excellent place to start is J. Alberto Coffa's *The Semantic Tradition from Kant to Carnap: To the Vienna Station* (1991). I have here presented Carnap's theory of meaning as if it were a straightforward truth-conditional semantics, which is both convenient for present purposes and true of many aspects and stages of his thought. However, in other respects his various emphases on meaning as determined by *rules*, particularly at the metalinguistic level, suggest a view of meaning that is closer in spirit to (and strongly influenced) Sellars' own 'non-relational' or functional role account of meaning.

5 It should be noted that (early) Frege, like Carnap, can also be interpreted (as by Brandom, for example) in ways that bring his views closer to the non-relational, inferentialist outlook defended by Sellars.

6 The appeal to possible worlds is a currently widespread way of pursuing the same broadly relational semantic strategy, and was in fact pioneered and explored in detail by Carnap himself in his *Meaning and Necessity* (1947). Such a formal semantics might attempt to effect a complete or partial 'extensionalist reduction' of intensional entities by showing how the latter may be defined in terms of sets of possible worlds. For example (let us assume that the number of planets in our solar system is nine), we can provide a logically impressive extensionalist semantics for the intensional proposition, 'necessarily, 9 > 7,' which neatly distinguishes its truth-conditions from the contingent proposition, 'the number of planets in our solar system > 7,' despite the co-reference to the same number, nine. Basically, the former is interpreted as holding in *all*, the latter only in *some* possible, worlds. Broadly speaking, in possible worlds semantics the intension of an expression is given a truth-conditional interpretation in terms of its extension across different possible worlds and occupants of those worlds.

7 One has to be careful in handling the slogan 'the meaning of a term is *use*.' Sellars will endorse the idea that the meaning of a term is its use in a "non-instrumental sense of 'use' " (*NAO* V.47), according to which, as he puts it, "the meaning of an expression is its 'use' (*in the sense of function*)" (*NAO* IV.64, italics added). In this sense, as he had earlier put it in 1950, the "linguistic meaning of a word is entirely constituted by the rules of its use" (LRB ¶22; note that *PPPW* in its 2005 printing ends Sellars' sentence with "uses" rather than "use" as in the original edition).

In his famous correspondence with Chisholm, however, Sellars also wrote: "I would be the last person to say that 'the meaning of a term is its use', for there is no sense of 'use' which *analyses* the relevant sense of 'means' " (ITM 525). Sellars' main concern in this connection is to carefully distinguish his functional-role-in-the-language account of 'use' from the sort of view that analyzes word-meaning in terms of people's *intentions to use* words (instrumentally) to achieve various ends of communication. For Sellars it is crucial to see that the former is conceptually prior to the latter, as we shall see in chapter 4.

See Jay Rosenberg's *Linguistic Representation* (1974), ch. 2, 'A Mentalist Theory,' for a detailed Sellarsian criticism of the arguably Cartesian explanatory priorities that are entailed by the 'agent-semantics' of Strawson, Austin, Grice, and Searle.

8 Sellars notes that it won't quite do to say that what (M) is asserting is the closely related claim:

   (M*) 'Und' functions in German as 'and' functions in English

   For instance, some Spanish speaker could happen to know that (M*) is true without knowing either English or German. Furthermore, in order to avoid certain technical objections having to do with Church's 'translation test,' it is important to stress that (M) presupposes that 'and' is in *our* language, i.e., (M) is addressed to another *user* of 'and,' one who already knows the functional role (the meaning) of 'and' in English (cf. ITM 532, CDCM 284).

9 See, for example, *NAO* IV.44n and IV.63n for Sellars' emphasis that it "is, of course, an over-simplification to speak of 'the' function of a certain expression in a given language. Classifications are always relative to a purpose," and "the use of such illustrating sortals is flexible, criteria of application shifting with context and purpose" (*NAO* IV.63n). Again, it "should be clear that in this reconstruction 'sameness of meaning' is simply the *extremum* of similarity of meaning. If to say what an expression means is to classify it, the relevant philosophical point is that classification requires criteria, and that the criteria for classification under a sortal are typically flexible" (TTP 296). See also *SM* V.37–47 for an application of these points to the case of conceptual change over time, for example in science (and see chapter 6, below).

10 Sellars marked the ambiguity involved in such quotations by also developing a device of star-quotation, where '*and*' is a common noun that picks out the range of *structural* sign-designs that count as cases of the English word 'and' (for example, 'and' in different font-styles), as opposed to the purely *functional* and cross-language common noun '•and•.'

11 Here we brush over some important questions concerning the nature of predication and the semantic function of predicates, for example in relation to Frege's distinction between objects and concepts – not to mention Sellars' own view of predicates as being in principle 'dispensable.' See the discussion of 'picturing' in chapter 6 below.

12 According to Kant, as Sellars plausibly reads him, such traditional metaphysical categorial concepts as those of *substance* and *causality* are ultimately second-order concepts that (roughly speaking) characterize those representational functions that any first-order sensory-cognitive conceptual system must realize if it is to succeed in representing an objective world of empirical objects (see in particular TTC and KTE).

13 Johanna Seibt (1990) offers a detailed examination of Sellars' thoroughgoing nominalism, emphasizing its importance throughout

Sellars' philosophy and comparing it favorably to other recent versions of nominalism such as Quine's.

14 A good place to start for further exploration of the technical adequacy of Sellars' theory of abstract entities is Loux 1977, 1978, and Seibt 1990.

15 See Loux 1978: 247 and Seibt 1990: 27 on Sellars and the platonism issue, including Seibt's attempted defense of Sellars. And for a recent defense of Sellars on the issues that divide him from Quine in relation to ontological commitment and the dispute concerning the 'objectual' vs. 'substitutional' interpretations of the quantifiers, see Lance 1996; but see also Sicha 1978 for an importantly different take on this latter issue in relation to Sellars.

16 See, for example, Quine 1981. It is interesting to note that debates concerning these competing conceptions of 'naturalism' go back a generation in American philosophy to debates that Sellars' father, Roy Wood Sellars, had with some of the naturalists associated with Columbia University. Roughly speaking, in recent discussions *methodological* naturalism is based on a rejection of 'First Philosophy' and on a conception of scientific method and good scientific theories (*whatever* kinds of entities this method and these theories end up positing); as opposed to naturalism as a *substantive* position in ontology and epistemology of a sort that would in principle be inconsistent with positing such 'supernatural' entities as gods, Cartesian souls, and real Platonic Forms or Essences. In the earlier debates Roy Wood Sellars felt that philosophers influenced by Santayana and Dewey (though not so much Dewey himself) were using 'naturalism' in a way that was consistent with positing just about anything as 'real,' as long as one could appeal to the new 'experimentalist' spirit of philosophy. Sellars' father thought of naturalism, rather, as a substantive thesis requiring the defense of a certain ontology (in his case, 'evolutionary naturalism' and 'physical realism'), backed up by a certain epistemology and philosophy of mind ('critical realism' and the 'double-knowledge approach' to the mind–body problem). Wilfrid Sellars carried on a defense of his father's more traditional substantive naturalism in all of these senses.

17 Note that Sellars here runs together such intensional abstract entities as propositions and attributes with such extensional abstract entities as classes or sets, while Quine distinguishes them and rejects the former on the grounds of their unclear identity conditions. But that point does not affect the present issue.

Chapter 4 Thought, Language, and the Myth of Genius Jones

1 For references and discussion of Sellars' account of intentions, volitions, and intentional action, see chapter 7 below.

2 It will turn out on Sellars' view that there are three importantly different senses in which linguistic behavior 'expresses' thoughts: (1) a

causal sense, (2) a logical or semantic sense, and (3) in some cases the sense of being the result of the deliberate *action* involved in intentional 'speech acts' (see LTC IX). (1) Inner thinkings will turn out to be causally 'prior in the order of being' to their linguistic *expression*₁ in speech and writing. (2) The appropriate verbal utterance 'that *p*' in a given language – which on Sellars' account will turn out to be 'prior in the order of our knowledge' to our conception of *inner* thinkings – *expresses*₂ the 'abstract,' i.e., cross-language, propositional content or role, •*p*•. And (3) we do on occasion engage in goal-oriented uses of language to *express*₃ our thoughts and achieve various aims by means of deliberate 'speech acts.' (The latter 'action' dimension of linguistic activity (3), while pragmatically and socially indispensable, is on Sellars' view both epistemologically and ontologically 'posterior' to dimensions (1) and (2).)

3 Jerry Fodor has vigorously defended semantic and conceptual atomism in the philosophy of mind, criticizing along the way a wide variety of holistic theses. See, for example, Fodor and Lepore 1992. The 'name-designates-object' approach to meaning that was briefly discussed in chapter 3, including the 'Augustinian' approaches to language that are criticized at the outset of Wittgenstein's *Philosophical Investigations*, are classical examples of atomistic as opposed to holistic approaches to meaning and conceptual content. Since the 1970s most atomistic approaches, such as Fodor's, have attempted to explain meaning and reference in terms of relations of *causal* covariance or counterfactual dependence obtaining between concepts and their objects.

4 The quotation is from *NAO* IV.29, originally from 'Meaning as Functional Classification' (1974) (which was reprinted in *Naturalism and Ontology*, chapter IV, sections I–VII and X).

5 In his various writings John McDowell (in particular in his *Mind and World*, chapter IV) has developed a notion of our 'second nature' conceptual capacities that plays a role within his own outlook that roughly corresponds to the role of socially acquired pattern-governed verbal behavior within Sellars' philosophy. A proper investigation of the similarities and differences between the views of Sellars and McDowell (and between each of those thinkers and Robert Brandom's explicitly Sellarsian 'inferentialist' theory of conceptual content) is outside the scope of the present work, although we shall have occasion to refer to the views of McDowell and Brandom again. These are lively and important topics of current philosophical controversy to be explored by anyone interested in Sellars' philosophy.

6 Those who are familiar with debates in modern philosophy of language will immediately call to mind the views of Austin, Strawson, Grice, or Searle.

7 Roughly speaking, as we shall see in chapter 7, on Sellars' view volitions (language exit transitions) are 'I shall do *A*' intentions that are *now* coming to fruition. Intentions are propositionally contentful thoughts ('I shall cross the road') that causally trigger corresponding

behaviors (my crossing the road) in anyone who has successfully acquired the •shall• role in any language. This parallels his account of perceptions in the reverse causal direction: perceptual knowings are propositionally and sensorily contentful thoughts ('I see the red table over there') that are causally triggered by corresponding states of affairs in the world (the presence of a red table).

I might note also for those who are familiar with disputes in the philosophy of action that Sellars' account of intentions and volitions as 'non-actions' enables him to avoid a classic regress objection to any account of action that involves appeal to volitions. The objection basically raises the question as to whether the acts of volition allegedly required for actions are themselves little inner actions that require prior volitions, thus leading to a vicious regress. Gilbert Ryle in *The Concept of Mind*, for example, attempted thereby to impugn the notion that there are such mental events as volitions at all. Sellars' functionalist account of intentions and volitions as mental acts or events that are *non-actions* is immune to that particular sort of objection.

For much more on Sellars' sophisticated theory of intentional action than I can cover in this introductory treatment, see Sellars' TA, VR, MP, and *SM* chapter 7, and references in chapter 7 below.

8 Or equivalently and more realistically, the child's dispositions are such that she will *not* move from '*x* is red all over' to '*x* is green.'

Material inferences are contrasted by Sellars with *formal* inferences (see, e.g., IM, SRLG, and ITSA). Formal inferences or primitive sentences are such that their validity does not depend on the contents of the terms or predicates they contain: for example, 'if *x* is a man and *x* is tall, then *x* is tall.' Material inferences or primitive sentences are such that their validity does depend on the particular contents of the predicates involved; for example: 'if *x* is copper, then *x* conducts electricity.' In the articles mentioned, Sellars argues that such material inferences, which roughly speaking amount to a standing permission to infer from '*x* is *A*' to '*x* is *B*' within a given conceptual framework, are an *irreducible* feature of any empirically meaningful conceptual framework.

In particular Sellars argues that such direct inferential connections between formal-logically distinct conceptual contents (*A* and *B*) are not best explained as being mere enthymemes the validity of which derives from corresponding formal arguments such as: 'All *A* are *B*. This *x* is an *A*. Therefore, this *x* is a *B*.' (For a detailed and systematic defense of central aspects of Sellars' conception of the irreducibility of material inferences, see Brandom 1994, especially chapter 2.)

This conception of material inferences is central to Sellars' entire theory of meaning, as was implicit in the discussion in chapter 3 (in ways that I have not had space to develop in detail in this introductory treatment). For example, as we saw, one does not grasp even the most basic of conceptual contents, such as •*x* is red•, unless one's linguistic dispositions are structured by such non-formal, material inference principles as 'if x is red, then x is colored.' And as the 'x is copper $\rightarrow$ x conducts electricity' example might suggest, Sellars' account of *causal laws* and of the modalities in general is also developed on the basis of his account of normatively sanctioned material inference principles conceived as 'rules of language' within a given conceptual framework: "[T]o say that it is a law of nature that all A is B is, in effect, to say that we may infer 'x is B' from 'x is A' (a *materially* valid inference which is not to be confused with the formally valid inference from 'All A is B *and* x is A' to 'x is B')" (SRLG §29; see Sellars' CDCM for a full discussion of this last important topic).

9 "The key to the concept of a linguistic rule is its complex relation to pattern-governed linguistic behavior. The general concept of pattern-governed behavior is a familiar one. Roughly it is the concept of behavior which exhibits a pattern, not because it is brought about by the intention that it exhibit this pattern, but because the propensity to emit behavior of the pattern has been selectively reinforced, and the propensity to emit behavior which does not conform to this pattern selectively extinguished. A useful analogy is the natural selection which results in the patterns of behavior which constitutes the so-called language of bees" (*NAO* IV.27).

10 On Wittgenstein and rule-following, see Kripke 1982 and the essays collected in Miller and Wright 2002. Specifically in relation to Sellars and rule-following, see Brandom 1994 and Rosenberg 1974.

11 As to this last anti-rationalist claim in relation to Wittgenstein's rule-following paradox, Sellars would perhaps agree with Kripke's various comments (though not with all of Kripke's contentions) in his *Wittgenstein on Rules and Private Language* that Noam Chomsky's conception of innate grammatical 'competence' does not by itself resolve the rule-following issue. For as Kripke remarks, "what *is* important here is that the notion of 'competence' is itself not a dispositional notion. It is normative, not descriptive," and consequently "our understanding of the notion of 'competence' is dependent on our understanding of the idea of 'following a rule' " (Kripke 1982: 31; cf. 72, 97–8).

12 For one among many places where Sellars makes connections between his 'language game' conception of meaning and the emphasis placed on *conduct* in the pragmatist tradition, see SRLG §§49–52.

13 However, for further difficulties that would have to be considered in relation to 'community norms' approaches to the rule-following puzzles, see Blackburn 1984. On norms, see also O'Shea 2006b.

14 The utterances that constitute thinking-out-loud are said to be 'spontaneous' in the sense that they are much like what Ryle in *The Concept of Mind* called "disclosure by unstudied talk" (Ryle 1949: 173ff.). There is a sense in which the normal and "natural thing to do is to speak one's mind" in a frank and unprepared manner, and we constantly rely upon such talk as our primary source of information about the states of mind of other people (Ryle 1949: 173ff.).

Of course, as we saw earlier, people are capable of more sophisticated, 'studied' uses of language: for example, when trying to mislead other people, or more generally when saying things with the intention of thereby performing a certain action, whether of lying, promising, marrying, communicating information to another person, giving an order, or choosing one's words carefully. But if one imagines constantly speaking one's everyday 'stream of consciousness' out loud, as imagined on the VB model, such intentional and sophisticated uses of language as those just mentioned would be seen to be built upon a more basic level in which one is simply *perceiving, inferring*, and *willing* (out loud) in the ways outlined earlier.

15 Sellars' account of 'Mentalese' or the so-called 'language of thought' will clearly differ in important respects from the 'neo-Cartesian' conception of the language of thought that was later famously developed by Jerry Fodor.

16 MEV §§4ff. is one particularly pertinent example of Sellars' use of this distinction, as is *SM* VI.34.

17 "And it is important to note," Sellars remarks, "that we all grant that there is such a thing as thinking-out-loud – though Cartesians give an account of it which presupposes the concept of non-verbal conceptual episodes" (SK II.52n). For a more recent discussion of the concept of 'thinking-out-loud,' see Gauker 1994.

18 For an insightful discussion of the status and central role of *myths* in Sellars' philosophy in general, see Kukla 2000.

19 Sellars' position is frequently misunderstood to entail that the pre-Jonesean Ryleans *lack any concept of the psychological*. Not so, as Sellars later explicitly clarified in his Correspondence with David Rosenthal (Letter of November 8, 1965, paragraph 3; available in Marras 1972: 461–503, and on A. Chrucky's website listed in the bibliography):

> Thus, pre-Jonesean psychological explanations are explanations in terms of what I have called 'thoughts-out-loud' and long- or short-term dispositions to have thoughts-out-loud. Of course, if we were to follow ordinary usage and restrict the phrase 'psychological explanation' to explanation in terms of thoughts (inner episodes) and dispositions to have them, then we would not speak of pre-Jonesean explanations of behavior as 'psychological', but rather as 'linguistic' or 'symbol-behavioral'. *But if the argument of EPM is sound, there is every reason to extend the term 'psychological' to cover pre-Jonesean explanations – provided the necessary distinctions are drawn.* (italics added)

For discussion of Sellars' myth of Jones and the Ryleans in relation to contemporary issues in cognitive science (such as the 'theory theory' vs. 'simulation theory' dispute concerning 'folk psychology'), see Rosenberg, 'Ryleans and Outlookers: Wilfrid Sellars on "Mental States" ' (in Rosenberg forthcoming); and also Garfield 1989, which brings these Sellarsian issues to bear on the 'eliminative materialism' of Richard Rorty (at one time) and Paul Churchland, and questions their affinities with Sellars' own views.

20 This well-worn issue is discussed in detail in the literature in the philosophy of mind under the related heading of belief/desire circularity objections to behaviorism. Note that Sellars has carefully constructed a position according to which the verbal behaviorist or Rylean VB model can be coherently conceived in principle without vicious circularity (otherwise its methodological autonomy would be a sham), but which threatens to collapse into circularity when pushed beyond its explanatory limits.

21 In this introductory account we cannot explore but should note certain theoretical challenges that face any functional or conceptual role theory of meaning in this regard. For example, Fodor and Lepore (2001) have argued that the general Sellarsian functional role account of meaning as recently articulated in particular in Robert Brandom's *inferentialist* view (1994) cannot give a plausible account of the *compositional* aspects of meaning (briefly mentioned in chapter 3 above). However, for recent defenses of Sellarsian approaches to this and other technical issues in the philosophy of language, see for a start Rosenberg 1974, Lance and O'Leary-Hawthorne 1997, Brandom 2000a, and Peregrin 2001.

22 This is true despite the fact that both of those thinkers in certain respects resisted the characterization of their views as 'behaviorist.' Wittgenstein's views on inner mental episodes have been open to many interpretations, which is not surprising given such famously enigmatic (but for Sellars, insightful) passages as the following from his *Philosophical Investigations*:

> 'But you will surely admit that there is a difference between pain-behaviour accompanied by pain and pain-behaviour without any pain?' – Admit it? What greater difference could there be? – 'And yet you again and again reach the conclusion that the sensation itself is a nothing.' – Not at all. It is not a something, but not a nothing either! (Wittgenstein 1953: §304)

Peter Geach in his 1957 book *Mental Acts* defended a view similar to Sellars' according to which inner mental acts or episodes are conceived by analogy with public linguistic behavior. Geach insisted that the "occurrence of mental acts, in my sense of the word, is not controversial. Wittgenstein did not, as some people think, wish to controvert it." Geach also, however, gives reasons "for rejecting Ryle's view that 'reports of mental acts', as I should call them, are really hypothetical or semi-hypothetical statements about overt behaviour" (Geach 1957: v). Sellars' view is that Ryle's behaviorist account of such avowals should be recognized to be conceptually on target (in the order of our knowledge) but ultimately explanatorily inadequate (in the order of being).

23 See Richard Rorty's *Philosophy and the Mirror of Nature*, chapter 2 for an interesting and detailed thought-experiment which is in certain respects Sellarsian in spirit (see Rorty 1979: 101–2n). Rorty follows Sellars in arguing in support of the intersubjective and linguistic origins of our privileged access to and avowals of our own 'states of consciousness.'

24 For a recent discussion of Sellars' account of privileged access in EPM which takes into account in particular Sellars' correspondence with Castañeda, see Lehrer and Stern 2000. For a comprehensive discussion of all of the topics discussed in this chapter from a Sellarsian perspective, see Aune 1967.

25 I have emphasized those aspects of conceptual cognition that Sellars holds are necessarily *acquired* within a socially maintained logical space of reasons. Sellars also grants, however, that such cognitive capacities are grounded causally in more basic features of evolved animal cognitive systems that function as quasi-propositional representations without yet being properly *logical* representations in the sense that pertains to knowledge (see MEV, and chapter 5 below).

26 This is yet another instance of the fundamentally *normative* turn to Sellars' naturalism, which we have seen to be central to his overall philosophical strategy from the beginning, and particularly as laid out in 'A Semantical Solution of the Mind–Body Problem' (1953).

   Sellars clarified his intentions regarding the primordial role of 'ought' language among the original prehistoric Ryleans – and hence their capacity to follow ought-to-be rules and ought-to-do rules in general, independently of the 'semantic enrichment' that involves their coming to apply prescriptive rules to *language* in particular – in a letter to Marras dated November 26, 1975, which includes the following: "My Rylean language [. . .] could perfectly well contain the *prescriptive* vocabulary of practical reasoning (and other passages in *EPM* imply that it does – see Section VIII, *passim*)." Hence "[. . .] Jones, from the beginning, is in a framework which includes the language of ought-to-be and ought-to-do. What he needs to do is not to *invent* this dimension of discourse, but, at most, to apply it to linguistic behavior." This letter is available on the Chrucky website, 'Problems from Wilfrid Sellars,' listed in the bibliography.

27 This assumes, of course, that Sellars is able to give a VB-compatible account of what it is to recognize, and be motivated to follow, an *ought*. He clearly thinks that he can do so, but we shall have to reserve discussion of Sellars' account of the meaning and force of normative *oughts* until the final chapter.

Chapter 5 Knowledge, Immediate Experience, and the Myth of the Given

1 To anticipate the upcoming discussion, one of Sellars' central concerns will be to analyze crucial ambiguities that he thinks plague the very notion of 'immediate experience.'

   Sellars will reject the idea of *'immediate'* or 'direct' perceptual knowledge when such notions are based on what he argues are mistaken conceptions of 'the given.' However, he will defend the idea that basic perceptual knowings are 'direct' in the sense of being *non-inferential*, for in normal cases, on Sellars' view, our perceptual judgments are appropriately reliable conceptual responses that are causally evoked in us by the (inner or outer) object or event itself – hence, 'directly' – rather than being the result of an inference from something else that we believe.

   The *'experience'* side of 'immediate experience' will also turn out to be crucially ambiguous, most notably between two different kinds of *content* that Sellars believes are involved in a perceptual knowing: the *non-conceptual* content of a *sensing* and the closely related *propositional* content of a *perceiving that* something is the case. All of this lies ahead.

2 Sellars makes a distinction between 'sense contents' (and 'sensa') as opposed to 'sense-data,' which I will not carefully observe in what follows. Basically, a sense-*datum* is an epistemic notion: it is a sense content or sensum that is conceived as *known* by the experiencer (as on Price's view, below). C. D. Broad (1923) introduced a notion of *sensa* in which sense contents were *theoretical posits*, and Sellars' own notion of 'sensa,' as he ultimately calls them, is influenced by Broad's view. Sellars, however, will go further than Broad in attempting to purge his theoretically postulated sensa of *any* epistemic givenness.

3 DeVries and Triplett in their helpful commentary on EPM have thus characterized knowledge of the given as a "positive epistemic status" that is both *"epistemically independent"* in not "being derived from some other epistemic state," and yet also *"epistemically efficacious"* in that "it can provide positive epistemic support to other elements within a person's epistemic system" (2000: xxvi). See also Rosenberg 2002, chapter 3: 'Immediate Knowledge: The New Dialectic of Givenness,' for a particularly insightful discussion of the myth of the given from a Sellarsian perspective.

4 It does not seem to be the case that Sellars regards all instances of the given that have been defended by philosophers as playing a *foundationalist* epistemological role. Philosophers have often taken the *nature* of various kinds of phenomena to be directly given without defending a foundationalist epistemology, indeed without having epistemological issues at the center of their attention at all. (Consider some recent discussions of ineffable *qualia* in the philosophy of mind; or consider

Sellars' own critique of ordinary language theories of appearance, mentioned below.) Underlying the idea of 'epistemically independent' knowledge, as we shall see, is arguably the more general notion of what Sellars in later writings characterized as the myth of the *categorial given* (see FMPP I.44–5).

5 As an aside, it is interesting to note that during Sellars' time at Oxford on a Rhodes Scholarship from 1934 to 1936 Price at one point was his tutor for his research on Kant's *Critique of Pure Reason* (AR 285).

6 Two good places to start in pursuing further study of earlier twentieth-century theories of sense-data and theories of the given more generally are Ross 1970 and the collected readings in Swartz 1965.

7 One central source of systematic ambiguity – though not the only one – results from considerations pertaining to the different standpoints of the manifest and scientific images, as Sellars makes clear in his 'Science, Sense Impressions, and Sensa: A Reply to Cornman' (SSIS 417): "For the point I wish to highlight is that in the Scientific Image, the move from 'Jones senses a red rectangle' to 'There is a red and rectangular item' will be valid, whereas it is not valid in the Manifest Image." Even within the manifest image, furthermore, 'Jones's theory' will involve a *sense-impression inference* which is closely related to but differs from the sense-datum inference (see the final section below).

8 I will be discussing Sellars' views on the myth of the given based on writings from all stages of his career. I will indicate any places where I believe his basic views underwent significant changes, but for the most part I believe that his views remained remarkably stable throughout his career.

9 The text of SRLG in *Science, Perception and Reality* in my edition has the mistaken ordering: '*sensation* and *inspection* respectively,' which is corrected by the editor at *SPR* 369.

10 DeVries and Triplett (2000) offer a useful formal characterization of Sellars' argument against the given on pp. 105–6. In a nutshell, the given conceived as a non-propositional item is epistemically inefficacious (as we have just seen), while the given conceived propositionally will turn out not to be epistemically independent. Therefore nothing turns out to be suited to play the role of the epistemic given.

11 At certain points in EPM Sellars might well appear to be blatantly begging the question against particular sense-datum theories. For example, in EPM I.3 he bluntly declares that "what is *known* [. . .] is *facts* rather than particulars" (that is, something with propositional form), but as the basis for an argument this would hardly impress Price or Russell, who held that there is 'knowledge by acquaintance' with *particulars*. Again, Sellars at times seems to assume that to do its intended work the sense-datum given must be conceived as *known*. However, this would not impress C. I. Lewis, who argued for a non-conceptual, non-cognitive conception of the given – the given is not itself known – which nonetheless, Lewis argued, plays a fundamental

role in our knowledge, a role which Sellars in the end wants to reject in its Lewisian form (see, e.g., FMPP I.85).

In what follows, however, I attempt to show within a brief space how Sellars' arguments considered as a whole, while not providing or even attempting to provide a knock-down argument, nonetheless do succeed in putting severe critical pressure on both sorts of sense-datum theory, and do so in a non-question-begging manner. In this way I would also argue that my analysis goes some way toward addressing some of the important objections that have recently been raised to Sellars' account of the myth of the given in the secondary literature, for example by Alston 2002, Bonevac 2002, Fales 1996, and Vinci 1998 (see also Koons forthcoming). The reader is encouraged to explore this literature further. The limitations of space for a manageable introductory volume do not permit me to explore this secondary literature directly here.

12 Price elsewhere puts the relationship between (non-propositional) sensing and (propositional) perceiving as follows:

> [T]here is not even a passage. The two states of mind, the acquaintance with the sense-datum and the perceptual consciousness of the tree, *just arise together*. The sense-datum is presented to us, and the tree dawns on us, all in one moment. The two modes of 'presence to the mind', utterly different though they are, can only be distinguished by subsequent analysis. (1932: 141, italics added)

C. I. Lewis, too, considers the objection that there is "no apprehension [. . .] without [conceptual] construction," but like Price he insists that this "implies no denial of the givenness of sense-data" (1929: 47). And Russell similarly cautions that while knowledge by acquaintance is "logically independent of knowledge of truths, [. . .] it would be rash to assume that human beings ever, in fact, have acquaintance with things without at the same time knowing some truth about them" (1912: 25).

13 "[W]hat I refer to as 'the given' in this experience is, in broad terms," says C. I. Lewis, "qualitatively no different than it would be if I were an infant or an ignorant savage" (1929: 50; cf. 119).

14 Sense-datum theorists might perhaps respond to Sellars' inconsistent triad by modifying (A) in the following way, while seeking to hold onto (B) and (C). For anyone with appropriately developed or acquired conceptual capacities, sensing a red sense-datum normally (other things being equal) gives rise to the companion conceptual knowledge of the fact that the sense-datum is red; or more realistically (since one presumably has to read some philosophy in order to acquire *the concept of a sense-datum*), it gives rise to the knowledge that something or other is or *looks* red – a tomato, for instance. This sort of concession, however, would have the effect of shifting the discussion, as Sellars wants to do, away from sense-data and toward the topics to be considered in the next section.

15 Brandom suggests in his commentary on EPM that Sellars does not himself share what he here calls "the nominalistic proclivities of the empiricist tradition" (EPM I.6); and by contrast Brandom characterizes what Sellars calls his 'psychological nominalism' as "rationalistic" (1997: 167, 169). The terms 'empiricist' and 'rationalist' are slippery, but in general I think Sellars regarded himself as defending a non-traditional, holistic empiricism by correcting it with rationalist insights. Sellars certainly *accepts* the following nominalistic proclivity that he ascribes to the empiricist tradition: namely, "that all classificatory consciousness [. . .] involves learning, concept formation, even the use of symbols" (EPM I.6).

The problem Sellars has with the traditional empiricists is that they have never fully and consistently applied their nominalistic insights to the knowledge of their own 'ideas,' 'perceptions,' or 'determinate sense-repeatables,' as Sellars himself, following the leads of Kant and Wittgenstein, will attempt to do (see EPM V–VII).

16 Referring to the awareness of 'determinate sense repeatables' such as *red* or *rectangular*, Sellars argues that "however much Locke, Berkeley, and Hume differ on the problem of abstract ideas, they all take for granted that the human mind has an innate ability to be aware of certain determinate sorts – *indeed, that we are aware of them simply by virtue of having sensations and images*" (EPM VI.28). This is an instance of the myth of the categorial given. Sellars' "psychological nominalism," by contrast, will be "the denial that there is any awareness of logical space prior to, or independent of, the acquisition of a language" (EPM VII.31), a thesis which we shall later see requires some careful qualification in order to be properly understood.

17 The entire skeleton of Sellars' philosophy requires a notion of 'conceptual frameworks' that is based on the theory of meaning and abstract entities examined above in chapters 3 and 4, and to be further elaborated in chapter 6. Some philosophers (notably Donald Davidson) hold that operating with the idea of alternative conceptual schemes or frameworks by itself imports the myth of the given as its correlative: what else could such frameworks 'shape' but the given? Sellars, however, argues that as long as our *conceptions* of the non-conceptual, receptive element in experience are themselves the product of ongoing and fallible conceptual (in particular, theoretical) construction, as suggested by his own myth of genius Jones, we can embrace the notion of conceptual frameworks while avoiding importing the sorts of directly revelatory encounters with the given that Sellars rejects.

18 This is not to suggest, absurdly, that such accounts of the given attribute to people an explicit awareness of the metaphysical categories under which their experiences fall. Rather, it is to say that such philosophical accounts of what people experience implicitly attribute to those people a direct awareness of what *sort* of thing it is that they are experiencing, simply in virtue of their undergoing the experience of it.

19   In all of this I am suppressing crucial considerations concerning conceptual change and the regulative ideal of a *fully* adequate conceptual scheme, or Peircean 'truth in the long run' – topics which will be considered in the next chapter.

On a separate but related matter, the reader is invited to compare Sellars' views on the myth of the *categorial given* with the currently much discussed views of John McDowell in his *Mind and World* (1994) and in his Woodbridge Lectures, 'Having the World in View: Sellars, Kant, and Intentionality' (1998). McDowell wants to defend a notion of the direct openness of the mind to the factual (or propositional, and hence categorial) structure of reality, when we are not misled by illusions, etc. Although this might seem like a clear instance of Sellars' myth of the categorial given, the matter is complicated by the fact that McDowell is a *holist* rather than an atomist with respect to our conceptual capacities (the 'logical space of reasons'). It is for this reason that he takes his own picture of the relation between mind and world to steer safely clear of the myth of the given. I must leave the detailed consideration of McDowell's subtle position to another occasion.

20   In technical terms, Sellars' theory of sensations or sense-impressions as non-conceptual representations will entail that they exhibit intensionality (with an 's') without being mental states with intentionality (with a 't') (though of course the perceptual judgments to which such sensations give rise will have intentional content). Roughly put, since a sensation of red will be an 'of red' type of sensation or manner of sensing ('sensing redly') in the sense that its *typical cause* is a red physical object out there, one can in this sense have a sensation *of* a red object without there in fact being any red physical object out there which one has sensed.

This gives sensory representations the intensionality which the rationalist and empiricist traditions both ran together (in opposite directions) with the intentionality of thought – as did Price and the sense-datum theorists. Sellars thinks Kant's distinction between understanding and sensibility was the first key step toward breaking this sensory–cognitive continuum, but that unfortunately it was a point that was lost on both Hegel and J. S. Mill as well as their twentieth-century descendents, necessitating "the slow climb 'back to Kant' which is still underway" (*SM* I.75).

21   The examples ought really to include shape as well color, as when one ostensibly sees that a building brick over there is red and rectangular on its facing side. As Sellars believes Berkeley correctly emphasized, the primary and secondary qualities of shape and color normally appear seamlessly together in our experience, as the form and matter of perceptual experience.

22   This problem represents one of those fundamental forks in the philosophical road, a controversy obviously closely related to the contemporary problem of *qualia* in the philosophy of mind. For Sellars, however, the issue will be stripped entirely of whatever *epistemic*

dimension it might have for current defenders of qualia. It would be the myth of the categorial given all over again to insist, for example, that we have immediate knowledge or awareness of qualia *as being non-physical*.

23   One basic form of the myth of the *categorial given* (and in direct contrast to Sellars' espousal of 'psychological nominalism') is the view of meaning which, after Wittgenstein's *Philosophical Investigations*, has come to be known as the 'Augustinian' picture of meaning and language acquisition. This is the idea, as Sellars puts it,

> that teaching a child to use a language is that of teaching it to discriminate elements within a logical space of particulars, universals, facts, etc., of which it is already undiscriminatingly aware, and to associate these discriminated elements with verbal symbols. And this mistake is in principle the same whether the logical space of which the child is supposed to have this undiscriminating awareness is conceived by *us* to be that of physical objects or of private sense contents. (EPM VII.30)

24   Various aspects of Sellars' endorsement account of 'looks' were in the philosophical air at the time (*circa* 1956). See for example Gilbert Ryle in 'Sensation' (1956) on appearance statements as "guarded statements of what I am tempted or inclined to judge to be the case, though I do not yet commit myself to their being the case" (in Swartz 1965: 195). See also Anthony Quinton in 'The Problem of Perception' (1955) and his proposal, wielded against sense-datum theories, that 'looks' statements are primarily "a modification of, an infusion of tentativeness into, the original claim, expressing a lack of confidence" (in Swartz 1956: 521).

25   See the commentary of deVries and Triplett (2000) on EPM, part III for a good discussion both of possible difficulties involved in the thought experiment concerning John in the necktie shop and of frequent misunderstandings of Sellars' conception of how propositional claims are involved in perception.

26   See Chisholm 1966 (and 3rd edn in 1989); and Sellars' discussion of Chisholm in Sellars' *ME*, chapter 6.

27   Robert Brandom's 1997 commentary on EPM is throughout very helpful on these anti-Cartesian points in EPM.

28   Note that one must distinguish between the particular sense in which *x looks F* is not making a claim (though it refrains from making one, namely that *x is F*), and the different but related claim that *x looks F to S*, where the latter is an unproblematic claim about perceiver S rather than a withheld claim about object *x*.

29   We might also add, with a further sense of philosophical relief, that this 'non-relational' endorsement conception of 'looks' also saves us from having to posit basic mental relations to *non-existent* (or non-actual) *entities*, which is a problem that plagues classical relational conceptions of appearance just as it plagues the classical relational

conceptions of meaning, thought, and intentionality discussed in previous chapters.

30   Let us follow Sellars in making the simplifying assumption for present purposes that there is some solution to the well-known and important problem of *Gettier cases* (as they are called, after Edmund Gettier's pioneering paper in *Analysis* in 1963, 'Is Justified True Belief Knowledge?'). Gettier counterexamples confront any view, of which Sellars' is a version, that knowledge is justified true belief (see SK III.1). As far as I can see, this assumption will not be harmful in that the current leading candidates for solutions to Gettier cases, whether internalist or externalist, will have analogues available to Sellars. At any rate, the problem we shall explore for Sellars' internalist view is a different one.

31   The epistemological *internalist* holds, roughly, that for one of subject S's beliefs B to be epistemically justified for S, the justification for B must be *accessible* to S herself (perhaps upon reflection). If S *has no idea* why her belief B is reliably true, then the internalist argues that it is absurd to credit S with knowledge. The epistemological *externalist* denies this 'internal accessibility' requirement, and holds that a belief B may be justified for S despite the fact that S herself may not be able to provide any justification for her belief B, even upon reflection. *Reliabilism* is a common position for an externalist: this is the view, again very roughly, that a belief B is justified (or constitutes knowledge) just in case it is the result of a reliable belief-forming process, where the latter is a (causal) process that tends to produce true beliefs. See Kornblith 2001 for recent work on this important contemporary debate.

32   Why might it be plausible to add the internalist requirement on justification, namely, that S is justified in believing that *p* only if S can herself (perhaps upon reflection) offer adequate reasons in support of *p*? Intuitively the idea is that one's beliefs are justified to the extent that one can offer good reasons in support of them and one has in other respects been a sufficiently epistemically responsible agent in relation to seeking out the available evidence in the given context. Furthermore, plausible counterexamples can be constructed which suggest that 'reliable discriminators' who have no (internalist) idea of how they are able to do what they do fail to qualify as knowers (see BonJour and Sosa 2003: 27ff.; Rosenberg 2002, ch. 3: 'Immediate Knowledge: The New Dialectic of Givenness').

On the other side of the debate, the externalist will point to the considerations introduced at the outset concerning the regress of justifications and suggest that our reason-giving justifications eventually terminate in certain basic beliefs, for example believing that *x* is green by *just seeing that x is green* (a causally reliable belief-forming process), which we take to be reliable and justified but which we do not usually support by means of any reasoning. In addition, very young children and sophisticated non-human animals are often plausibly regarded as having such perceptual knowledge without being in the reason-giving game at all.

So there are intuitive considerations supporting both the internalist requirement and the opposing externalist notion that perceptual reliability without the additional internalist requirement can be sufficient for epistemic justification. Sellars wants to defend a strong internalist requirement on knowledge by displaying its virtues and showing that it does not have any counterintuitive consequences.

33 Sellars had raised a structurally parallel difficulty for his earlier account of 'looks' in EPM, part III. Recall that Sellars' analysis of the *is/looks* conceptual connection involved the idea that "the ability to recognize that something *looks green*, presupposes the concept of *being green*," which in turn "involves knowing in what circumstances to place an object if one wishes to ascertain its color" (EPM III.18). The problem will be that the latter *'is/looks'* contrast-knowledge of standard and non-standard conditions amounts to general reliability knowledge [PR] that itself could have been acquired (it seems) only if one *already* possessed *particular* observational knowledge such as that *x is green* [P]. Hence, put brusquely, [P] presupposes [PR] yet [PR] presupposes [P], threatening vicious circularity.

34 Recall our discussions of language learning and language entry transitions in chapters 3 and 4, which likewise involved distinguishing between, on the one hand, utterances of 'this is red' which do not yet satisfy the holistic, inferential requirements that enable any •this is red• language entry transition to have genuine conceptual content and, on the other, those which later do.

35 Sellars' strong internalist requirement itself might seem to result in an absurdly over-intellectualized account of perception (cf. Alston 1989 and 2002). Can it seriously be maintained that no one can see (observe, perceptually know) that an object is green unless they also have the meta-knowledge that their own observational beliefs are generally reliable indicators of green physical objects? Who reasons in *that* way about the general reliability of their perceptions, apart from a handful of epistemologists?

However, what Sellars' view really entails that Jones must know in relation to his perceptual reliability is essentially the *is/looks* connection and the basic *being/seeming* contrasts discussed in the previous section. This knowledge would be expressed in such ordinary, non-technical epistemic appraisals as: 'What do you mean by asking how I know that this object, right here, is green? We're looking at it in broad daylight; I'm not colorblind; it's a large object right in front of my eyes; and I know what "green" means!' These are the sorts of statements that evince one's ordinary knowledge, when called upon, of the reliability of one's own judgments of color in certain standard conditions and not in various other kinds of conditions. Child Jones's proto-perceptual responses are not yet embedded within these other sorts of acquired conceptual capacities.

Sellars' account therefore does not require that one be able to launch into perceptual epistemology if one is to be able to see that something is green. It does, however, distinguish between, on the one hand, those who are perceptual knowers within a conceptual framework of reason-giving to the extent that they can, *if called upon* by circumstance or by criticism, make at least some minimal distinctions concerning the sorts of conditions in which their color judgments are reliable or unreliable and, on the other hand, those proto-perceivers who cannot (or cannot yet) do so.

36   In relation to the sorts of objection now to be considered, see in particular Sosa 1997 and 2003, as well as Alston 1989 and 2002. For responses in defense of Sellars on these points, see Williams 2001, ch. 15 and Rosenberg, 'Sellarsian Seeing: In Search of Perceptual Authority' (in Rosenberg forthcoming). For further discussion of this issue, see deVries and Triplett 2000, ch. 8. See also Williams 1999 and 2003.

37   Note the following remark of Sellars':

> It might be thought that the question as to how the theory [of persons as representers of themselves-in-the-world] was 'arrived at' is one which belongs to the 'order of discovery' *rather than* 'the order of justification'. But reflection on the fact that to answer a question of the form 'Is x justified in φ-ing?' requires taking x's historical situation into account should give one pause. (MGEC II.37)

The mentioned theory of 'persons as representers of themselves-in-the-world' will take center stage in a moment.

38   Such animal representations, if sufficiently functionally integrated with each other and with the animal's basic habitual modes of goal-seeking behavior, provide the animal (ultimately due to natural selection) with basic cognitive maps of itself-in-its-environment; and Sellars argues plausibly that these representational elements can have proto-propositional form (referring to objects and characterizing them as F) despite lacking the subject–predicate structure, logical operators, and quantifiers afforded by natural languages. Sellars thus holds that the "concept of innate abilities to be aware *of* something *as* something, and hence of pre-linguistic awareness is perfectly intelligible" (MEV 336). However, while in these senses Sellars grants that "propositional form is more primitive than logical form" (MEV 336), he also argues that only representational systems incorporating *logical* (and hence linguistic) representations can reason in the normative sense that involves following rules in the pattern-governed manner we have investigated in the previous two chapters.

39   Regarding the issues about to be explored, Sellars remarked in 'The Structure of Knowledge' (1975/1971) that a "similar point was made less clearly" in EPM VIII.32–9, which includes the passages concerning Jones's dubious inductive justification of his perceptual reliability. See

similar remarks on the general need for clarification of his earlier views on the myth of the given at the outset of FMPP; and see MGEC for Sellars' general recognition that an inductive account will not answer the fundamental justificatory question to be discussed below.

40   For a full development of related Kantian themes within a deeply Sellarsian outlook, see Jay F. Rosenberg's *One World and Our Knowledge of It* (1980). See also his more recent *Thinking About Knowing* (2002) for broadly Sellarsian treatments of the epistemological topics discussed in this chapter.

41   See the useful recent collections of material by Sellars on Kant, *KPT* and *KTM*, including Jeffrey Sicha's substantial introduction to *KTM*.

42   To take just one other pertinent example, Sellars argues in 'More on Givenness and Explanatory Coherence' that "since agency, to be effective, involves having reliable cognitive maps of ourselves and our environment, the concept of effective agency involves that of our IPM [i.e., introspective, perceptual, and memory] judgments being likely to be true, that is, to be correct mappings of ourselves and our circumstances" (MGEC IV.82). For criticism of these later moves by Sellars, see Sosa 2003 (esp. 122–3), who argues that the mere fact that we "want effective agency" will not *epistemically* justify whatever principles might be necessary for such agency (such as [PR]). Sosa's challenge is well taken, and a reply on Sellars' behalf would require a full defense of his claim that the perceptual reliability principle and associated *is/looks* contrasts are necessary for the possibility of any conceptual cognition and (hence) any practical agency at all, not merely for the possibility of desirably effective agency.

43   Note that neither Sellars nor Kant is "attempting to prove that there is empirical knowledge, but to articulate its structure" (KTE 60; ¶45), and to display the fundamental epistemic principles such as [PR] that are entailed by "the concept of empirical knowledge" in general (KTE 58; ¶38).

44   For a brief overview of twentieth-century attempts similar to Sellars' to appropriate Kantian transcendental arguments within an analytic context, see O'Shea 2006a. See also Sicha's substantial introduction to *KTM*.

45   For a well-known recent discussion of problems pertaining to consciousness, see Chalmers 1997. Sellars would perhaps regard Chalmers as properly 'taking consciousness seriously,' whatever other important disagreements there are in the epistemological and theoretical details of their resulting positions.

Chapter 6 Truth, Picturing, and Ultimate Ontology

1 What is a 'basic' or 'atomic' proposition? And what makes a proposition a 'matter-of-factual' or 'empirical' one? Philosophical difficulties surround all of these notions, but for present purposes we
may say that an *atomic* proposition is one which contains no logical
constants or quantifiers, in contrast to 'compound' or 'molecular'
propositions, which are built up out of other propositions either by
using truth-functional connectives (such as 'and,' 'or,' 'if–then') or
by quantifying over 'some' or 'all' items in a given domain. The
notion of 'matter-of-factual' or 'empirical' truth will be clarified further
on.

2 Once again our methodological focus, following Sellars, will be on
language. In accordance with the argument of chapter 4, however, the
distinctions articulated in this chapter are meant to apply at an ontologically more basic level to inner episodes as well, based on substantive analogical theory construction, etc.

3 Sellars' reference to "such information as these [semantical] rules may
require" would in this case presumably include the information that
there is indeed a red apple nearby to Smith, as a necessary condition
of his perceptual claim's being *correctly* semantically assertible. We
saw in chapter 5 that a similar 'external' condition, in conjunction with
a further 'internalist' condition, is required if Smith is to have perceptual *knowledge* that there is a red apple in front of him. Sellars accordingly needs his notion of truth as semantic assertibility to walk a rather
fine normative line, as Sellars himself acknowledges at one point in
passing (see *NAO* IV.94n). For one thing, "there is a weaker sense of
semantically correct in which a well-formed but false sentence can be
said to be semantically correct. It might therefore be intuitively more
plausible to explicate truth in terms of semantical correctness *and
success*" (*NAO* IV.94n). However, since 'true' does not mean '*known* to
be true,' correct semantic assertibility had better itself be a weaker
notion than that of being "assertible with good reason or warrant"
(*NAO* IV.95). Furthermore, one might also worry that the stronger
'success' condition on correct assertibility will amount to a *truth* condition, thus threatening Sellars' assertibility account of truth with
circularity.

  In response to the circularity worry, Sellars' normative account of
the 'truth move' from " '*p*' is true" to the authorized performance of
asserting that *p* will be intended to show how truth assertions do have
a distinctive role to play in relation to the simple information or assertion that *p*, with which they are of course intimately related. And the
question of *epistemic warrant* on Sellars' view does raise distinctive
questions concerning justification and reliability that appropriately go
beyond, but are also tightly connected with, the weaker notion of
semantic correctness. However, it would, I think, certainly be a non-

trivial task to spell out in detail just how a 'correct assertibility' account of truth is supposed to handle all of these distinctions.

4   As indicated in chapter 3, Sellars is in this connection taking a particular (broadly constructivist) stand in the philosophy of mathematics, which is beyond our scope to examine here. The nature of *moral* truths will be considered in chapter 7.

5   For the meaning of 'recursive,' recall our brief discussion of Carnap and *truth-conditional* approaches to meaning in chapter 3 (Carnap adopted and developed Tarski's 'semantic' analysis of truth). To say that Tarski's definition of truth is *recursive* means, very crudely, that by applying the same formal rules or definitions repeatedly – for example, the rules that specify the truth-conditions for the logical operators 'or,' 'and,' 'if–then', and so on – you can generate all the true sentences of the language on that basis. The question of how to understand the truth of the 'base class' or bottom-level atomic sentences not surprisingly emerges as one key place where philosophical perplexities arise, and such sentences will be central to Sellars' account of the picturing or correspondence dimension of truth.

6   Or as Tarski puts it more generally and formally:

> In other words, the following equivalence holds:
>
> (T) X *is true if, and only if, p.*
>
> We shall call any such equivalence (with '*p*' replaced by any sentence of the language to which the word '*true*' refers, and '*X*' replaced by a name of this sentence) an '*equivalence of the form* (T).' (Tarski 1944: section IV)

7   In his correspondence with Harman, which is available on the 'Problems from Wilfrid Sellars' website (see Chrucky in the bibliography), Sellars also explains how the right-to-left implication is to be accounted for on his view of truth as S-assertibility.

8   For a sophisticated development of a theory of truth within an avowedly Sellarsian inferentialist semantic framework, but one which also makes use of technical devices from the 'prosentential' and 'anaphoric' approaches to truth, see Brandom 1994, ch. 5 or the more brief version in Brandom 2000a, ch. 5. On Brandom's normative terminology, roughly speaking S's assertion that '*p*' is true amounts to S's *undertaking a commitment* to the claim that *p*, as well as S's *endorsing* that claim when made by others. Broadly speaking, it is Sellars' social-normative account of truth in terms of the authorization to assert a claim that is a predecessor of Brandom's more recent account. The *picturing* dimension in Sellars' account of empirical truth plays no part in Brandom's story, however.

9   Ruth Millikan is one well-known philosopher and former student of Sellars' who argues that there are important insights contained in his conception of picturing (see Millikan 2005 for her most recent

statement). For a more detailed earlier account of linguistic picturing from a Sellarsian perspective, see Jay Rosenberg's *Linguistic Representation* (1974), chapters VI and VII, as well as his updated account of 'Sellarsian Picturing' (in Rosenberg forthcoming).

10 See also the extended 'super-inscriber' thought-experiment at TC 219–24, as well as Sellars' discussion of maps and of 'smart missiles' in *NAO* ch. V.

11 See Shepard and Chipman 1970. A related 'homomorphic' conception · of sensory consciousness has been developed in recent years by David Rosenthal, as part of his influential 'Higher-Order Thought' conception of consciousness (see Rosenthal 2005, especially pp. 167–74 in relation to Sellars). (In mathematics, a homomorphism is in effect a partial or 'many–one' isomorphism between two relational structures; roughly put, all the structures in one system are reflected in corresponding structures of the other system, but not necessarily vice versa. I shall use the more familiar term 'isomorphism' to cover both cases hereafter.) Rosenthal credits Sellars with the initial insights and reflections on the structural isomorphism that they both contend is involved in our inner sensory representations of objects. However, Rosenthal disagrees with Sellars' and others' so-called 'relocation' account of sensory consciousness and the sensible qualities of objects (see below).

12 The key to Sellars' own account of picturing will be to replace Hume's 'perceptions,' considered as particular kinds of 'individual existences' or image-like objects in the mind, with what Sellars calls *natural-linguistic objects* (TC 212). The latter are propositionally structured items, such as sentences (or by analogy, inner thoughts) considered naturalistically in terms of their causal, structural, and other empirical properties. Our cognitive representings for Sellars, as for Kant and unlike Hume, have *propositional form*. (They do not necessarily have 'subject–predicate' form, however. See the discussion of 'Jumblese' below, and see Sellars' MEV on 'animal representational systems,' which brings out the insights and limitations of the Humean account.)

13 For a helpful discussion of Sellars' notion of a *world story* both as it appears in his early writings and how this develops into the later account of *picturing*, see Jeffrey Sicha's introduction to his collection of Sellars' early essays, *Pure Pragmatics and Possible Worlds* (*PPPW*), pp. xlvff.

14 Is it any wonder that Hilary Putnam's lucid discussions of *Turing machine functionalism* in the early 1960s found a wide audience among analytic philosophers (see Putnam 1975), while Sellars' insightful contemporaneous contributions to the question of how mental representations might be realized in complex physical systems were not as influential? In retrospect, however, there is arguably much to prefer in Sellars' way of approaching the problem of mental representation and its realization in physical systems.

15 While there are of course differences between the two approaches, it would be interesting to compare Sellars' discussion here in 1960 with Daniel Dennett's later well-known conception of the *intentional stance* in relation to the 'design stance' and the 'physical stance,' including Dennett's similar emphasis on the 'engineering' standpoint.

16 The use of single 'scare-quotes' throughout this discussion, following Sellars, reflects the fact that for our immediate purposes we need not commit ourselves on the question as to whether or not our android qualifies as a genuine thinker.

17 There are notorious philosophical controversies here which would have to be pursued in a more extended discussion of this topic. Theories of reference have undergone enormous changes since Kripke's *Naming and Necessity* and Putnam's 'The Meaning of "Meaning" ' in the early 1970s. Loosely put, for Sellars the reference of a proper name within any given context would be determined – to put it in the terms of these debates – by associated senses, criteria, or descriptions. To many philosophers this would seem to render his view implausible in light of the influential *causal* theories of reference deriving from Kripke and Putnam.

   However, in his discussion of picturing, Sellars himself is offering an account of the underlying causal dimension of picturing that is a necessary presupposition of our empirical referential practices. The crucial difference between Kripke and Sellars is that for Sellars, *at any given stage of inquiry*, the normative-epistemic and causal-representational dimensions of reference will necessarily track one another due to the fact that the causal uniformities required for picturing are a reflection of the given community's espousal of the corresponding meaning rules. Consequently the famous modal thought experiments offered in support of Kripke's notion of *rigid designation* (for example, it is conceivable that the historical Socrates will turn out not to have been a philosopher at all), which seem to drive a metaphysical wedge between the epistemic and the causal dimensions of reference, must on any Sellarsian account be handled by taking the pragmatist turn and *'going diachronic.'* That is, built into our concept of reference in both its normative and causal aspects is a distinction between our here-and-now epistemic resources and those of improved successor frameworks that are generated by ongoing inquiry (for example, concerning future discoveries as to who Socrates really was). Sellars' accounts of picturing and conceptual change are thus crucial to his own account of reference, as we shall see later on.

   For a detailed discussion of how a Sellarsian theory of meaning and reference might accommodate the insights contained in the new theories of reference, see Jay Rosenberg's *Beyond Formalism: Naming and Necessity for Human Beings* (1994), especially chapter 5. Robert Brandom's social 'score-keeping' account of *de re* reference is another Sellarsian, diachronic pragmatist approach to these issues.

18   A more detailed account would have to be careful with tenses. Sellars suggests that in such contexts we read the 'is' in 'Socrates is wise' as 'is, was, or will be.'

19   The platonist, of course, will argue that 'having a certain character' in turn requires a reference to an abstract entity. Sellars, however, provides a complex ontological analysis according to which *qualified particulars* are the basic entities, ultimately without requiring any reification of shared qualities as platonic entities. For those up to the task, see Sellars' 'Particulars' (P, 1952, reprinted in *SPR*) and 'On the Logic of Complex Particulars' (LCP, 1949, reprinted in *PPPW*). See chapter 3 above for an introduction to Sellars' nominalism, and see Seibt 1990 and 2000 for a deeper investigation of many of the ontological matters discussed in this chapter.

20   Interestingly, Sellars appeals to a notion of 'psycho-sociological-historical' relations in different but related ways in both his first and one of his last published articles (PPE 1947, §41n, pp. 198–9; TTP 1985).

21   Sellars' letter to Gilbert Harman, February 26, 1970, available on Andrew Chrucky's website 'Problems from Wilfrid Sellars' listed in the bibliography.

22   Here my account apparently disagrees with that of deVries, although these issues are quite complex (see also deVries 2005, ch. 10). DeVries argues that Sellars' explication of "the reduction relation as an identity relationship" is in tension with Sellars' Kantian 'appearance vs. reality' account of the relationship between the manifest image and the scientific image. As he puts it, "the appearance–reality relationship is supposed to be asymmetrical; it is not a form of identity" (deVries 2005: 160). However, my account of Sellars' views on counterpart concepts and conceptual change shows the consistency, and in fact the necessary connection, between the two Sellarsian tenets just mentioned. This issue is also important for correctly sorting out the relationship between the manifest and scientific images within Sellars' ideal synoptic 'fusion' (more on this below and in chapter 7).

23   There is an important ongoing philosophical controversy that bears directly on Sellars' account of conceptual change, and which ultimately traces back to fundamental disputes in the theory of meaning. Some contemporary philosophers influenced by Quine's rejection of the analytic/synthetic distinction also reject any principled distinction between *changes in concept* and *changes in belief* such as that on which Sellars' account of conceptual change depends. See Sellars' 'Conceptual Change' (CC) for an explicit discussion of this issue. For a recent example of the dispute, see 'Naturalism and the A Priori' by Penelope Maddy, who defends the broadly Quinean outlook, and 'Transcendental Philosophy and A Priori Knowledge: a Neo-Kantian Perspective' by Michael Friedman, who defends a relativized conception of a priori principles and of conceptual change that would, it seems to me, have been broadly congenial to Sellars. Both articles are contained in Boghossian and Peacocke (2000).

24 Here I omit, among other things, the more complex considerations concerning attributive senses and individual senses that would have to be discussed in order to explain Sellars' cross-framework conception of *existence* (see *SM* V.95–7).

25 For a more detailed examination than Sellars himself provides of the possibilities and challenges for a Sellarsian-Peircean 'convergence' account of truth in the long run of inquiry, see Rosenberg 2002, ch. 6 and 'Comparing the Incommensurable: Another Look at Convergent Realism' (in Rosenberg forthcoming).

26 Sellars' futuristic 'anthropoid robot,' for example, were it successfully programmed in accordance with the categories of the ideal SI, would be forming pictures that directly 'map' its environment *exclusively* in the representational 'vocabulary' of that same microphysical SI. Incidentally, nothing in this account of the ideal SI implies that "ideal matter-of-factual truth [need] be conceived of as one complete picture existing in simultaneous splendour. The Peirceish method of projection must enable picturings (by observation and inference) of *any* part, but this does not require a single picturing of *all* parts" (*SM* V.76).

27 There are some important controversies addressed in previous chapters that I will not revisit here, although they bear directly on the issues at hand. For instance, in chapter 2 we discussed Sellars' grounds for rejecting instrumentalist, empiricist, and other more recent 'quietist' and pluralist approaches to the fundamental clash of the images (e.g., recall the discussion of Strawson). I shall also take the significant liberty of assuming that chapter 5 has addressed Sellars' grounds for rejecting the general idea that the phenomenology of perceptual consciousness might adequately be accounted for on various influential 'intentionalist' accounts of sensory content (e.g., functionalist, information-processing, topic-neutral, disjunctivist, and other 'belief' approaches to the problem of 'qualia').

However, I believe that one's position on the latter, wider dispute is ultimately crucial for assessing the general plausibility of Sellars' controversial views on sensory consciousness and 'sensa' to be discussed below. If any such intentionalist account could adequately account for – or show that one can plausibly do without – what Sellars characterizes as the 'actual,' 'intrinsic,' 'occurrent' pinkness that he takes to be 'undeniably' involved in the vivid hallucination of a pink ice cube, then a properly naturalistic synoptic vision of sensory consciousness would arguably be in reach without pursuing Sellars' further lines of argument below. Whether any such functionalist/intentionalist account of 'qualia' is plausible is currently a wide open and vigorously debated question. Several well-known philosophers of consciousness who are otherwise quite sympathetic to Sellars' philosophical views explicitly depart from him on just this issue: for example, William Lycan (1987, ch. 8, and in unpublished work), David Rosenthal (2005, e.g. ch. 6), and, in a slightly different way, Daniel Dennett (1981, comments on Sellars' Carus Lectures).

See also for substantive critical examinations of Sellars' views along these general lines, Clark 1989 and Hooker 1977. For a defense of Sellars' views on sensings as developed in the Carus Lectures of 1981, see Wright 1985. On these issues, see also Muilenberg and Richardson 1982 as well as Rubenstein 2000.

28 To be more precise, Sellars has several highly complex stories to tell about the various philosophical moves involved in considering colors as *ingredient-contents* as opposed to as *attributes* of physical objects. These accounts span across an imposing array of actual and possible conceptual frameworks from the "pre-pre-Socratics" (as Willem deVries [2005] helpfully explores in his chapter eight on 'Sensory Consciousness'), Plato, Aristotle, genius Jones, the early modern philosophers, Kant, Russell, and ultimately Sellars' own quasi-logical atomist account of 'particulars' as logically constructed out of *quality-instances* each of which exhibits a *single quale* (in LCP and P). The last on this list is an ontological precursor of Sellars' ultimate ontology of *absolute processes* to be discussed below.

29 After quoting this remark from Sellars, Dennett comments as follows: "I guess I must grit my teeth and disagree with this proclamation of the obvious. It is seldom obvious what is obvious, and this strikes me as a prime case of a dubiously obvious claim" (Dennett 1981: 104). Dennett argues that the phenomena can be accounted for along broadly functionalist (and in some respects instrumentalist) lines without the 'occurrent volume of pink' that Sellars takes to be undeniable (see note 27).

30 Jay Rosenberg's 'The Place of Color in the Scheme of Things: A Roadmap to Sellars's Carus Lectures' (in Rosenberg forthcoming) remains the best exposition of Sellars' views on the complex set of issues we are considering in this section. Seibt 2000 is a rich and complex exploration of the 'projective' process metaphysics that she argues is defended in, and exhibited by, Sellars' Carus Lectures (FMPP).

31 The issue of normativity presents its own unique difficulties, of course, some of which will be discussed in chapter 7.

32 As Sellars later briefly restated the import of the distinction: "Roughly, those features of objects are physical^2, which are, in principle definable in terms of attributes exemplified in the world before the appearance of sentient organisms, i.e., attributes necessary and sufficient to describe and explain the behavior of 'merely material' things. Physical^1, features, on the other hand, are any which belong in the causal order" (FMPP III n15).

33 Among the earlier sketches of the role of 'sensa' in the projected scientific image are EPM XVI, PSIM 34–7, PH 95–105, *SM* VI.44–64, and IAMB.

34 After his 'Perspectives Lecture' late in his career in 1986, Sellars remarked during the question and answer session: "Until I go on to develop a more accurate account of the Heraclitean [i.e., absolute

process] ontology, I would just go back to logical atomism. Basically, at heart, I am a logical atomist." Here I rely upon the dating and titles of audio recordings of Sellars' lectures available from the Notre Dame Archives (ADPL A1672 (20823), CD disk 4, track 7).

Incidentally, earlier during the same talk (tracks 1 and 2 respectively) Sellars makes several other interesting remarks in passing that bear on the interpretation of his views offered in this chapter. For example, of his 'picturing' account of linguistic representation, cognitive mapping, and the truth of atomic matter-of-factual statements, he remarks: "This is the correct version of the correspondence theory of truth." And in relation to the same topic, he also remarks that what is needed is "an adequate causal theory of reference," regarding which he comments that some interesting work has been done but that it "has never been worked out with a clear awareness of what its task was." These warm remarks by Sellars on logical atomism, on truth as correspondence, and on the need for a causal theory of reference might come as a surprise to those who know Sellars only through recent discussions of his views on the 'myth of the given,' but they fit smoothly with the interpretation of Sellars offered throughout this chapter.

35 The text of the Carus Lectures is badly corrupted here at FMPP III.121–2 in the original *Monist* 1981 printing. The last word "process" of III.121 is omitted, *as is the entire crucial single sentence paragraph III.122*, except for a ghostly command left lingering from its final three words: "be nomologically autonomous"! A corrected version is available on the Chrucky website cited in the bibliography. I thank Jay Rosenberg and Bill deVries for confirming the wording of the original version from Sellars' own typescripts.

36 For a detailed critical discussion of Sellars' 'Grain Argument,' see Lycan 1987, chapter 8, sections 5–10.

Chapter 7 A Synoptic Vision: Sellars' Naturalism with a Normative Turn

1 The well-known philosopher and former student of Sellars' Hector-Neri Castañeda wrote that "Wilfrid Sellars has proposed one of the most profound and comprehensive meta-ethical theories. This has not been fully appreciated by his contemporaries" (Castañeda 1975b: 27). Unfortunately we shall only scratch the surface of Sellars' views on ethics and practical reason here. For good overviews, however, see also deVries 2005, ch. 9, Solomon 1977, Gutting 1977, Hurley 2000, and Aune 1975.

2 Robert Brandom has recently explored in detail the Sellarsian parallels between perception and action in his *Making It Explicit* (1994, ch. 4) and in the shorter version, *Articulating Reasons* (2000a). Note that during the early 1950s Sellars was thus already developing an account

of intentions according to which an agent's *reasons* can also be *causes*, thus anticipating central aspects of Donald Davidson's later and more influential view.

3　Sellars develops his theory of action in detail in 'Thought and Action' (TA) and many other places, e.g. *SM* ch. 7, FD, VR, AAE, MP, SE, ORAV, and IIO. In chapter 4 it was noted that volitions are not themselves quick or tiny little 'actions.' They are 'acts' not in the sense of being themselves intentional actions but in the sense of being mental acts or actualities, i.e., mental events, conceptual thinkings.

4　Sellars is using '*p* implies *q*' in a stronger sense than the merely truth-functional 'if *p*, then *q*,' for example as presupposing the truth of *p* (*SM* VII.14, 57).

5　Here in particular Sellars' own detailed discussions in the works cited must be consulted in relation to the necessary qualifications required before the following brief remarks concerning normativity and 'ought's can be made plausible. Here I am focusing on his most sustained published account of 'the moral point of view,' in *Science and Metaphysics*, chapter 7: 'Objectivity, Intersubjectivity and the Moral Point of View'; but see also the more introductory treatment in 'Science and Ethics' (SE).

6　In relation to some of the issues raised in this case by the required '*ceteris paribus*' qualifications (which themselves generate well-known philosophical controversies that are currently much discussed), Sellars offers a complex account of the phenomenon of weakness of will in 'On Knowing the Better and Doing the Worse' (KBDW).

7　For the mid-twentieth-century *locus classicus* in relation to contemporary discussions of the 'internal ought,' see W. D. Falk's collected papers in Falk 1986. For more recent references and for a good overview of the meta-ethical issues involved, see Smith 1994.

8　Sellars' letter to David Solomon of June 18, 1976 (available on the Sellars website, listed under Chrucky in the bibliography) is quite helpful on the various features of "logically sharable intentions and the moral point of view."

9　I believe (though I shall not attempt to document that claim here) that certain tendencies in Kant interpretation over the last few decades ought to generate increased interest in Sellars' particular analysis of

> how 'teleological' and 'deontological' themes are harmonized in Kant's ethics. Specific moral principles are categorical oughts, but the categorical validity of the intersubjective intentions, that any rational being in a certain kind of circumstance do a certain kind of action, is derivative from the categorical validity of the intersubjective intentions that our welfare be maximized. Thus, when Kant speaks in the *Metaphysical Elements of Ethics* of the happiness of others as a categorical end, what he says is in no way inconsistent with his claim that the ought of moral principles is categorical rather than the hypothetical ought which pertains to the relation of means to ends. (*SM* VII.147)

10 In a footnote in 'Language, Rules and Behavior' in 1950, following a
    discussion of the nature of rule-governed behavior, Sellars had
    noted:

> The historically minded reader will observe that the concept of rule-
> regulated behavior developed in this paper is, in a certain sense, the
> translation into behavioristic terms of the Kantian concept of Practical
> Reason. Kant's contention that the pure consciousness of moral law can
> be a factor in bringing about conduct in conformity with law, becomes
> the above conception of rule-regulated behavior. However, for Kant's
> conception of Practical Reason as, so to speak, an intruder in the natural
> order, we substitute the view that the causal efficacy of the embodied
> core-generalizations of rules is ultimately grounded on the Law of
> Effect, that is to say, the role of rewards and punishments in shaping
> behavior. (LRB fn3)

11 For a different but thought-provoking and insightful account of the
    final synoptic matters discussed in this chapter, see the final chapter
    of deVries 2005, entitled 'The Necessity of the Normative.' My own
    way of sorting out these rather speculative matters concerning the
    details of Sellars' final synoptic vision has relied heavily upon the
    theory of conceptual change, the account of basic matter-of-factual
    picturing at the ideal scientific level, and the complex diachronic rela-
    tionships between SI and MI generally that were examined above in
    chapter 6.

Bibliography

Works by Wilfrid Sellars

This partial bibliography of Sellars' works is based on the complete one in Jeffrey F. Sicha (ed.), *Kant's Transcendental Metaphysics* (*KTM* below), with the year of publication in parentheses. It contains corrections from Dr. Andrew Chrucky's website on Sellars (*http://www.ditext.com/sellars/bib-s.html*).

AAE   (1973) 'Actions and Events,' *Nous* 7: 179–202. Reprinted in *EPH*.

AE   (1963) 'Abstract Entities,' *Review of Metaphysics* 16: 627–71. Reprinted in *PPME*. (All text references are to this reprint.)

AR   (1975) 'Autobiographical Reflections (February, 1973).' Published in Castañeda 1975a.

ATS   (1975) 'The Adverbial Theory of the Objects of Sensation,' in *Metaphilosophy* 6, ed. Terrell Bynum (Oxford: Basil Blackwell): 144–60.

BBK   (1960) 'Being and Being Known,' *Proceedings of the American Catholic Philosophical Association*: 28–49. Reprinted in *SPR*.

BLM   (1980) 'Behaviorism, Language and Meaning,' *Pacific Philosophical Quarterly* 61: 3–30.

CAE   (1963) 'Classes as Abstract Entities and the Russell Paradox,' *Review of Metaphysics* 17: 67–90. Reprinted in *PPME* and in *EPH*.

CC   (1973) 'Conceptual Change,' in P. Maynard and G. Pearce (eds), *Conceptual Change*, Dordrecht: D. Reidel, 77–93. Reprinted in *EPH*. (All text references are to this reprint.)

CDCM   (1957) 'Counterfactuals, Dispositions, and the Causal Modalities,' in Herbert Feigl, Michael Scriven, and Grover Maxwell (eds), *Minnesota Studies in the Philosophy of Science*, Vol. II, Minneapolis: University of Minnesota Press, 225–308.

CE   (1956) 'The Concept of Emergence' (with Paul Meehl), in Herbert Feigl and Michael Scriven (eds), *Minnesota Studies in the Philosophy of Science*, Vol. I, Minneapolis: University of Minnesota Press, 239–52.

CIL   (1948) 'Concepts as Involving Laws and Inconceivable without Them,' *Philosophy of Science* 15: 287–315. Reprinted in *PPPW*.

DKMB   (1971) 'The Double-Knowledge Approach to the Mind–Body Problem,' *The New Scholasticism* 45: 269–89.

EAE   (1963) 'Empiricism and Abstract Entities,' in Paul A. Schilpp (ed.), *The Philosophy of Rudolf Carnap (The Library of Living Philosophers)*, Chicago: Open Court, 431–68. Reprinted in *EPH*. (All text references are to this reprint.)

ENWW   (1947) 'Epistemology and the New Way of Words,' *Journal of Philosophy* 44: 645–60. Reprinted in *PPPW*.

EPH   (1974) *Essays in Philosophy and its History*, Dordrecht: D. Reidel.

EPM   (1956) 'Empiricism and the Philosophy of Mind' (presented at the University of London in Special Lectures in Philosophy for 1956 under the title 'The Myth of the Given: Three Lectures on Empiricism and the Philosophy of Mind'), in Herbert Feigl and Michael Scriven (eds), *Minnesota Studies in the Philosophy of Science*, Vol. I, Minneapolis: University of Minnesota Press, 253–329. Reprinted in *SPR*, in Brandom 1997, and in deVries and Triplett 2000. All references are to 'part.section,' e.g., 'EPM III.17.'

FD   (1966) 'Fatalism and Determinism,' in Keith Lehrer (ed.), *Freedom and Determinism*, New York: Random House, 141–74.

FMPP   (1981) 'Foundations for a Metaphysics of Pure Process' (The Carus Lectures) *The Monist* 64: 3–90.

GE   (1960) 'Grammar and Existence: A Preface to Ontology,' *Mind 69*: 499–533. Two lectures delivered at Yale University, March 1958. Reprinted in *SPR*. Also reprinted in Charles Landesman (ed.), *The Problem of Universals*, New York: Basic Books, 1971.

GEC   (1973) 'Givenness and Explanatory Coherence' (presented at a symposium on Foundations of Knowledge at the 1973 meeting of the American Philosophical Association [Eastern Division]). An abbreviated version is in *Journal of Philosophy* 70 (1973): 612–24.

I   (1972) '. . . this I or he or it (the thing) which thinks,' the presidential address, American Philosophical Association

(Eastern Division), for 1970, *Proceedings of the American Philosophical Association* 44 (1972): 5–31. Reprinted in *EPH* and in *KTM*.

IAMB   (1965) 'The Identity Approach to the Mind–Body Problem,' *Review of Metaphysics* 18: 430–51. Presented at the Boston Colloquium for the Philosophy of Science, April 1963. Reprinted in *PPME*.

IIO   (1963) 'Imperatives, Intentions, and the Logic of "Ought," ' in Hector-Neri Castañeda and George Nakhnikian (eds), *Morality and the Language of Conduct*, a collection of essays in moral philosophy, Detroit: Wayne State University Press, 159–214.

IKTE   (1978) 'The Role of Imagination in Kant's Theory of Experience,' The Dotterer Lecture 1978 in Henry W. Johnstone, Jr. (ed.), *Categories: A Colloquium*, Pennsylvania State University, 231–45. Reprinted in *KTM*.

IM   (1953) 'Inference and Meaning,' *Mind* 62: 313–38. Reprinted in *PPPW*.

ITM   (1957) 'Intentionality and the Mental,' a symposium by correspondence with Roderick Chisholm, in Herbert Feigl, Michael Scriven, and Grover Maxwell (eds), *Minnesota Studies in the Philosophy of Science*, Vol. II Minneapolis: University of Minnesota Press, 507–39. Reprinted in Marras 1972. (All text references are to the 1957 original.)

ITSA   (1953) 'Is There a Synthetic A Priori?,' *Philosophy of Science* 20: 121–38. Reprinted in a revised form in Sidney Hook (ed.), *American Philosophers at Work*, New York: Criterion Press, 1957; also published in Italy in translation. Also reprinted in *SPR*. (All text references are to *SPR*.)

IV   (1964) 'Induction as Vindication,' *Philosophy of Science* 31: 197–231. Reprinted in *EPH*.

KBDW   (1970) 'On Knowing the Better and Doing the Worse,' *International Philosophical Quarterly* 10: 5–19. The 1969 Suarez Philosophy Lecture delivered at Fordham University. Reprinted in *EPH* and *KTM*.

KPT   (2002) *Kant and Pre-Kantian Themes: Lectures by Wilfrid Sellars*, ed. P. V. Amaral, Atascadero, CA: Ridgeview Publishing Co. In addition to Sellars' Kant lectures, this volume includes lectures on Descartes, Locke, Spinoza (with an introduction by the editor), and Leibniz.

KTE   (1967) 'Some Remarks on Kant's Theory of Experience,' *Journal of Philosophy* 64: 633–47. Presented in a symposium on Kant at the 1967 meeting of the American Philosophical Association (Eastern Division). Reprinted in *EPH* and in

KTM; page references to KTE in text are to *EPH*; paragraph references are to its reprinting in *KTM*.

KTI (1976) 'Kant's Transcendental Idealism' (presented at an International Kant Congress at the University of Ottawa). Published in volume 6, *Collections of Philosophy*: 165–81. Reprinted in *KTM*.

KTM (2002) *Kant's Transcendental Metaphysics: Sellars' Cassirer Lectures and Other Essays*, edited and introduced by Jeffrey F. Sicha, Atascadero, CA: Ridgeview Publishing Co.

LCP (1949) 'On the Logic of Complex Particulars,' *Mind* 58: 306–38. Reprinted in *PPPW*.

LRB (1949) 'Language, Rules and Behavior,' in Sidney Hook (ed.), *John Dewey: Philosopher of Science and Freedom*, New York: The Dial Press, 289–315. Reprinted in *PPPW*. Page references are to the original 1949 article, together with the paragraph number.

LT (1961) 'The Language of Theories,' in Herbert Feigl and Grover Maxwell (eds), *Current Issues in the Philosophy of Science*, New York: Holt, Rinehart, and Winston, 57–77. Reprinted in *SPR* and in E. A. McKinnon (ed.), *The Problem of Scientific Realism*, New York: Appleton-Century-Crofts, 1972. (All text references are to *SPR*.)

LTC (1969) 'Language as Thought and as Communication,' *Philosophy and Phenomenological Research* 29: 506–27. Reprinted in Paul Kurtz (ed.), *Language and Human Nature*, St. Louis, MO: Warren H. Green, 1971. Also reprinted in *EPH*. (All text references are to the original 1969 article.)

ME (1989) *The Metaphysics of Epistemology: Lectures by Wilfrid Sellars*, ed. P. V. Amaral, Atascadero, CA: Ridgeview Publishing Co.

MEV (1981) 'Mental Events,' *Philosophical Studies* 39: 325–45. Contributed to a symposium of that title at the 1980 meeting of American Philosophical Association (Western Division).

MFC (1974) 'Meaning as Functional Classification (A Perspective on the Relation of Syntax to Semantics)' (with replies to Daniel Dennett and Hilary Putnam), *Synthese* 27: 417–70. Reprinted in J. G. Troyer and S. C. Wheeler, III, *Intentionality, Language and Translation*, Dordrecht: D. Reidel, 1974. Also reprinted in chapter IV of *NAO*.

MGEC (1979) 'More on Givenness and Explanatory Coherence,' in George Pappas (ed.), *Justification and Knowledge*, Dordrecht: D. Reidel, 169–82.

MP (1969) 'Metaphysics and the Concept of a Person,' in Karel Lambert (ed.), *The Logical Way of Doing Things*, New Haven:

Yale University Press, 219–52. Reprinted in *EPH* and in *KTM*.

NAO   (1980) *Naturalism and Ontology*, Atascadero, CA: Ridgeview Publishing Co. The John Dewey Lectures for 1973–4. Reprinted with corrections in 1997. (Chapter IV includes all of MFC; chapter V includes a reprinting of the final section of TC; and the Appendix contains Sellars' correspondence with Loux on abstract entities.) All references are to 'chapter. paragraph', e.g., 'II.16.'

NI   (1964) 'Notes on Intentionality,' *Journal of Philosophy* 61: 655–65. Presented in a symposium on intentionality at the 1964 meeting of the American Philosophical Association (Eastern Division). Reprinted in *PPME* and in Marras 1972.

NS   (1962) 'Naming and Saying,' *Philosophy of Science* 29: 7–26. Reprinted in *SPR*.

OAFP   (1988) 'On Accepting First Principles,' in James E. Tomberlin (ed.), *Philosophical Perspectives, 2, Epistemology*, Atascadero, CA: Ridgeview Publishing Co., 301–14. This paper was written in the sixties but first published here. Reprinted in *KTM*.

ORAV   (1980) 'On Reasoning About Values,' *American Philosophical Quarterly* 17: 81–101. One of three Tsanoff Lectures presented at Rice University, October 1978.

P   (1952) 'Particulars,' *Philosophy and Phenomenological Research* 13: 184–99. Reprinted in *SPR*.

PH   (1963) 'Phenomenalism,' in *SPR*, 60–105.

PPE   (1947) 'Pure Pragmatics and Epistemology,' *Philosophy of Science* 14: 181–202. Reprinted in *PPPW*.

PPHP   (1977) *Philosophical Perspectives: History of Philosophy*, Atascadero, CA: Ridgeview Publishing Co.

PPME   (1977) *Philosophical Perspectives: Metaphysics and Epistemology*, Atascadero, CA: Ridgeview Publishing Co.

PPPW   (1980) *Pure Pragmatics and Possible Worlds: The Early Essays of Wilfrid Sellars*, ed. and introduced by Jeffrey F. Sicha, Atascadero, CA: Ridgeview Publishing Co.

PR   (1955) 'Physical Realism,' *Philosophy and Phenomenological Research* 15: 13–32. Reprinted in *PPME*.

PRE   (1954) 'Presupposing,' *Philosophical Review* 63: 197–215. Reprinted in E. D. Klemke (ed.), *Essays on Bertrand Russell*, Urbana: University of Illinois Press, 1970.

PSIM   (1962) 'Philosophy and the Scientific Image of Man,' in Robert Colodny (ed.), *Frontiers of Science and Philosophy*, Pittsburgh: University of Pittsburgh Press, 35–78. Reprinted in *SPR*. (All text references are to this reprint.)

RD   (1975) 'Reply to Donagan,' *Philosophical Studies* 27: 149–84.

RM   (1973) 'Reply to Marras,' *Canadian Journal of Philosophy* 2: 485–93. Reprinted in *EPH*. (All text references are to the original 1973 article.)

RNWW   (1948) 'Realism and the New Way of Words,' *Philosophy and Phenomenological Research* 8: 601–34. Reprinted in Herbert Feigl and Wilfrid Sellars (eds), *Readings in Philosophical Analysis*, New York: Appleton-Century-Crofts, 1949. Reprinted in *PPPW*. (Paragraph numbers refer to *PPPW*.)

SE   (1960) 'Science and Ethics,' given at the Phoebe Griffin Noyes Library Association, printed in *PPME*.

SK   (1975) 'The Structure of Knowledge: (I) Perception; (II) Minds; (III) Epistemic Principles,' The Matchette Foundation Lectures for 1971 at the University of Texas. Published in Hector-Neri Castañeda (ed.), *Action, Knowledge and Reality: Studies in Honor of Wilfrid Sellars*, Indianapolis: Bobbs-Merrill, 295–347. All references are to 'lecture.section,' e.g., 'III.33.'

SM   (1967) *Science and Metaphysics: Variations on Kantian Themes*, The John Locke Lectures for 1965–6, London: Routledge and Kegan Paul. Re-issued in 1992 by Ridgeview Publishing Co. (Atascadero, CA). All references are to 'chapter.paragraph', e.g., 'II.16.'

SPR   (1963) *Science, Perception and Reality*, London: Routledge and Kegan Paul. Re-issued in 1991 by Ridgeview Publishing Co. (Atascadero, CA).

SRII   (1965) 'Scientific Realism or Irenic Instrumentalism: A Critique of Nagel and Feyerabend on Theoretical Explanation,' in Robert Cohen and Max Wartofsky (eds), *Boston Studies in the Philosophy of Science*, Vol. II, Atlantic Highlands, NJ: Humanities Press, 171–204. Reprinted in *PPME*. (All text references are to this reprint.)

SRLG   (1954) 'Some Reflections on Language Games,' *Philosophy of Science* 21: 204–28. Reprinted in *SPR*.

SRT   (1976) 'Is Scientific Realism Tenable?' (presented at a symposium at the 1976 Philosophy of Science Association Meeting in Chicago). Published in Volume II, *Proceedings* of *PSA*: 307–34.

SSIS   (1971) 'Science, Sense Impressions, and Sensa: A Reply to Cornman,' *Review of Metaphysics* 25: 391–447.

SSMB   (1953) 'A Semantical Solution of the Mind–Body Problem,' *Methodos* 5: 45–82. Reprinted in *PPPW*.

SSOP   (1982) 'Sensa or Sensings: Reflections on the Ontology of Perception,' *Philosophical Studies* 41 (Essays in Honor of James Cornman): 83–111. Presented at a Colloquium at the University of North Carolina, October 1976.

TA   (1966) 'Thought and Action,' in Keith Lehrer (ed.), *Freedom and Determinism*, New York: Random House, 105–39.

TC   (1962) 'Truth and Correspondence,' *Journal of Philosophy* 59: 29–56. Reprinted in *SPR*. (All text references are to this reprint.)

TE   (1963) 'Theoretical Explanation,' in Bernard Baumrin (ed.), *Philosophy of Science: The Delaware Seminar*, Vol. II, New York: John Wiley, 61–78. Reprinted in *PPME* and in *EPH*. (All text references are to *PPME*.)

TTC   (1970) 'Towards a Theory of the Categories,' in Lawrence Foster and Joe William Swanson (eds), *Experience and Theory*, Cambridge: University of Massachusetts Press, 55–78. Reprinted in *KTM*.

TTP   (1985) 'Towards a Theory of Predication,' in James Bogen and James McGuire (eds), *How Things Are*, Dordrecht: D. Reidel), 285–322. Presented at a conference on predication at Pitzer College in April 1981.

TWO   (1962) 'Time and the World Order,' in Herbert Feigl and Grover Maxwell (eds), *Minnesota Studies in the Philosophy of Science*, Vol. III, Minneapolis: University of Minnesota Press, 527–616.

VR   (1976) 'Volitions Re-affirmed,' in Myles Brand and Douglas Walton (eds), *Action Theory*, Dordrecht: D. Reidel, 47–66. Presented at a conference on action theory at Winnipeg, May 1975.

Works by other authors

Alston, William (1989) *Epistemic Justification: Essays in the Theory of Knowledge*, Ithaca, NY: Cornell University Press.

Alston, William (2002) 'Sellars and "The Myth of the Given",' *Philosophy and Phenomenological Research* 65: 69–86.

Aune, Bruce (1967) *Knowledge, Mind, and Nature*, Atascadero, CA: Ridgeview Publishing Co.

Aune, Bruce (1975) 'Sellars on Practical Reason,' in Castañeda 1975a.

Benacerraf, Paul (1973) 'Mathematical Truth,' *Journal of Philosophy* 70: 661–80 (also reprinted in Paul Benacerraf and Hilary Putnam (eds), *Philosophy of Mathematics: Selected Readings*, 2nd edn, Cambridge: Cambridge University Press, 1983).

Blackburn, Simon (1984) 'The Individual Strikes Back,' *Synthese* 58: 281–301 (also reprinted in Miller and Wright 2002).

Boghossian, Paul, and Peacocke, Christopher (eds) (2000) *New Essays on the A Priori*, Oxford: Oxford University Press.

Bonevac, Daniel (2002) 'Sellars vs. the Given,' *Philosophy and Phenomenological Research* 64: 1–30.

BonJour, Laurence, and Sosa, Ernest (2003) *Epistemic Justification*, Oxford: Blackwell.

Brandom, Robert (1994) *Making it Explicit: Reasoning, Representing, and Discursive Commitment*, Cambridge, MA and London: Harvard University Press.

Brandom, Robert (1997) 'Study Guide,' in Wilfrid Sellars, *Empiricism and the Philosophy of Mind* (with an introduction by Richard Rorty), Cambridge, MA and London: Harvard University Press.

Brandom, Robert (2000a) *Articulating Reasons: An Introduction to Inferentialism*, Cambridge, MA and London: Harvard University Press.

Brandom, Robert (2000b) 'Sellars, Wilfrid Stalker,' *American National Biography* (online at *http://www.anb.org/articles/20/20-01795.html*), American Council of Learned Societies, Oxford University Press.

Broad, C. D. (1923) Scientific Thought, London: Routledge and Kegan Paul.

Broad, C. D. (1933) *Examination of McTaggart's Philosophy*, London: Cambridge University Press.

Carnap, Rudolf (1934) *The Logical Syntax of Language*, trans. Amethe Smeaton, International Library of Psychology, Philosophy and Scientific Method, London: Kegan Paul, 1937.

Carnap, Rudolf (1939) 'Foundations of Logic and Mathematics,' in Otto Neurath, Rudolf Carnap, and Charles Morris (eds), *International Encyclopedia of Unified Science*, Chicago: University of Chicago Press. Page references to the paperback reprint of this work by the same press under the title *Foundations of Logic and Mathematics* by Rudolf Carnap.

Carnap, Rudolf (1947) *Meaning and Necessity: A Study in Semantics and Modal Logic*. Chicago: University of Chicago Press, enlarged edn 1956.

Carnap, Rudolf (1950) 'Empiricism, Semantics, and Ontology,' *Revue Internationale de Philosophie* 4: 20–40 (also reprinted in Carnap's *Meaning and Necessity: A Study in Semantics and Modal Logic*, Chicago: University of Chicago Press, 1956).

Carnap, Rudolf (1956) 'The Methodological Character of Theoretical Concepts,' in Herbert Feigl and Michael Scriven (eds), *Minnesota Studies in the Philosophy of Science*, Vol. I, Minneapolis: University of Minnesota Press, 38–76.

Carnap, Rudolf (1966) *Philosophical Foundations of Physics: An Introduction to the Philosophy of Science*, ed. Martin Gardner, New York: Basic Books, Inc. (from lectures given in 1958).

Castañeda, Hector-Neri (ed.) (1975a) *Action, Knowledge, and Reality: Critical Studies in Honor of Wilfrid Sellars*, Indianapolis: Bobbs-Merrill.

Castañeda, Hector-Neri (1975b) 'Some Reflections on Wilfrid Sellars' Theory of Intentions,' in Castañeda 1975a.

Chalmers, David (1997) *The Conscious Mind: In Search of a Fundamental Theory*, Oxford University Press.

Chisholm, Roderick (1950) 'The Theory of Appearing,' in Swartz 1965.

Chisholm, Roderick (1957) 'Intentionality and the Mental' (included in Sellars ITM, correspondence with Sellars), in Herbert Feigl, Michael Scriven, and Grover Maxwell (eds), *Minnesota Studies in the Philosophy of Science*, Vol. II, University of Minnesota Press, 507–39 (also reprinted in Marras 1972).

Chisholm, Roderick (1966) *The Theory of Knowledge*, Englewood Cliffs, NJ: Prentice-Hall (and also subsequent heavily revised edns in 1977 and 1989).

Chisholm, Roderick (1986) 'The Myth of the Given,' in P. K. Moser (ed.), *Empirical Knowledge: Readings in Contemporary Epistemology*, Totowa, NJ: Rowman and Littlefield Publishers, Inc., 55–75. Reprinted from Roderick Chisholm, *Philosophy*, Englewood Cliffs, NJ: Prentice-Hall, 1964.

Chrucky, Andrew, website 'Problems from Wilfrid Sellars,' containing works by and on Sellars, and many other resources: *http://www.ditext.com/sellars/index.html*.

Church, Alonzo (1951) 'The Need for Abstract Entities in Semantic Analysis,' in *Proceedings of the American Academy of Arts and Sciences* 80: 110–12.

Clark, Austen (1989) 'The Particulate Instantiation of Homogeneous Pink,' *Synthese* 80: 277–304.

Coates, Paul (forthcoming) *The Metaphysics of Perception: Wilfrid Sellars, Critical Realism and the Nature of Experience*, London: Routledge.

Coffa, J. Alberto (1991) *The Semantic Tradition from Kant to Carnap: To the Vienna Station*, ed. L. Wessels, Cambridge: Cambridge University Press.

Delaney, C. F., Loux, Michael J., Gutting, Gary, and Solomon, W. David (eds) (1977) *The Synoptic Vision: Essays on the Philosophy of Wilfrid Sellars*, Notre Dame, IN and London: University of Notre Dame Press.

Dennett, Daniel (1974) 'Comment on Wilfrid Sellars,' in Sellars' MFC (*Synthese* 27: 439–44).

Dennett, Daniel (1981) comments on Sellars in Sellars' FMPP.

Dennett, Daniel (1987) *The Intentional Stance*, Cambridge, MA: Bradford Books/MIT Press.

Descartes, René (1641) *Meditations on First Philosophy*, in *The Philosophical Writings of Descartes*, Vol. II, trans. John Cottingham, Robert Stoothoff, Dugald Murdoch, and Anthony Kenny, Cambridge: Cambridge University Press, 1991.

deVries, Willem A. (2005) *Wilfrid Sellars*, Chesham, Bucks: Acumen.

deVries, Willem A., and Triplett, Timm (2000) *Knowledge, Mind, and the Given: Reading Wilfrid Sellars's 'Empiricism and the Philosophy of Mind'* (including the complete text of Sellars's essay), Indianapolis and Cambridge: Hackett Publishing Co.

Eddington, A. S. (1931) *The Nature of the Physical World*, New York: Macmillan.

Eddington, A. S. (1938) *The Philosophy of Physical Science*, Lectures given to Trinity College, Cambridge, Easter Term 1938, Ann Arbor: University of Michigan Press, 1978.

Fales, Evan (1996) *A Defense of the Given*, New York: Rowman and Littlefield Publishers, Inc.

Falk, W. D. (1986) *Ought, Reasons, and Morality*, Ithaca, NY: Cornell University Press.

Firth, Roderick (1964) 'Coherence, Certainty, and Epistemic Priority,' *Journal of Philosophy* 61/19, 545–57 (also reprinted in Jonathan Dancy (ed.), *Perceptual Knowledge*, Oxford: Oxford University Press, 1988).

Firth, Roderick (1981) comments on Sellars, in Sellars' FMPP.

Fodor, Jerry, and Lepore, Ernest (1992) *Holism: A Shopper's Guide.* Oxford: Blackwell.

Fodor, Jerry, and Lepore, Ernest (2001) 'Brandom's Burdens: A Review of Robert B. Brandom's *Articulating Reasons*,' *Philosophy and Phenomenological Research* 63: 465–82.

Frege, Gottlob (1892) 'Sense and Reference,' in *Translations from the Philosophical Writings of Gottlob Frege*, trans. Peter Geach and Max Black, Oxford: Basil Blackwell, 1960.

Friedman, Michael (2000) 'Transcendental Philosophy and A Priori Knowledge: A Neo-Kantian Perspective,' in Boghossian and Peacocke 2000.

Garfield, Jay L. (1989) 'The Myth of Jones and the Mirror of Nature: Reflections on Introspection,' *Philosophy and Phenomenological Research* 50: 1–26.

Gauker, Christopher (1994) *Thinking Out Loud: An Essay on the Relation Between Thought and Language*, Princeton, NJ: Princeton University Press.

Geach, Peter (1957) *Mental Acts*, London: Routledge and Kegan Paul.

Gettier, Edmund L. (1963) 'Is Justified True Belief Knowledge?,' *Analysis* 23: 121–3.

Gutting, Gary (1977) 'Philosophy of Mind: Action and Freedom,' in Delaney et al. 1977.

Gutting, Gary (1982) 'Scientific Realism vs. Constructive Empiricism: A Dialogue,' *The Monist* 65: 336–49.

Hempel, Carl G. (1958) 'The Theoretician's Dilemma,' in *Aspects of Scientific Explanation and other Essays in the Philosophy of Science*, New York: Free Press, 1965.

Hempel, Carl G. (1966) *Philosophy of Natural Science*, Englewood Cliffs, NJ: Prentice-Hall.

Hooker, C. A. (1977) 'Sellars' Argument for the Inevitability of the Secondary Qualities,' *Philosophical Studies* 32: 335–48.

Hume, David (1739) *A Treatise of Human Nature*, ed. L. A. Selby-Bigge (2nd edn, P. H. Nidditch), Oxford: Clarendon Press, 1978.

Hume, David (1748) *An Enquiry concerning Human Understanding*, ed. Tom L. Beauchamp, Oxford: Oxford University Press, 1999.

Hurley, Paul (2000) 'Sellars' Ethics: Variations on Kantian Themes,' *Philosophical Studies* 101 (a special issue on Sellars): 291–324.

Kant, Immanuel (1787) *A Critique of Pure Reason*, trans. Paul Guyer and Allen Wood, Cambridge: Cambridge University Press, 1997.

Kim, Jaegwon (2003) 'The American Origins of Philosophical Naturalism,' in *Philosophy in America at the Turn of the Century*. APA Centennial Supplement, *Journal of Philosophical Research*. Charlottesville, VA: Philosophy Documentation Center.

Koons, Jeremy Randel (forthcoming) 'Sellars, Givenness, and Epistemic Priority,' in Mark Lance and Michael P. Wolf (eds), *The Self-Correcting Enterprise: Essays on Wilfrid Sellars*, Amsterdam and New York: Rodopi.

Kornblith, Hilary (ed.) (2001) *Epistemology: Internalism and Externalism*, Oxford: Blackwell.

Kripke, Saul A. (1980) *Naming and Necessity*, Oxford: Blackwell, and Cambridge, MA: Harvard University Press. (Edited version of three lectures given at Princeton in 1970. First published in Gilbert Harman and Donald Davidson (eds), *Semantics of Natural Language*, Dordrecht: D. Reidel, 1972.)

Kripke, Saul A. (1982) *Wittgenstein on Rules and Private Language: An Elementary Exposition*, Cambridge, MA: Harvard University Press.

Kukla, Rebecca (2000) 'Myth, Memory and Misrecognition in Sellars' "Empiricism and the Philosophy of Mind," ' *Philosophical Studies* 101: 161–211.

Lance, Mark Norris (1996) 'Quantification, Substitution, and Conceptual Content,' *Nous* 30: 481–507.

Lance, Mark Norris, and O'Leary-Hawthorne, John (1997) *The Grammar of Meaning*, Cambridge: Cambridge University Press.

Lange, Marc (2000) 'Salience, Supervenience, and Layer Cakes in Sellars's Scientific Realism, McDowell's Moral Realism, and the Philosophy of Mind,' *Philosophical Studies* 101: 213–51.

Lehrer, Keith, and Stern, David G. (2000) 'The "Dénouement" of "Empiricism and the Philosophy of Mind," ' *History of Philosophy Quarterly* 17: 201–16.

Leibniz, Gottfried (1714) *The Monadology*, in *Philosophical Essays*, ed. and trans. Roger Ariew and Daniel Garber, Indianapolis: Hackett, 1989.

Leplin, Jarrett (ed.) (1984) *Scientific Realism*, Berkeley: University of California Press.

Lewis, Clarence Irving (1929) *Mind and the World Order*, New York: Dover.

Loux, Michael J. (1977) 'Ontology,' in Delaney et al. 1977.

Loux, Michael J. (1978) 'Rules, Roles, and Ontological Commitment: An Examination of Sellars' Analysis of Abstract Reference,' in Joseph C. Pitt (ed.), *The Philosophy of Wilfrid Sellars: Queries and Extensions. Papers Deriving from and Related to a Workshop on the Philosophy of Wilfrid Sellars Held at Virginia Polytechnic Institute and State University 1976*. Dordrecht: D. Reidel.

Lycan, William G. (1987) *Consciousness*, Cambridge, MA: Bradford Books/MIT Press.

Lycan, William G. (forthcoming) 'Recent Naturalistic Dualisms,' in Armin Lange, Eric Meyers, and Randall Styers (eds), *Light Against Darkness: Dualism in Ancient Mediterranean Religion and the Contemporary World*, Leiden: Brill Academic Publishers.

McDowell, John (1994) *Mind and World*, Cambridge, MA: Harvard University Press; reissued with a new introduction, 1996.

McDowell, John (1998) 'Having the World in View: Sellars, Kant, and Intentionality' (the Woodbridge Lectures for 1997), Journal of Philosophy XCV: 431–91.

Maddy, Penelope (2000) 'Naturalism and the A Priori,' in Boghossian and Peacocke 2000.

Marras, Ausonio (ed.) (1972) *Intentionality, Mind, and Language*, Urbana: University of Illinois Press.

Marras, Ausonio (1973a) 'Sellars on Thought and Language,' *Nous* 7: 152–63.

Marras, Ausonio (1973b) 'On Sellars' Linguistic Theory of Conceptual Activity' and 'Reply to Sellars,' *Canadian Journal of Philosophy* 4: 471–501 (includes Sellars' 'Reply to Marras').

Maxwell, Grover (1962) 'The Ontological Status of Theoretical Entities,' in Herbert Feigl and Grover Maxwell (eds), *Minnesota Studies in the Philosophy of Science*, Vol. III, Minneapolis: University of Minnesota Press.

Miller, Alexander and Wright, Crispin (eds) (2002) *Rule-Following and Meaning*, Chesham, Bucks: Acumen.

Millikan, Ruth (2005) 'The Son and the Daughter: On Sellars, Brandom, and Millikan,' in *Language: A Biological Model*, Oxford: Clarendon Press.

Muilenberg, G., and Richardson, R. C. (1982) 'Sellars and Sense Impressions,' *Erkenntnis* 17: 171–212.

Nagel, Ernest (1961) *The Structure of Science: Problems in the Logic of Scientific Explanation*, New York: Harcourt, Brace & World, Inc.

O'Shea, James R. (2002) 'Revisiting Sellars on the Myth of the Given,' *International Journal of Philosophical Studies* 10: 490–503.

O'Shea, James R. (2006a) 'Conceptual Connections: Kant and the 20th-Century Analytic Tradition,' in Graham Bird (ed.), *A Companion to Kant*, Oxford: Blackwell.

O'Shea, James R. (2006b) 'On the Structure of Sellars' Naturalism with a Normative Turn,' delivered July at University College London, conference in honor of the fiftieth anniversary of Sellars' delivery of the EPM lectures in London. (Available online at: *http://philosophy.sas. ac.uk/Empiricism_Mind_Sellars.htm*.) Publication forthcoming.

O'Shea, James R. (forthcoming) 'American Philosophy in the Twentieth Century,' in Dermot Moran (ed.), *The Routledge Companion to Twentieth-Century Philosophy*, London: Routledge.

Peregrin, Jaroslav (2001) *Meaning and Structure*, Aldershot: Ashgate.

Pitt, Joseph C. (1981) *Pictures, Images and Conceptual Change: An Analysis of Wilfrid Sellars' Philosophy of Science* (Synthese Library Vol. 151), Dordrecht: D. Reidel.

Plato (1961) *The Collected Dialogues of Plato*, ed. Edith Hamilton and Huntington Cairns, Princeton, NJ: Princeton University Press.

Price, H. H. (1932) *Perception*, London: Methuen & Co. Ltd.

Putnam, Hilary (1974) 'Comment on Wilfrid Sellars,' in Sellars' MFC (*Synthese* 27: 445–55).

Putnam, Hilary (1975) *Mind, Language and Reality* (Philosophical Papers, Vol. 2), Cambridge: Cambridge University Press.

Quine, W. V. O. (1980) 'Sellars on Behaviorism, Language and Meaning,' *Pacific Philosophical Quarterly* 61: 26–30.

Quine, W. V. O. (1981) 'Five Milestones of Empiricism,' in *Theories and Things*, Cambridge, MA: Harvard University Press.

Quinton, Anthony (1955) 'The Problem of Perception,' in Swartz 1965.

Robinson, Howard (1994) *Perception*, London: Routledge.

Rorty, Richard (1979) *Philosophy and the Mirror of Nature*, Princeton, NJ: Princeton University Press.

Rosenberg, Jay F. (1974) *Linguistic Representation*, Dordrecht: D. Reidel.

Rosenberg, Jay F. (1980) *One World and Our Knowledge of It*, Dordrecht: D. Reidel.

Rosenberg, Jay F. (1994) *Beyond Formalism: Naming and Necessity for Human Beings*, Philadelphia: Temple University Press.

Rosenberg, Jay F. (2002) *Thinking About Knowing*, Oxford: Clarendon Press.

Rosenberg, Jay F. (forthcoming) *Wilfrid Sellars: Fusing the Images*, Oxford: Oxford University Press. (A collection of Rosenberg's articles on Sellars' philosophy, including several previously unpublished essays.)

Rosenthal, David M. (2005) *Consciousness and Mind*, Oxford: Oxford University Press.

Ross, Jacob Joshua (1970) *The Appeal to the Given: A Study in Epistemology*, London: Allen and Unwin.

Rubenstein, Eric M. (2000) 'Sellars Without Homogeneity,' *International Journal of Philosophical Studies* 8: 47–72.

Russell, Bertrand (1912) *The Problems of Philosophy*, Oxford: Oxford University Press, 1998.

Ryle, Gilbert (1949) *The Concept of Mind*, London: Penguin, 2000.

Seibt, Johanna (1990) *Properties as Processes: A Synoptic Study of Wilfrid Sellars' Nominalism*, Atascadero, CA: Ridgeview Publishing Co.

Seibt, Johanna (2000) 'Pure Processes and Projective Metaphysics,' *Philosophical Studies* 101: 253–89.

Seibt, Johanna (2006) *Wilfrid Sellars*, Berlin: Mentis Verlag.

Sellars, Roy Wood (1916) *Critical Realism: A Study of the Nature and Conditions of Knowledge*, Chicago: Rand-McNally and Co.

Sellars, Roy Wood (1922) *Evolutionary Naturalism*, New York: Russell & Russell, 1969.

Sellars, Roy Wood (1932) *The Philosophy of Physical Realism*, New York: Macmillan.

Shepard, Roger N., and Chipman, Susan (1970) 'Second-Order Isomorphism of Internal Representations: Shapes of States,' *Cognitive Psychology* 1: 1–17.

Sicha, Jeffrey (1974) *A Metaphysics of Elementary Mathematics*, Amherst: University of Massachusetts Press.

Sicha, Jeffrey (1978) 'Logic: The Fundamentals of a Sellarsian Theory,' in Joseph C. Pitt (ed.), *The Philosophy of Wilfrid Sellars: Queries and Extensions. Papers Deriving from and Related to a Workshop on the Philosophy of Wilfrid Sellars Held at Virginia Polytechnic Institute and State University 1976.* Dordrecht: D. Reidel.

Smith, Michael (1994) *The Moral Problem*, Oxford: Blackwell.

Solomon, W. David (1977) 'Ethical Theory,' in Delaney et al. 1977.

Sosa, Ernest (1997) 'Mythology of the Given,' *History of Philosophy Quarterly* 14: 277–86.

Sosa, Ernest (2003) 'Knowledge, Animal and Reflective: A Reply to Michael Williams,' *Aristotelian Society Supplementary Volume* LXXVII: 113–30.

Stebbing, L. Susan (1937) *Philosophy and the Physicists*, New York: Dover, 1958.

Strawson, P. F. (1979) 'Perception and its Objects,' in G. F. Macdonald (ed.), *Perception and Identity: Essays Presented to A. J. Ayer*, London: Macmillan (also reprinted in Jonathan Dancy (ed.), *Perceptual Knowledge*, Oxford: Oxford University Press, 1988; all text references are to the 1979 original).

Strawson, P. F. (1992) *Analysis and Metaphysics: An Introduction to Philosophy*, Oxford: Oxford University Press.

Swartz, Robert J. (ed.) (1965) *Perceiving, Sensing, and Knowing*, Los Angeles: University of California Press.

Tarski, Alfred (1944) 'The Semantic Conception of Truth and the Foundations of Semantics,' *Philosophy and Phenomenological Research* 4: 341–76 (also reprinted in Leonard Linsky (ed.), *Semantics and the Philosophy of Language*, Urbana: University of Illinois Press, 1952).

van Fraassen, Bas C. (1975) 'Wilfrid Sellars on Scientific Realism,' *Dialogue* 14: 606–16.

van Fraassen, Bas C. (1976) 'On the Radical Incompleteness of the Manifest Image' (a response to Sellars' SRT), Lansing, MI: *Proceedings of the Philosophy of Science Association* (PSA) 2: 335–43.

van Fraassen, Bas C. (1980) *The Scientific Image*, Oxford: Oxford University Press.

Vinci, Thomas C. (1998) 'The Myth of the Myth of the Given,' located on the Chrucky website on Sellars (listed above), *http://www.ditext.com/vinci/mmg.html*.

Williams, Michael (1999) *Groundless Belief*, 2nd edn, Princeton, NJ: Princeton University Press.

Williams, Michael (2001) *Problems of Knowledge: A Critical Introduction to Epistemology*, Oxford: Oxford University Press.

Williams, Michael (2003) 'Mythology of the Given: Sosa, Sellars and the Task of Epistemology,' *Aristotelian Society Supplementary Volume* LXXVII: 91–112.

Wittgenstein, Ludwig (1922) *Tractatus Logico-Philosophicus*, trans. C. K. Ogden, London: Routledge and Kegan Paul Ltd, 1983.

Wittgenstein, Ludwig (1953) *Philosophical Investigations*, trans. G. E. M. Anscombe, Oxford: Basil Blackwell, 1963.

Wright, Edmond L. (1985) 'A Defence of Sellars,' *Philosophy and Phenomenological Research* 46: 73–90.

Index

absolute processes *see* pure processes
abstract entities 4, 49–50, 53, 55, 58,
    61, 63–76, 116, 160
  abstract ideas 211n16
  abstract singular terms 64, 66–7,
    70, 75
  as changing 72, 161
  as metalinguistic 67, 69–70, 72
  conceptualism 63–4
  linguistic universals 70
  platonism (platonic realism) 50,
    63–7, 69–71, 73–7, 156
  universals 63, 107
  see also conceptual role;
    distributive singular terms;
    mathematics; nominalism;
    rules
actions (intentional, rational) 11, 18,
    22, 44, 48, 78–80, 102, 178–87,
    217n42, 203n7
  construed in scientific terms in the
    ideal scientific image 187–8
  perceptions, inferences, and
    volitions are not actions
    80–1
  see also intentions; language entry/
    inference/exit patterns
adverbialism *see* sensing
Alston, William 210n11, 215n35,
    216n36
analogy (analogical) *see* models
analytic philosophy 5, 7, 49–50

animal representational systems *see*
    representation
anti-realism 15
appearance 108, 118, 120–5, 129–30
  and conceptual change 159–60
  endorsement (epistemic appraisal)
    dimension of 121–4, 136
  generic looks 123
  is/looks contrast principle (priority
    of *is* to *seems*) 108, 119, 121–2,
    129–30, 133, 137, 215n33
  '*looks* is not a relation' 124,
    213n29
  qualitative vs. existential 119, 123
  theories of 209n4
  vs. the epistemic priority of 122–3,
    129
  see also ostensible seeing;
    perception; phenomenology
Aquinas, St. Thomas 90
Aristotle; Aristotelian 90, 114, 165,
    193n2, 224n28
Aune, Bruce 207n24, 225n1
assert vs. convey 50, 56, 61, 124, 177,
    188
  see also presupposition
atomism
  logical 144, 146, 171, 197n24,
    218n1, 219n5, 224n28
    'Basically, at heart, I am a
    logical atomist'
    (Sellars) 225n34

Made in United States
North Haven, CT
17 November 2023

44163177R00148